WHY INNOVATION FAILS

The 7 keys to succes

JOACHIM DE VOS

Lannoo
Campus

D/2021/45/273 – ISBN 978 94 014 7846 5 – NUR 800

Cover design: Adept vormgeving
Interior design: Peer De Maeyer
Translation: Ian Connerty
Visuals: Dieter Paternoster
Key Illustrations: Kristof Braekeleire

© Joachim De Vos & Lannoo Publishers nv, Tielt, 2022.

LannooCampus Publishers is a subsidiary of Lannoo Publishers,
the book and multimedia division of Lannoo Publishers nv.

LannooCampus Publishers
Vaartkom 41 box 01.02   P.O. Box 23202
3000 Leuven   1100 DS Amsterdam
Belgium   Netherlands
www.lannoocampus.com

CONTENTS

PREFACE

Preface by Herman Van Rompuy,
President Emeritus of the European Council

Preface
By Joachim De Vos

"There is no doubt that the way we live will be different in the future."

BILL GATES

"There is no doubt that the way we live will be different in the future. The advances in PC technology and low-cost communications are bringing a revolution that we all talk about today as the information superhighway. I think that the impact that is coming in the next twenty years will be very dramatic. So, I think it's very wise for us to start exploring what it all means. A project like this one where you are brainstorming about what is possible and you are getting people to come in, look at this and that, and think about what this all means... It's fantastic that this is happening early on. I was certainly impressed with what I saw. And I'm very pleased to be here. Thank you."

These were the words of Bill Gates on 16 March 1995 at the opening of Living Tomorrow, the first project that I worked on with heart and soul to build a better future. It also marked the start of my professional career. He told me that he was impressed with the vision that we had for that future. Today, 27 years later, the time has come to look back, but also to look forward. This is a book about how I experienced innovation in hundreds of different organisations, both great and small. About how I learnt to predict the future, so that I and others could be prepared for it in the best possible way. Above all, it is an honest and frank account of how I saw innovation succeed and fail, often because the drastic nature of change had been underestimated. This is truer now than it has even been: "The next twenty years will be very dramatic."

INTRODUCTION
WHAT DOES THIS BOOK HAVE TO OFFER?

Returning to normal after Covid-19 is an illusion

Covid-19 was the 'black swan' that surprised us all by its intensity and scale. No one could have imagined that something as ordinary as a bat would catapult the globalised world a quarter of a century back in time, with several large-scale lockdowns that paralysed both society and the economy, with millions of deaths as a result. Yet in spite of everything, the pace of technological progress did not slacken. Quite the reverse. There was also significant societal change. Covid-19 caused us to fundamentally question the way we look at the world and our role in it. António Guterres, the secretary-general of the United Nations, issued the following stern warning: "I am here to sound the alarm. Our world has never been more threatened..."

In the old normal, we used to spend hours in traffic jams, rushing from one meeting to the next, but scarcely making an active contribution when we got there. We attempted to pass on our knowledge to our children by making them sit for hours in overfull auditoria, where there was little or no interaction. We organised events that were only viable if attended by huge numbers of people and we were able to fly around the world for less than the price of a decent meal.

Until everything suddenly ground to a halt: total lockdown. We were imprisoned – happily or unhappily – in our own bubbles, only being allowed out of doors for 'essential travel'. Our lives changed drastically. Never before in the history of mankind had there ever been such a massive change experiment that affected our habits and our way of living and working. But people soon grew tired of accepting the rules that had been imposed upon them. Soon there was a growing number of dissenting voices, shouting in unison: "Let's get back to normal, as soon as possible." And that is what we did, as far as we could. As a result, we are now once again sitting in traffic jams, flying around the world and buying things like it is going out of fashion. So, we need to ask the question: has innovation failed?

In the meantime, we are also being confronted with the downside of the rapid recovery of the economy, which finds expression in a shortage of materials and energy. This further contributes to the level of harmful emissions, while the weather continues to become increasingly capricious, with blisteringly hot summers in some parts of the world and devastating floods in others. But this is just the beginning, and the further development of these trends will force us to change almost constantly. To make this possible, innovation will need to play a key role in helping to provide the structural change that is so desperately needed.

What if we all travelled less?
What if we all worked online, wherever possible, instead of commuting?
What if we all generated our own energy?
What if we recycled and reused things, and consumed less?

How can we change our objective from 'getting back to normal' to 'finding a way forward'? How can we learn to embrace change fully, even in the face of the uncertainties it presents? This will be the great challenge in the coming century, both for individuals and organisations. Why does innovation so often remain just a one-off project? When I ask companies to tell me about the recent innovations that make them feel proud, they usually answer with something like: "Well, Eric and his team did something great last year" or "We had a fantastic hackathon back in 2020". But after these 'great' and 'fantastic' initiatives, things suddenly went quiet. There was no follow-up. The idea of non-stop innovation failed to catch on. Things simply went 'back to normal'. 'Business as usual' is the order of the day.

So what is going wrong? Why do we find it so hard to innovate in the way we should? Why are we unable to convert innovation into an integrated process that continues to produce success after success?

Wanting to tackle these questions was one of my main reasons for writing this book. Having said that, I am the first to admit that I do not have all the answers.

That would be presumptuous in the extreme in a domain as volatile as innovation. What I can do, however, is to share the lessons I have learnt from a life that has been devoted to innovation. Sometimes these insights were gleaned from success; sometimes from the scars of painful failure. Yet whatever their origin, they always led to greater clarity and understanding.

What will your approach be? Will you let change just happen to you? Or will you seek to shape it?

My life dedicated to innovation and the future

My professional life has been driven by a boundless passion for the future and the innovation that will be necessary to get us there. As a child, I was given an encyclopaedia about technological progress. I soon knew its contents by heart. During my engineering studies, my interest was captured most forcefully by 'what must come'. In 1995, we built the House of the Future – Living Tomorrow – in Brussels, so that we could imagine what life would be like in the 21st century, surrounded by new technologies, products and services. A living glass dome, the purpose of which was to stimulate and communicate innovation. It was a huge success. Since then, millions of people have visited one of our six generation projects; hundreds of millions, if you count our virtual visitors. In the intervening years, I have worked closely with more than a thousand organisations to develop new products and services. Together with them, I have been able to think about the challenges that will need to be met to secure all our futures. This has become an international open science project of which I am immensely proud, as I am of the many people who help – and continue to help – to make it possible each day.

When Living Tomorrow was launched in 1995, Bill Gates was one of our main guests. On the evening of the launch, we walked together through the House of the Future, admiring its many radical new ideas, like a kitchen computer integrated seamlessly into one of the work surfaces. As a result, daily products could be ordered automatically and you could fun-shop via a virtual supermarket, so that you could organise your next house party quickly and easily. Your virtual assistant – "My name is Franz and I'm going to help you organise your evening" – knew your preferences, which made choosing from an endless range of products so much simpler. At the same time, demotics ran everything in your home and you could even let the delivery man into your house from a distance, watching on camera while he put everything away neatly in your fridge.

In addition to our many 'ordinary' visitors, a number of my idols also found their way to Brussels, such as Nicholas Negroponte, Pattie Maes, Ray Kurzweil, the Chinese premier Zhu Rongji, Zaha Hadid and Chief Raoni Metuktire – one of the chiefs of the Kayapo people, who fought together with Sting to combat deforestation. We have also been fortunate that former European Council president Herman van Rompuy has regularly chaired our international round-table meetings to discuss future thinking and innovation.

At the heart of the future that surrounds us, we had and still have the most fascinating discussions. People start to dream about what might be; they see the future and decide to think and act differently.

Many of the things we demonstrated later came onto the market. Sometimes as long as 20 years later. We often saw the magic unfold right before our eyes. Dozens of products and services, which we had helped to co-create, either through design or the building of prototypes, have become a huge success: household automation with voice interaction became Google Home and Alexa; e-commerce became Bertelsmann Online and later bol.com and Amazon; the virtual travel planner became Tripadvisor; video meetings became Zoom and Skype; delivery box became DHL packing stations; the automatic doorbell that lets in delivery people became Amazon Ring; the streaming jukebox became Spotify. And that is to name only a few.

At the same time, it needs to be remembered that many innovations failed; far more than ever succeeded. Some never made it out of the lab. Others failed to catch on in the market, often because they were ahead of their time or insufficiently adjusted to the needs of the moment. We introduced speech technology far too early in 1999. Job matching (active collaborative filtering), used by Randstad as long ago as 1998, also arrived two decades too soon. The idea of an intelligent 'kitchen board' – offering a range of smart services and communicating with smart packaging and kitchen devices – dates back to 2007, but only looks set to make a big breakthrough in the next ten years. The smartwatch – which tells sportsmen and women when they need to top up their energy levels and what energy bar they should eat, before automatically adjusting their dietary profile, thanks to the biochips contained in the bar – was first developed as a concept back in 2010 and is now available as an aid to help people follow their medication correctly. The intelligent mirror, which also functions as a virtual doctor, is only now starting to become popular after six years, through the use of apps like SkinVision and Doktr.

Imagining what the future will be like excites passionate emotions, both in terms of the innovations themselves and their adoption by consumers. I can remember weekends in the House of the Future when we had intense and sometimes heated discussions with our visitors. Some people thought our ideas were madness and saw us as demons who were determined to introduce an artificial, technocratic world that needed to be resisted at all costs!

A screen in every room? How dare you suggest such a thing! A screen that you can carry in the palm of your hand? Never! Discussions of this kind are still being conducted today, but the themes have moved on from screens and smartphones to Artificial Intelligence (AI), self-driving cars, brain-computer interfacing and other similar possibilities.

Your mirror on the future

Like the House of the Future, this book is intended to serve as your guide to discover the future and how you can best prepare for it. Above all, you will also learn how you can innovate with the future in mind and how you can increase the likelihood of turning your innovative projects into repeatable successes in both the short and the long term, not only for yourself but for your customers as well.

> This book will be your mirror on the future,
> your guide for your own future,
> and for the future of your children,
> your company, your customers and your partners.

Whether you are an incumbent, a start-up, a family business, a major company, a government authority or an educational or care institution, this book will offer you a number of practical tools and instruments that will help you to make your innovation more successful and more meaningful. But on its own this will not be enough. The saying "a fool with a tool remains a fool" contains more than a grain of truth. Successful innovation requires much more than just the right people and the right tools. It also requires a clear vision of the kind of future that you want to build, and I hope that this book will show you how best to do this. Having a clear vision, supported by the right people, tools and processes, will make it possible for you and your organisation to remain relevant in the future. That is the ultimate goal of successful innovation. This future is something that should interest and fascinate us all: after all, we are going to spend the rest of our life there! But it begins here. And it begins now.

Innovation: the new religion

'Innovation' is one of the buzzwords of the modern business world. You see it and hear it everywhere. The hype around new products and services continues to increase. It has also been suggested that the Covid-19 pandemic has not only further intensified this urge to innovate, but has familiarised it as well. Development of a Covid-19 vaccine put mRNA biotechnology in the public spotlight, while contact tracing did much the same for Bluetooth. We all Zoomed from our front rooms instead of commuting into the office. Air travel was replaced by video conferencing. Museums and galleries were visited virtually rather than physically, thanks to the ingenuity of VR glasses.

Without innovation, it is possible that the effects of the pandemic might have been insurmountable for the economy and perhaps even for mankind as a whole. Recent innovation has drastically changed our lives in many different ways. And I am not talking about robots, drones or AI, linked to our brains or not. In spite of the pandemic, things continued to grow. Innovative companies continued to make their way inexorably to the top. Look at the stock market explosion that took place in the middle of 2020. With an estimated value of 2,500 billion dollars, Apple became as large as the entire British or French economy. Tesla is now worth more than the three largest German car manufacturers and the rest of the top ten put together. Elon Musk has become the richest person in the world. This is a seismic shift. Successful innovation on a massive scale.

Innovation is doing something new.

Change is taking place faster than ever before. Technology is booming. The world is being shaken by the scruff of its neck. When I started my career in future thinking at the age of 25, I can remember a visit made to Living Tomorrow by the top man at Intel. The title of his speech to a packed hall of CEOs was short and to the point: "Innovation. The quick and the dead!" It was quite a performance, but in 1995 people felt that they could still afford to laugh at his words. They are not laughing now.

As an organisation, you need to innovate. You have no choice. As a result, countless new initiatives are launched: idea boxes, participation platforms, R&D labs, accelerators, incubators, venture capital starters, innovation boards, skill learning programmes, culture programmes, open innovation, partnership programmes, intrapreneur bootcamps, hackathons, innovation tours, innovation cafés, disruption boards, etc., etc. I see this happening week after week in our event spaces and during my location visits, or when I am invited as an 'inspirational speaker' to fire up people's creative energy. Please don't misunderstand me: these are all noble and worthwhile initiatives, but they seldom lead to positive results. They lack structure. There is no connection between the different projects. No vision. No follow-up system. Each innovation is an end in itself, rather than a springboard to something bigger and better. Innovation of this kind is a waste of time. It can be done better. It must be done better.

Every level of society is fixated on innovation. Since the early 2000s, we have learnt to worship a quadrumvirate of new gods: Google, Apple, Facebook and Amazon, collectively known as GAFA. More recently, this constellation has been expanded and reformed to create MATAMA (Microsoft, Apple, Tesla, Amazon, Mega and Alphabet). These super-organisations all have the most charismatic leaders: Steve Jobs, Mark Zuckerberg, Jeff Bezos, Satya Nadella and Elon Musk. Fortunately, there are also a number of women among them: Susan Wojcicki, the CEO at YouTube, and Gwynne Shotwell, the COO at SpaceX, to name but two. Even so, the very top of the business world is still far too male-dominated. Where do these 21st century divinities come from? Some of them are from the promised land of Silicon Valley, but others have emerged from China, a country that we thought (until recently) had embraced capitalism, resulting in organisations like Alibaba, Tencent, Neo and TikTok, led by innovative entrepreneurs like Jack Ma. With their army of innovation teams, unlimited budgets, radical technology and out-of-this-world business models, they rapidly created a business value of a kind that has never previously been seen, running into trillions and trillions of dollars. The world seemed to be theirs for the taking, until they were called to a halt by President Xi.

Unbridled techno-optimism?

Here are some questions to consider. In this turbulent age, how should I organise myself and my company to have the best chance of a successful future? Sadly, I am not part of a MATAMA organisation, so how can I innovate successfully with only a millionth of the innovation budget available to these business giants? Or should I simply admit defeat and try to sell my company as quickly as possible? Or perhaps pass the problem on to the next generation, to see if they can do any better? These are not simple choices. But one thing is certain: you will solve nothing by engaging in what professor Steve Blank refers to as 'innovation theatre'.

There is no point in pretending to be innovative. In fact, it can even be counter-productive, since it often leads to a reaction against too much unbridled techno-optimism and the ceaseless urge to innovate. Some people even abandon innovation altogether, claiming that we have reached the so-called Great Tech Stagnation, the point at which technological breakthroughs no longer contribute to the economy or change people's lives in the way they once did. There are no longer any revolutionary and life-enhancing inventions, such as the light bulb or the refrigerator in the 20th century. New products seldom succeed in creating a significant and sustainable added value for the globalised world market as a whole. "Let's get back to normal" is their cry, in much the same way that people are anxious to revert to their old way of doing things after the Covid-19 pandemic. Or that, at least, is how it seems on the surface.

The believers in the Great Tech Stagnation argue that all the major steps forward in terms of life extension, electrification, construction, transport, etc. have all been made.

So, the million-dollar question is this: are they right or are they wrong?

I want to build a bridge between today and tomorrow

Whenever I start a conversation in organisations about innovation and the future, I am usually confronted with the supporters of both points of view: those who are enthusiastic to explore what the future might hold and those who are equally convinced that a focus on the present must be the priority. How do you deal with this kind of situation? How can you set everyone's sights on the future without neglecting the present? How can you get everyone to support the same objectives, without losing some of the doubters along the way? These are the questions that I want to answer in this book.

Innovation is something living. Understanding how innovation evolves helps us to look at the challenges of a changing future with greater insight. I will start by analysing what has already happened in the past in terms of industrial innovation and then invite you to reflect in a responsible, realistic but ambitious manner on what the future might have in store for us during the next 20 years. My aim is to show you – whether you are a leader in the world of business, politics, care, education, mobility or the environment – how to build that future in a way that benefits us all.

So how can you gain insight into the secrets of the future, into the universe of tomorrow?

We will explore this together on the basis of three fundamental questions:

- Why innovation? Why do we need to focus our attention on the future?

- What innovation? To analyse the future and build it on strong foundations, we need to understand innovation through and through. What is it? What is it not?

- What if innovation fails? Where can innovation go wrong? And why does it go wrong?

To this, we will add a fourth question:
What are the keys to success?
How can you increase the likelihood that your innovation will be successful?

PART 1
WHY INNOVATION?

'Innovation is the ability to see change as an opportunity, not a threat.' STEVE JOBS

In this first part, you will discover why innovation is necessary and how it manages to bring about creative destruction: the process by which the new replaces the old. In chapter 1, I will refute the argument that we have reached the Great Tech Stagnation, as some people claim. On the contrary, the speed of change continues to increase, which is harmful to the life expectancy of organisations. Well-known and successful organisations disappear, to be replaced by the new kids on the block. This is not only a consequence of digital disruption, but also of antiquated business models that have not been updated over time. The route that leads to a billion-dollar company looks very different today than it did 50 years ago. In part, this can be attributed to the law of increasing entropy. I will demonstrate this by offering a concise summary of the different phases of this evolution. I will also describe a number of mega-trends that form the basis for important innovations like blockchain, 4D-printing and mRNA.

In chapter 2, I will seek to answer the question 'what is innovation?'. I will analyse the three phases of the innovation cycle and examine the six major waves of innovation that have already taken place. Why do I do this? Because preparing effectively for the future is only possible by understanding the past.

In chapter 3, I will use an in-depth study of the Kodak case to illustrate the pitfalls and the cost of failing to innovate.

Chapter 4 will explain the importance of inside-out, systemic and open innovation for any organisation that wishes to be successful in the future. I will demonstrate this with reference to the case of the Creative Conversion Factory within Philips.

THE FUTURE FITNESS FORMULA

To discover to what extent your organisation is ready to meet the challenges of the future, you can use my Future Fitness Formula, which combines four key parameters:

$$\text{Future Fitness Formula} = \frac{\text{Vision x Speed x Agility}}{\text{Experience}}$$

This formula will be discussed occasionally in part 1, but will be examined in greater depth in Key 2 in part 2.

1
INNOVATION AS THE ANSWER TO CHANGE

The speed of change will only continue to increase

We are currently standing on the threshold of a new technological-industrial revolution. This revolution will change the foundations of our society for good, in part through the introduction and wide-scale use of world-shaking, super-intelligent and invisible nano-robots and bionic beings. Mankind, together with the AI likenesses it has created of itself, is poised on the eve of a new century of space exploration, during which the existence of extra-terrestrial life will be confirmed for the first time. Perhaps this will not happen during the next 20 years, but it is unquestionably the path that we are destined to follow.

> *We are not only living in an age of change,*
> *but also in a change of age.*

We are privileged to experience this process. Even more importantly, we are privileged to be a part of the process and to have the opportunity to help construct it. However, this will only be possible if we approach the future from a realistic perspective and with a clear vision in mind. This book will teach you how to build that future. It offers you a basis for the formulation of an innovation doctrine, an ideological creed explaining why your organisation must innovate.

I will analyse the past and look forward into the future. I will reveal the guiding principle that I have exploited with success during the past 25 years. This principle is my mirror into the future, my crystal ball to gain insight into the likely development of crucial new technologies, not only today, but also in the decades to come. I have only rarely been surprised by new discoveries and inventions, because I was able to predict most of them. In contrast, I was frequently surprised by how and by whom these discoveries and inventions were brought to market, as well as by the speed or slowness with which this happened.

The only constant throughout this period has been the acceleration of the speed of change. From the end of the Second World War in 1945 until the 1970s, many organisations were able to sail through relatively calm waters. There were still technological innovations, but companies had the necessary time to integrate these innovations into new and improved production processes, resulting in new and improved products that still offered a sufficiently good margin to bring them to market. Notwithstanding the shock waves created by the first worldwide crises, such as the oil crisis of 1974, organisations found themselves operating increasingly in a globalised economy in an atmosphere of relative political stability, at least in the West and in part thanks to the further expansion of a united Europe.

If, for example, we now look back at the development of the first transistor computer and the emergence of the PC, it all seems to have happened so slowly. This is probably what the young Steve Jobs and Bill Gates must have thought, and so they set about changing it.

The resulting acceleration in the speed of technological innovation made it more difficult for many organisations to adjust. Such adjustments not only required significantly more resources – to get the right people on board and to create large-scale research labs, such as the Bell Labs, the Philips NatLab, the Xerox PARC and the HP Labs – but also demanded greater creativity and 'guts' to successfully launch new products onto the market. There are legendary stories about how the young Steve Jobs was amazed by what he saw during his visits to the Xerox PARC, totally new things that he had never seen before: the mouse for the PC, the graphic interface, etc. Jobs immediately saw the possibilities offered by these innovations, whereas the engineers who had actually created them failed to see their revolutionary potential. Working with Steve Wozniak, Jobs quickly adapted, improved and elaborated these ideas, laying the foundations for the creation of the Apple empire.

These and other subsequent innovations were so rapid and so far-reaching that by the turn of the century even established names like Xerox, HP and IBM were finding it hard to keep up and in the following decades found themselves increasingly pushed to the margins by the new starters in the Valley. At the time of writing, Apple is probably the first company ever to have achieved a value of

3,000 billion dollars. Microsoft is worth 2,000 billion dollars. This means that both companies are fifteen times more valuable than the combined values of HP ($41.3 billion) and HPE ($20.8 billion), IBM ($120 billion) and Xerox ($4.1M billion)! No, this is not a misprint: fifteen times more. Apple's value alone is equivalent to 13% of American GDP and almost 20% of Chinese GDP.

Today's leading companies are nothing like the leading companies of yester-year. The problems at Blackberry and Nokia and the challenges faced by Twitter, Yahoo, Xerox and so many others are all illustrative of the fact that the process of 'creative destruction' – a concept first introduced by Joseph Schumpeter in the 1940s – is not only still relevant, but is increasing in speed and importance.

This obviously has an impact on the life expectancy of organisations. Nowadays, they come and they go. In this respect, an important research study that serves as a wake-up call and helps to shed light on how things might develop in the future is the Creative Destruction study by Innosight, the results of which are supported by an analysis of the changing composition of the list of the world's top five companies during the past two decades.

The changing life expectancy of our organisations

Innosight is a spin-off founded by the late Clayton Christensen, professor of disruption studies at Harvard. He investigated the longevity of organisations in the S&P 500 and came to the disconcerting conclusion that their life expectancy is consistently and quickly decreasing in a succession of waves. It seems as though the business jungle is continually producing a rapid growth of new and powerful young trees.

At the start of the 1960s, the average life expectancy of an organisation was 60 years. Professor Stéphane Garelli of IMD saw a parallel with the laws of thermodynamics. The first of these laws relates to the conservation of energy and states that energy remains constant within a closed system. This is how big companies used to work in the past: there was an interaction between generating heat (sales), the conversion of that heat into work (R&D) and the transfer of the resulting energy (to create and market new products with profit). This all seemed to take place without too much effort. It was a kind of perpetual motion: all the energy remained confined within the organisation's closed system. You converted one form of energy into another, and then back again.

In thermodynamics, this first law was subsequently investigated and supplemented by the work of Thompson, Planck and Clausius, resulting in the addition of the concept of increasing entropy, which can be summarised as:

> *Energy is required to maintain order;*
> *otherwise, order will be irrevocably converted into disorder.*

This means, for example, that it is impossible to keep a system in operation indefinitely without the addition of new energy. This applies equally to the development of organisations: entropy eventually kills large companies. The very size of such companies makes them more complex and more vulnerable. It takes ever increasing amounts of energy to keep their systems functioning. In the end, they spend more time and resources managing themselves, rather than trying to manage their customers and to manage the innovation that they need to survive. As a result, their systems lose energy, entropy (disorder) sets in and the company dies. There are examples enough: we all know what happened to Kodak, Nokia and BlackBerry (providing we were born in the last century).

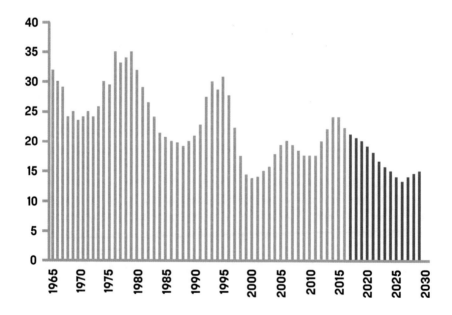

Figure 1 – *The average lifespan of organisations is decreasing.* SOURCE: INNOSIGHT

By the time the 1980s arrived, average organisational life expectancy had fallen to 35 years. The perpetual motion effect still seemed to be working and not even the oil crisis of 1974, the first major economic crisis since the Second World War, had any immediate impact. The same could not be said, however, for the rapid progress being made in the field of information and communication technology – ICT as it was then known. This was the period that saw the breakthrough of the personal computer: the Apple Macintosh was launched in 1984 and Windows 1.0 in 1985. By this latter year, average longevity had dropped to 20 years. The dot.com crisis of 2000 caused the downfall of a further swathe of companies, including some from the new economy, such as AltaVista, Wang and Compaq. By 2010, average life expectancy was hovering around 17 years. By 2030, this is expected to decrease still further, to around 10 to 12 years.

Of all the companies that were listed in the Fortune 500 six decades ago, only 52 can still be found in the list today. The remaining 448 no longer exist: they were either too small, or too large (so that they needed to be sliced up), or were simply pushed out of the market by disruptive business models that made them superfluous.

MATAMA on cloud nine

If the changing composition of the top 500 companies speaks volumes, so too does the changing composition of the top five.

Immediately after the dot.com crisis, the world's largest companies came from the 'classic' sectors: banking, retail and consumer goods. There was just a single oil company, Exxon, and a single IT company, Microsoft, which had what amounted to a software monopoly in home and office computing. The combined stock market value of the top five amounted to roughly 300 billion dollars.

For the first five years of the new century there was very little change. A second oil company, Total, pushed its way into the list, since the re-emerging economy was crying out for oil as it sought to recover from the dot.com debacle. Whereas huge amounts of risk capital had been pumped into the software industry in the run-up to 2000, following the crash this investment largely dried up. It was once again the classic economic motor, driven by oil, that was the main focus

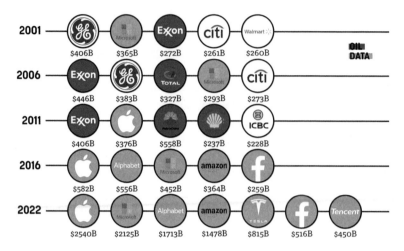

2001	GE	Microsoft	Exxon	citi	Walmart		OIL DATA
	$406B	$365B	$272B	$261B	$260B		
2006	Exxon	GE	TOTAL	Microsoft	citi		
	$446B	$383B	$327B	$293B	$273B		
2011	Exxon	Apple	PetroChina	Shell	ICBC		
	$406B	$376B	$558B	$237B	$228B		
2016	Apple	Alphabet	Microsoft	amazon	f		
	$582B	$556B	$452B	$364B	$259B		
2022	Apple	Microsoft	Alphabet	amazon	Tesla	f	Tencent
	$2540B	$2125B	$1713B	$1478B	$815B	$516B	$450B

Figure 2 – As of 2016, data companies dominated the top 5 largest companies in the world.
SOURCE: YAHOO FINANCE

of attention, with the banks lending heavily to the construction and manufacturing sectors.

By 2011, the hegemony of the oil companies had been strengthened still further, with the addition of Shell to the top five. The banking crisis of 2008 hit financial institutions like Citibank very hard, while the shale oil and gas extraction of the energy giants once again fuelled economic recovery. Even so, the first signs of what was to come were starting to be seen. Thanks to the massive success of the iPhone (2007) and the iPad (2010), Apple effectively created a new economic reality that allowed it to burst into the top five at the expense of Microsoft, which at that time was seeking to rediscover itself. The reaction of Microsoft top man Steve Ballmer when he first learnt about the iPhone has become the stuff of business legend: "What? 500 dollars for a phone that doesn't even have a keyboard? Who the hell is going to buy that?" The answer was... everyone! Underestimating the iPhone and failing to recognise that the PC era was coming to a close almost proved fatal to the company.

By 2016, Microsoft was back on track and back in the top five – and the recent Covid-19 pandemic has helped the communication and data-based companies to tighten their stranglehold over the business world even more. Satya Nadella, one of Ballmer's successors as CEO of Microsoft, said of this period: "We saw two years of digital transformation in just two months." The pandemic has indeed given the tech industry wings. As a result, the proportion of the total value of the S&P 500 contributed by Microsoft, Apple, Amazon, Mega and Alphabet has increased from 17.5% to 22%. In October 2021, Tesla also broke through the magical 1,000-billion-dollar mark, so that MATAMA was born. This sextet now represents half of the value of the 50 largest companies in the United States. Tech is now dominating all other rival industries, but internecine rivalry among the tech companies themselves is also starting to increase: competing cloud services, video conference tools, lower margins in the app stores, etc. Apple is focusing more on customer privacy, so that Facebook and Google are earning less revenue from data analysis, while new players like Snap, Zoom and TikTok are knocking ever more loudly on the door. In short, after two years of Covid-19 the tech industry is more cloud-based, more hardware-based (sensors, chips, etc.) and, above all, more turbulent and more aggressive. Fascinating times!

The radical change in our daily lives...

 If you are now in your mid-fifties, there is a good chance that back in 1992 your average day might have looked something like this:

6.30 a.m. The alarm clock rings. Today is an important day. I have a meeting with one of our major customers in a town 70 kilometres from here. Yesterday, I printed off directions using Microsoft Autoroute, which I bought recently on a CD-ROM. It's really useful. I've just got time for a cup of coffee before I leave. Damn, my answering machine is flashing. Who is it? Ah, it's John, one of my friends, and he has left a message: "Fancy going to a concert this evening? Give me a call." I quickly dial his number, but he doesn't pick up. I'll try again later, but now I really have to get going, because I don't want to be late! With luck, there won't be too much traffic on the roads. And hopefully my bloody car will start: the battery is always a bit dodgy in freezing weather. Okay: lights off, heating off, door closed, door locked. Ready to go! I'll have to stop somewhere for petrol; I forgot that the tank is nearly empty. Fortunately, there is a petrol station on the motorway. I stop, get out and fill the tank. God, it's cold this morning! Quickly into the shop to pay at the cash desk and then I am on my way again. The traffic slows down, slows down some more and then stops. We sit there for half an hour. What on earth has happened? To find out, I have to wait for the traffic summary on the radio after the 8 o'clock news. "It a busy morning on the roads, with

300 kilometres of tailbacks and a serious accident on the E40 motorway." On no, that's my motorway! Never mind: it is what it is. By the time I arrive at the customer's office, I am 15 minutes late. Thankfully, I can see a parking space not far from the main entrance. I press the intercom next to the car park barrier and the receptionist lets me in. I rush upstairs and find that everyone is already waiting for me in the meeting room. "Good morning, ladies and gentlemen. Sorry I'm late!" I quickly hand out my business cards and pull my presentation discs from my briefcase. Next problem: there is no suitable PC for playing my discs in the meeting room! It's just as well that I printed off a few hard copies last night. I pass them around, so that people can share them and follow what I am saying.

Happily, things go well and they decide that they are interested in working with our company. They will draw up a contract and send it to me by post. Once I have read and approved it, I will add my signature and send it back to them by fax, so that they can also sign it and then fax a duplicate copy back to me. Just another two weeks and we should be able to start our col- laboration! By now, it is already late in the afternoon. Time to call it a day. The receptionist gives me a token to open the car park barrier and I set off for home. I think I know the route by heart, until I suddenly see an orange 'diversion' signboard blocking the road. I keep following the orange boards, but fifteen minutes later I find myself back at the point where I started! I try a different direction and eventually get myself back on the right road. Sud- denly, I remember that I need to phone John about the concert. Can I find a telephone box somewhere? Good, there is one over there on the corner. I park the car. But have I got some coins? Again, I am in luck. "Hello, John? Thank goodness I've caught you at home. Are we still on for the concert to- night? Yes, I'd love to go. And you? Great! Have you got tickets already? No? Okay, I'll call in at the Fnac on my way home. I should get them there."

When I arrive, the Fnac is still open, but there is a long row of 20 people waiting for tickets. "Patience," I tell myself, "patience." At last, it is my turn and they still have two tickets. Hooray! I phone John from the pay phone outside to let him know, but he doesn't answer so I leave a message on his answering machine. Hopefully, he will hear it in time. As I open my car, I see a piece of paper under the windscreen wiper. Oh no, a parking ticket! I forgot to display my parking disc! Blast! No time to worry about that now. I get in the car and make the 30-minute drive to John's apartment. By now, it is 7 o'clock. We have a quick bite to eat and then set off to the concert hall. It can be pretty busy, so we want to get there early. We queue up for 15 minutes and then we are inside. But here we find another queue, this time for drink vouchers. "Have you got some cash, John? I'm all out." I'll get some money from the cash dispenser later on, so that I can pay him back. The concert starts. Great group, with great new numbers. Afterwards, I decide to buy one of their CDs. In the foyer we bump into one of John's neighbours, who has a really cool girl with him. I really like her but we don't have much time to talk, because I still have a long drive home. It's a shame I didn't ask for her number. Maybe John can get it for me next week? I arrive home. It is cold, but it doesn't matter, because I am going straight to bed, anyway. I have to be up early again in the morning to take my car into the garage for its three-monthly maintenance check. I hope they give me a replacement. Nighty night, sleep tight!

If you were 25 years old in 1992, this might well have been an average working day. But if you were born in 1997, so you are now 25 years old, your average working day will probably look more like this:

6.00 a.m. My alarm clock slowly increases the amount of light in my bedroom. It is earlier than I had planned, but my connection with Waze has let me know that there is heavy traffic on my route. I will have to leave by 7 o'clock at the latest, if I want to arrive at the customer's place on time. The bathroom and the kitchen are deliciously warm, because my smart thermostat knew I would be getting up. My electric car will have fully charged itself during the night, using the stored solar energy in my home battery, and it will warm itself up before I set off. The auto-pilot will take over the driving as soon as we reach the motorway, because it already knows where it needs to go. My favourite Spotify list – the same one that is on my alarm clock and home hub – is now playing in the car. I check the time on my smartwatch, which will count my steps and the calories I burn throughout the day, as well as checking my heart rate. A new message from my friend John comes in on the watch, asking me if I am interested in going to a concert this evening. I use the phone to speak to him and tell him that I would love to go. The rendezvous is noted automatically in my diary. With a click on the link in John's message, the tickets are automatically purchased, paid for and stored in our respective wallets. While the car is held up by traffic, I use LinkedIn to check on the people I will see in the meeting. It is always interesting to have a quick look at the CVs of the people you will be dealing with.

Yes, I know, you are not supposed to take your hands off the wheel when you are driving, even with the auto-pilot, and certainly not to use your apps, but everybody does it. I arrive at the customer's premises exactly on time. I sent them the number of my car in advance, so that I am immediately recognised and the car park barrier opens automatically. After the usual introductions, I give my wireless multimedia presentation on a large screen, using my smartphone and the cloud. The meeting goes well and they want to do business with us! We download and amend a standard contract, which we then validate with facial recognition. Our collaboration starts tomorrow! During my journey home, I hear in a podcast that a new book by Harari is now available, so I ask my Google assistant to read something from it. The assistant hires the e-book and seconds later the voice text booms through my car speakers. As our batteries are getting low, the car automatically turns off the motorway to find a fast-charger where it knows that a space will be available. I can charge up for free, because I gave my referral code to a friend who bought the same brand of EV. After 20 minutes the batteries will be full again, which leaves me just enough time to finish looking at the Netflix film I started last night. My car delivers me to a free parking space near John's apartment, but my smartwatch tells me that I haven't really had enough exercise today and suggests a little sporting activity before the concert. I can see that the same applies to John, since we share our exercise data as a way to encourage and motivate each other. We agree to go for a 20-minute jog in the park, resulting in plenty of 'kudos' from my other online sporting friends. After a shower and a bite to eat, we set off to the concert hall. The tickets appear automatically on our smartwatch, so that we can walk straight into the auditorium and take up our reserved places. The concert starts.

My Shazam function recognises all the songs and automatically stores them in a new playlist with the title 'concert with John', so that I can listen to them again on my way home. At the bar after the concert, we bump into one of John's neighbours, Gerry, together with one of his friends, a great girl called Inga. It's a shame there wasn't much time to get to know her, but I still have a long drive ahead of me. When I arrive at my house, the garage door opens automatically and the lighting turns itself on. Inside, the virtual assistant has already warmed up the bathroom, so that I can take another shower in comfort before I climb into bed. I keep on thinking about Inga. She was a really nice girl and it was dumb of me not to ask for her contact details... Wait a minute! I once contacted Gerry by Facebook. Maybe if I check his list of friends...? Yes, there she is, Inga! I send her a friend request. Let's hope she gives me a thumbs up! Before going to sleep, I decide to check on my Tinder account. Bummer, no matches today. Might Inga be on Tinder as well? Yep, I've found her! Swipe 'yes'. Seconds later, I get a match! Inge again. So it wasn't just me who was impressed! Super! I'll get in touch with her tomorrow, so that we can plan to meet again. A great end to a great day!

Go on, admit it! For many of us, this is how some of our days look now. Technology plays a far greater role in our life than we sometimes realise. In this respect, the difference between 1995 and today can be summed up in just two words: 'radical change'. Behind every step in the contrasting scenarios given above, there is a fundamentally different product, service and business model, provided by a company or official authority that needs to organise itself in a completely different way from 25 years ago to make this possible.

NEW

Google (1998)

P PayPal (1998)

TESLA (2003)

Spotify (2006)

TikTok (2012)

(2013)

Figure 3 – Most globally dominant companies have emerged recently

DISAPPEARED

KODAK (2012)

NOKIA (2013)

RadioShack. (2015)

Sears Good life. Great price. (2018)

ToysЯus (2018)

Figure 4 – Even well-known, robust companies are disappearing because of the rapid change.

Look at the biggest newcomers who have appeared in the top indexes during the past 25 years. Many of them did not even exist when we first started the House of the Future: eBay was founded in 1995, Netflix in 1997, Google in 1998, PayPal in 2000, Tesla in 2003, Facebook in 2004.

Only Amazon was already in business, but only just: it was set up in 1994. At first, Jeff Bezos and his small team ran an online bookstore from his garage and organised business meetings in Barnes & Noble's outlets. Every time something sold well, Bezos noted what it was, where it was, why it was and how it was. The first great explosion of sales came during the Christmas period in 1998. The company soon realised that it was seriously undermanned and took on numerous seasonal workers to make good the shortfall, which is something that it still does today. Other online packaging services soon followed, and the rest, as they say, is history. Europe later followed the successful online Amazon approach, resulting in a new series of internet giants, such as Zalando and Spotify, founded in 2008.

The pathway leading to a billion-dollar company has also radically changed...

One thing is crystal-clear: the business models of the 'new' top companies are also radically different from the business models of their 'old' predecessors. These new models are not only based on new technologies (internet and data), but are also extremely customer-centric.

In 1989, Queen already knew what the future would bring: "I want it all and I want it now."

What a contrast with the companies of yesteryear

During the past quarter of a century, many companies have disappeared out of the S&P 500 for a variety of reasons, but primarily because they failed or were too slow to react to the changing circumstances in their environment. Consider, for example, the case of Blockbuster, which has gone out of business and been replaced by Netflix. Or Nokia replaced by Apple. Or Barnes & Noble replaced by Amazon.

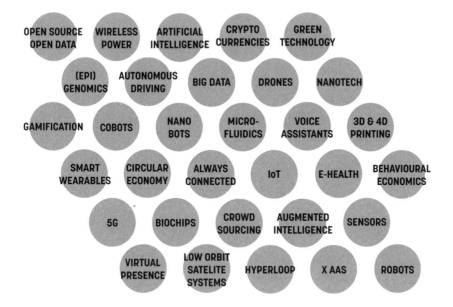

Figure 5 – *Technology is driving the accelerating change*

Driven by the technological revolution

In 1995, hardly anyone was using the internet to go online and 'surf the web'. I can still remember the first basic ICQ chat sessions at a virtual table. The ICQ channel #antwerpen was very popular in Belgium and was the most widely used forum. In the mid-1990s, some of the users occasionally used to meet in the physical world at a pub in the centre of Antwerp. Just imagine: internet buddies who actually met in person! In the year 2000, just 7% of the world population had access to the internet. Today that figure has risen to 60%, with 90% of these connections being by smartphone. At the time of writing, there are some 6 billion smartphones in the world, which is almost as many as the number of people. The greatest level of penetration (97%) is in Northern Europe. The time spent on using online devices has risen to an average of 6 hours per day. Worldwide, one out of every three people uses Facebook, while one in six is on WhatsApp and one in seven, on Instagram. In October 2021, these three platforms shut down for a period of six hours. Communication throughout the world ground to a halt. The value of Facebook shares immediately fell by 5%, meaning that Zuckerberg (virtually) lost something like 6 billion dollars of his personal wealth in a matter of minutes. These figures illustrate the extent to which connected technology has changed our world since the dot. com crisis. Nowadays, we are, all online beings, who are actively connected for six hours a day, which is more than a third of our waking life. And this only refers to the time we spend on the internet and mobile communication devices. Every few months a new piece of technological wizardry is launched, each of which has the potential to initiate a paradigm shift in our daily existence. These new tech phenomena do not necessarily need to be spectacular. Sometimes they can be simple and easy to implement, so that they can quickly create a shock effect.

The many changes in our society have been – and are still being – accelerated by technology. It is impossible to be an expert in each of these domains. In this respect, it is always an interesting exercise to sit around a table with your organisation's leadership and assess which technologies play an important role in your business today, which ones will play an important role tomorrow, and what you intend to do about it.

Some of the future developments that you certainly need to keep an eye on in the coming decade are the developments that the richest people in the world and their organisations already have in their sights: the metaverse, space tourism, low-orbit satellite communication, humanoid robots, self-driving vehicles, life expectancy-enhancing innovations, meat substitutes and cultivated meat, quantum computing, brain-computer interfaces, cryptocurrencies, NFTs (non-fungible tokens) ... In fact, enough to write a separate book about! If we think that recent technological innovations have already fundamentally changed our lives and our societies, wait until the full effect of these new innovations is felt. Our world will change beyond all recognition.

In a nutshell

In this chapter, I have described how the speed of technological change and the creative destruction it initiates continue to have an ever-increasing impact on everything and everyone. One of the knock-on effects is that the average life expectancy of organisations has been drastically reduced, with established players being driven out of business by new names, who quickly grow to become billion-dollar organisations.

Now that I have explained *why* innovation is so important, it is time to look at the core of what innovation involves.

2
WHAT IS INNOVATION?

In the previous chapter, I primarily looked back at the past and examined the major change phenomena that had taken place in recent times: the innovation revolutions. We saw that these were the result of both product-based and technology-based innovations (driven by new inventions), process innovations (driven by new ways to do things faster and more efficiently), and business-model innovations (often driven by changes in human needs and expectations). We saw that business-model innovations above all played a key role in the final waves of innovation, whereas technological innovations tended to generate major shock effects during the earlier innovation waves.

In other words, innovation in one form or another was a recurring theme, and therefore one that deserves to be looked at in more detail. Moreover, it is a crucial term for defining what is meant by future progress. Innovation can mean different things in different contexts. New companies often venture into unexplored territory; for existing organisations, innovation is a way to ensure that they remain relevant.

A definition

Innovation is concerned with the exploration of new ideas that result in the creation of successful products, services, processes or profitable business models.

In my opinion, this is the most complete definition. 'New ideas' is a term that covers a very broad area, embracing, amongst other things, products, services, methods of working, partnerships and profit models. The word 'successful' is crucial to the definition, because innovation is only worth that name if it creates economic, ecological and/or social added value. Of course, I often hear other definitions of innovation. For that reason, I would also like to make clear what innovation is not.

Innovation is not the same as creativity

This is one of the most serious misunderstandings: namely, that if you are creative, you will also innovate. This is the wrong way of looking at things.

Innovation is not the same as inventing

Innovation is often measured on the basis of intellectual property (IP). In other words, the number of patents and copyrights held by your organisation. Is this a good yardstick for innovation? No, it is not. An extensive IP portfolio simply proves that an organisation is inventive, but not all inventions are successful. Some organisations almost seem to make a sport out of collecting patents and then seek to exploit this through the marketing of their rights (patent royalties) or through their protection (patent fencing). That being said, the real value of intellectual property is something that is being increasingly questioned in our rapidly evolving technological world. There are hundreds of R&D laboratories around the world full of patented inventions that are gathering dust. Maintaining a patent portfolio is one thing; the necessary follow-up and market exploitation is extremely expensive and labour intensive.

Of course, I understand why knowledge institutions continue to register their inventions: part of their income is derived from technology transfer. Their fundamental research is translated into market applications, for which they need to be recompensed, not in the least because public funding for this kind of research, which was once so readily available, is now in short supply.

Innovation is not the same as book wisdom or procedural methodology

There is no shortage of innovation principles: lean start-up, blue/red ocean, studio venturing, outcome-driven innovation, etc., etc. These principles encourage you to seek further insights and give you the energy and passion to start something new. Yet when all is said and done, they are still no more than tools. They are not objectives.

The innovation cycle of an organisation

It often happens that organisations adopt a protectionist approach in an effort to try to preserve their competitive advantage. They only innovate within the scope of their familiar activities. Because an innovation trajectory always follows the pattern of a learning curve, such organisations frequently end up repeating what they know and what they can do. This explains why new 'outsiders' often display a higher degree of innovation than established names. Do you remember the mRNA story I mentioned earlier?

The change cycle usually passes through three main phases, which are all related to understanding the needs of consumers and creating a dominant design, as a result of which a single player becomes the 'winner-takes-all' in a particular market. In the course of these three phases, the organisation will change tack between product/service innovations and process innovation.

The development of an innovation starts with a fluid phase, during which numerous prototypes are made. At this stage, the true needs and wishes of the

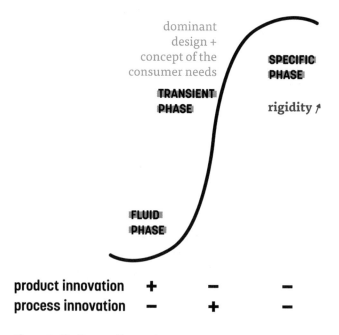

Figure 6 – *The S-curve of innovation.* SOURCE: ABERNATHY & UTTERBACK, TECHNOLOGY REVIEW, 1978

end-user are not yet fully understood, so a process of trial-and-error and/or other flexible methods are used to refine the design as perfectly as possible. This phase is characterised by a rapid succession of product versions. In the past, these were often named alpha, beta, etc. or RTM (ready-to-manufacture) 1, 2, etc. Today, it is more common to talk of an MVP (minimum viable product). The prototype will generally be not quite good enough to allow the testing of its basic functionalities with the public in real-world conditions. In this phase, little attention is devoted to process innovation. Instead, organisations work in a series of short sprints with a BML (build-measure-learn) method, such as Eric Ries' Lean Start-up. There are, however, a number of potential pitfalls to this approach, which I will return to later.

The second phase is known as the transient phase. During this phase, repeated tests are carried out, leading to a product or service that is ready to be brought to market. By now, the organisation fully understands its customers' needs and uses these insights to create what it hopes will be a dominant design. If it can do this successfully, there is a good chance that the organisation will be able to conquer the entire market, thanks to first-mover advantage. Other market rivals react too slowly and are unable to follow. They have less knowledge about the consumer/end-user and are less able to develop new and better prototypes with the necessary speed. For organisations that are able to develop a dominant design, the interest in new product development subsequently starts to decrease. Instead, the focus shifts to the protection of profit margins. As a result, this automatically leads to more attention to operational excellence and process innovation.

This applies not only to production companies, but also to platform models that provide online services, where the network effect plays a role in this phase. Think, for example, of Facebook, a company where more users mean more value. Once again, the 'winner-takes-all' principle holds good, because you are competing worldwide and only one organisation can be the biggest and the best. This explains why, after nine years of spectacular growth, the most successful Dutch social network site, Hyves, was finally forced out of the market in 2013 by Facebook. There is, however, a caveat that needs to be borne in mind with regard to the 'winner-takes-all' principle; namely, the increasing importance of local network effects that deviate from the 'more is better' principle. In this case, it is the quality provided by the local network that is key. Uber and Airbnb are classic examples. There is no point in attracting a hundred million extra users to their platforms if there are not enough local Uber drivers or

Airbnb accommodation outlets to service these users. Adjusting the process to match the right user needs is the main consideration.

The third phase of innovation is the specific phase, which is typified by a low level of both product innovation and process innovation. The company that has the dominant design reacts rigidly to change and seeks to maintain its dominant position. The outcome of the Future Fitness Formula – which we will look at more closely later in the book – is very low, in part because the need for speed and agility has declined, and in part (and often primarily) because their teams have acquired a huge amount of experience (5, 10, 20 years) and therefore have a tendency to block new ideas along the lines of 'been there, done that'. This automatically leads to reduced interest in genuinely new ideas. As a result, important new opportunities are missed, which may signal the start of the organisation's decline. Once again, the mRNA story is a good case in point, but the same can also be seen in numerous other sectors, including electric vehicles, novel foods (for example, cultivated meat), banking and digital wallets.

Hence the importance of Schumpter's 'creative destruction' theory: to ensure survival, old assumptions need to be eradicated, so that they can be replaced by new ways of thinking and a new approach. This means that in this phase organisations need to look beyond their current market and activities.

The major waves of innovation

Economic growth and technological innovation have always been closely related to each other. The changes that they have created over the centuries tended to come in waves, which we refer to as waves of innovation. These waves were marked by important breakthroughs in terms of efficiency, new products and services, and globalisation. Throughout history, they have formed the basis for huge paradigm shifts in the social, economic, technological and (also often) political fields of human endeavour. If we want to look forward meaningfully to the future, it is necessary to understand the past and to observe the changes that change itself has undergone. In this way, for example, each new age of innovation has been fired by a different 'fuel' (from wood through coal, oil and electricity to hydrogen) and facilitated by new forms of transport (boat, train, plane, ICT, etc.) that ensured the rapid distribution of new products and services. Innovations in the field of medicine were also made possible thanks to new accelerators; from medicinal herbs, through fungi (like penicillin), chemical substances (chemotherapy) and radiology to the more recent advances of mRNA or CRISPR. Before we turn our attention to the present and the future, it may be useful to look briefly these major waves of innovation in the past.

The first wave of innovation: the first industrial revolution (1785 – 1845)

The first industrial revolution came about following the use of wood and water power to process textiles and iron. The looms in the cotton mills were mechanised and the iron foundries were industrialised. In the first instance, production was concentrated on the things that people needed on a daily basis, such as clothes and tools. Innovations in transport were achieved through perfecting the performance of sailing ships and improvements in the conservation of food, which made longer voyages possible. As a result, the costs of both production and transport (import/export) fell rapidly. Above all, it was the European countries that profited from this revolution, allowing some of them – the United Kingdom, the Netherlands, Spain and France – to acquire worldwide empires.

The second wave of innovation: the age of steam (1830 – 1900)

The mining of coal as a new source of energy made possible the emergence of the steam engine. This in turn made possible the development of a new and fast means of transport: the steam train. Railways were built on a massive scale, opening up new markets to a wider range of products making use of the improved supply of raw materials. The steam ship eliminated reliance on the wind and slashed the time necessary for maritime transport. Mass production began to appear, primarily for foodstuffs, cotton goods and clothing. This led to a rapid fall in prices that increased the general level of prosperity.

The third wave of innovation: the age of electricity (1880 – 1960)

The discovery and exploitation of electricity changed the world forever. Electric motors, dynamos and turbines powered countless new machines, new applications and a new generation of trains and trams. The development of the combustion engine led to a new boom in the mobility of goods and people, on land, at sea and in the air. Radio, television and the electric printing press offered new promotional channels, which gave a massive boost to the demand for products. At the same time, new and more efficient methods of production were developed, resulting in the dramatic lowering of prices, thereby laying the foundations for the next wave of innovation.

The second and third waves of innovation are generally known as the second industrial revolution.

The fourth wave of innovation: mass production (1950 – 1990)

Oil played a crucial role in increasing the scale and scope of mass production. After the Second World War, new and experimental materials were derived from the petrochemical industry. Thanks to the development of plastics and other electrochemical inventions (tube lamps, transistors, etc.), the electronics industry came into being. Oil used as a fuel helped to speed up the process of globalisation by making long-distance air travel quick, reliable and affordable. The number of trains and motor vehicles increased exponentially. Assembly lines made possible the production of cars and consumption goods on a gigantic scale never previously seen at increasingly lower prices. Electronics and the need for greater worldwide contact paved the way for the start of the fifth wave of innovation.

The fifth wave of innovation: the age of information and communication (1980 – present day)

The development of new information systems not only generated new forms of communication, but also made the organisation of production and distribution far more efficient. Data and information were now raw materials. The new means of transportation for these materials was the internet. New industries emerged as a result of the miniaturisation of the professional computer into the personal computer. This was followed by the digitalisation of internal processes. The internet brought the world into people's homes. Greater digitalisation and greater connectivity also had huge benefits for the business world, allowing the efficient maximisation of profits. The software industry became the fastest growing sector, along with internet companies that provided for worldwide communication and e-commerce platforms.

The fourth and fifth waves of innovation are generally known as the third industrial revolution.

Are we standing on another new threshold today? A double threshold of the sixth wave of innovation, which will herald the fourth industrial revolution? Yes, we probably are. But before we look at this prospect, I would first like to say something more about the current fifth wave of innovation.

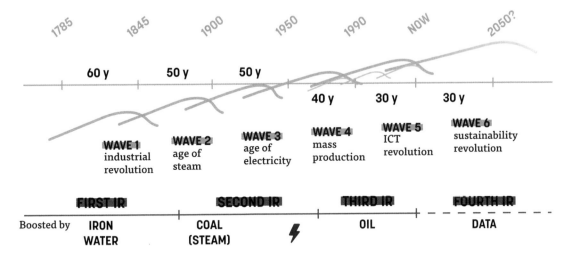

Figure 7 – *Total overview of all innovation waves.*

The previously mentioned research by Innosight into organisational longevity and dominant design focused primarily on the experiences of companies during this fifth wave, the ICT wave. This wave is still very much in progress and, in my opinion, actually consists of three sub-waves, the third of which is now starting to unfold. I call these waves the three IT waves, which have brought about far-reaching change to industry, organisations and their products and services. In turn, this change has digitalised and increasingly connected society, transforming its nature completely.

The 3 IT sub-waves of the fifth wave of innovation: the ICT revolution

It is noteworthy that the pivotal moments in the fifth wave – excluding the dot. com crisis in 2000 and the financial crisis in 2008 – coincided with the first two IT sub-waves. The third IT sub-wave will also have a dramatic effect on the life expectancy of large organisations, including some of today's leading names, like Facebook, Apple, Amazon and Google.

The first IT sub-wave (1975 – 1995): the digitalisation of internal processes
Large mainframes were replaced by mini-computers, which in turn made way for the personal computer. Soon, every desk had its own PC, which was able to communicate with other PCs via a network connection. This signalled the end

for written communication and the traditional typewriter. At the same time, internal processes became increasingly digitalised, making possible more efficient SCL (supply chain and logistics). This not only meant that raw materials and semi-finished products could now be delivered to the right production facilities in the shortest possible time, but also that finished products could be delivered with equal speed and cheapness to the end-user. MRP (material requirements planning) improved dramatically during the 1970s and 1980s. The demand for raw materials grew exponentially, and this needed to be accurately planned and monitored. This improvement in turn led to the emergence of ERP (enterprise resource planning), which looked beyond materials alone and also considered matters such as timing and bottlenecks in the machine park and transport. During the 1990s, the widespread fear that existing systems might not be able to cope with the transition to the new millennium resulted in the large majority of these systems being upgraded to APS (advanced planning and scheduling) software, which now linked internal processes to the outside world of suppliers, customers and co-producers. The JIT (just-in-time) principle was applied rigorously to reduce the costs associated with storing goods unnecessarily, which created a huge explosion in freight traffic.

Figure 8 – The mini-computer set the IT subwaves in motion, the IT revolution was a fact.

The introduction of ERP (enterprise resource planning) and the arrival of CNC (computer numerical control) machines made the planning and production processes in organisations much easier. It took much less energy to achieve the same level of excellence. However, this came as a great shock to many companies, which were taken by surprise. The companies that reacted quickly were able to adjust to the new reality easily, which increased their efficiency and allowed them to stand head and shoulders above the companies that attempted to persist with their old and cumbersome systems. This was well illustrated by a now legendary promotional film that was launched by Apple at the time, which contrasted the stolid, grey IBM computer with its playful and colourful Apple counterpart. In the offices where IBMs were used, the film showed lights burning until late into the evening, while the offices where Macs were used were shrouded in darkness, because people had already finished work and gone home. An exaggeration, of course, but it really hit the mark – and it perfectly encapsulates the significance of the first IT-wave: the old heavyweight champions being outmanoeuvred by new, faster, more creative and more flexible challengers. Many organisations wasted huge amounts of energy by trying to survive without embracing this progress, but they were doomed to failure and gradually disappeared from the radar, one by one. Consider, for example, the fate of Wang Laboratories. Founded in 1951 and focusing primarily on personal computers with word-processing, by the 1980s it had achieved a turnover of some 3 billion dollars and employed 33,000 people. However, the company failed to make the transition to general purpose PCs, which were much more cost efficient, so that Wang eventually went bankrupt in 1992.

Another example? PanAm was the largest airline company in the United States. It was a company well known for its willingness to innovate. They invented air traffic control, flight procedures, weather control, etc., and were also the first to take flying boats and jet liners into service, including the iconic Boeing 707. Likewise, PanAm was first to introduce both economy class and a worldwide network of destinations. In 1970, they carried no fewer than 11 million passengers and were the undisputed number one in the aviation sector. But then, in 1974, the oil crisis struck. The price of kerosene increased by 400%, so that the market for long-distance flights collapsed. New cost-efficient companies specialised in domestic flights and investing heavily in automation began to emerge. PanAm tried to rival them but found it difficult to reconcile its self-created image as a national flagship airline, famed for its focus on grandeur, service and old-world luxury, with the new need to economise and automate. As a result, it began to fall behind its competitors. The final nail in the coffin was the Lockerbie disaster. On 21 December 1998, a bomb exploded on board PanAm flight 103 as it flew over the Scottish village of Lockerbie. All 259 passengers and crew were killed, along with 11 villagers on the ground. This was a human tragedy but also an economic catastrophe for the company. It was charged with negligence for failing to invest sufficiently in security and digitalisation for the screening of its passengers and was eventually obliged to pay a 350 million dollar fine. It was the beginning of the end for what had once been the most powerful airline in the world. PanAm finally went bust in 1991.

The second IT sub-wave (1995 - 2007): digitalisation of external transactions

The second IT sub-wave was set in motion by the internet; more particularly, by the world wide web. As a result, this period was characterised primarily by external communication. The availability of public internet from 1991 onwards ushered in the next wave of innovation. Internet systems were now connected with external partners like customers, suppliers and accountants. This was the new age of CRM (customer relationship management). Suddenly, everything became more efficient than it had ever been before. The days of ordering by fax and manually following up logistical processes were gone. JIT (just-in-time) delivery reached new levels of sophistication. The internet took on the role that had been played by the internal network in the first IT phase and the worldwide TCP/IP protocol provided both a standard and a solid base for its operations. After the year 2000, this second phase developed further in the di-

Figure 9 – *The second ICT subwave was characterised by the internet, everything was connected.*

rection of social communication, which saw the appearance of the first social media, which made possible the large-scale grouping of customers in powerful platforms. New companies like Amazon, Google and Facebook emerged, using the new technology to bind customers in a completely different way. And so the online platform model was born, in which the amount of collected information about customers helped to determine the value of the system: the more customers who used the platform, the more valuable it became.

Once again, many companies were left behind by these evolutions. Some failed to innovate sufficiently; others missed the train completely. This created a gulf between the 'haves' and the 'have nots'. Those who failed to surf on this second IT sub-wave were briefly able to hold their head above water, but not for long. A well-known example is Blockbuster, which completely misjudged the 'internetisation' of video. In 2000, the company had the option to buy Netflix for just 50 million dollars, but did not believe that the internet would play an important role in the video world. They were convinced that their model was perfectly constructed and 100% safe against cannibalisation. They were wrong. Blockbuster no longer exists and Netflix is currently worth 230 billion dollars or 5,600 times more than it could have been bought for in 2000. Talk about a missed opportunity...

The third IT sub-wave (2007 -): the internet of people and things, always connected
We are currently in the third IT sub-wave of the fifth wave of innovation, which will soon open the door to a new sixth wave of innovation: the age of sustainability (more about this later). This third sub-wave is typified by products like the iPhone and the Tesla. These were products that were totally different from anything that had gone before and were initially thought to be inferior to their rivals. Many competitors actually laughed at them. Do you remember the comments about the iPhone made by Microsoft CEO, Steve Ballmer, which I mentioned earlier?

Thanks to a series of updates, the quality and performance of the iPhone quickly improved. Later, the same was also true of Tesla cars. Faults were filtered out in a manner and at a speed that their rivals could not follow. In terms of ease of use, the new products increasingly matched what customers wanted. As a result, they became the dominant design and the 'winner-takes-all' in their sectors. The enormous quantities of data that were collected and analysed during this process gave Apple and Tesla very clear insights into what was right and what was wrong about their products; what could be improved still further and what needed to be eliminated. This gave them a huge competitive advantage. It was the first time during the period of the IT sub-waves – in fact, the first time during any of the innovation revolutions – that immediate feedback could be given directly from the users to the designers, the R&D teams and the production managers. Data was the new holy grail. Its importance cannot be underestimated. It made (and makes) possible things that were never possible before.

Nowadays, if Tesla becomes aware of a particular problem, a solution is sent via an over-the-air update to all its cars on the road. At the same time, new features are constantly being added, some of which are more necessary (an auto-pilot or a signal if you leave a window/door open, or a dashcam that automatically records what is happening if you sound your horn) than others (new games on Netflix to make your wait during supercharging more pleasant). Customers seem to like this kind of thing and they are happy to provide Tesla with gigabytes and gigabytes of feedback. The company then processes this mass of data with AI to develop new improvements and guidelines that are transmitted directly from the design department to the products already in operation with the end-users. In this way, the system remains constantly up to date, a continually improving version of itself.

One of the classic examples of this process in operation occurred at the end of 2013. One of the first Tesla S models burst into flames after a collision on a motorway. Tesla examined the data it received from the car's sensors, battery pack and cameras. It was established that a fire could be started in the battery pack when the base plate is impacted at high speed and/or damaged through contact with the road surface or other debris. At this time, the batteries were positioned under and not above the base plate. This could be made safer by raising the position of the batteries by just a few centimetres to give better ground clearance. If a 'normal' car brand was faced with this kind of problem, its correction would involve a huge and expensive operation that necessitated the call-back and the mechanical adjustment of each individual car. But not with Tesla. From one day to the next all its S models were automatically raised by the necessary centimetres using the car's pneumatic suspension system, thereby eliminating both the possibility of contact with the road or debris and the possibility of fire. At the same time, all new Tesla models were fitted with a three-layered bottom plate in titanium under the batteries as an additional safety feature, while the owners of existing vehicles could ask to have the plate

fitted the next time their car was in the garage for routine maintenance.* The
cost that this saved Tesla in relation to other companies that do not innovate in
the same way is what I refer to as 'the cost of not innovating' – which is something we will return to in a later chapter.

In previous waves of innovation, R&D was strictly separated from production
and marketing. The finished product was launched onto the market – often
with huge amounts of advertising and promotion – and feedback was obtained
from consumers through the extensive use of questionnaires and market research. In the past, it was commonplace to receive phone calls from car brands
to ask how satisfied you were with your vehicles, its servicing, etc. These were
golden times for market research bureaus, which attempted to identify customer needs so that the next generation of products could be improved before
being brought to market.

Not any longer, of course. Nowadays, this all happens in real time. Almost
every component in a Tesla is linked to intelligent networks in Tesla's headquarters, where artificial intelligence makes use of this mass of data to make
these components smarter and more performant, also in real time. This is the
crucial difference between Tesla and other car manufacturers. It is also the
reason why Tesla attaches less importance to the four-yearly updating of its
cars, which has been the practice of the classic car brands for decades. Tesla
prefers to implement incremental upgrades as soon as they become available.
The extending of this same principle to other sectors explains why some new
generation products now only need to be 'good enough' to bring to market. Initial perfection is no longer required, because a constant stream of incoming
feedback and data in real-life conditions makes it possible to further improve
the products in situ. The most important gain for the end-user is to be found in
these over-the-air updates, which make the original product better and better.

Many start-ups and companies with an innovation culture now make use of
these processes. It is generally known as the 'lean start-up' approach: you start
with a semi-finished product and gradually build up its capabilities and performance by learning from the needs of its users. This reduces the risk of bringing
something to market in which you have invested huge amounts of time and

* https://www.tesla.com/en_CA/blog/tesla-adds-titanium-underbody-shield-and-aluminum-deflector-
  plates-model-s

resources but actually fails to meet consumer expectations. In the past, during the first two IT sub-waves, this was a common practice. Think, for example, of the first generation of smartphones, such as the Microsoft Zune, or many of the software products of the 1990s and 2000s.

However, the third IT sub-wave has taken this a stage further, by initiating what is known as 'design thinking' product development, where the product is conceptualised with the end-user in mind. As soon as you have a product that is good enough, you launch it onto the market. The numerous sensors it contains provide you with a constant stream of feedback that allows you to perfect your product almost instantly. This 'lean' method puts you miles ahead of your competitors, who may have a better initial product but do not have access to the mass of 'improving' data that allows you to quickly overtake them. This is what the third IT sub-wave has made possible for some products and it is destined to become the dominant design principle. The emergence of 5G, 6G and 'low-orbit' will ensure that this 'always connected' strategy is cheap, simple and super-fast. IoT (the internet of things) will make this possible in many different fields: smart buildings, smart cars, smart packaging, smart wearables and even smart implants that will monitor our health. These developments are only just beginning, but every organisation that wishes to remain relevant will need to move in this direction – and they had better start preparing now. The crucial first step is to have an ambitious vision for your digital transformation.

Will change happen to you or be led by you? That is the question.

The sixth wave of innovation: the age of sustainability (202x - ?)

In my opinion, the third IT sub-wave will also form the basis of the sixth wave of innovation. This is the sustainability wave, which has already begun. The next generation of business models will be founded on smart services. Data, artificial intelligence, connectivity, robotics, automation, nano dimensions, etc. will be the key factors. In addition to the use of data as fuel, there is also another new driver: the growing awareness of the finite nature of our planet.

I define sustainability as coping successfully with the five great scarcities that we all share: food, health, water, energy and natural resources.

We need to deal sparingly with each of these fundamentals, which is something that we failed to do during the previous waves of innovation. Michio Kaku has said that the innovative power of the human race can be described in terms of the number of times it is capable of reviving the planet on which it lives. We are currently using more resources than the planet can offer. At the present time, we actually need 1.75 planets to satisfy our existing consumption. By 29 June (Earth Overshoot Day), we had already used up all the ecological resources and services that our world is capable of reproducing in a year. The number of planets that we need to survive is calculated by dividing our ecological footprint by the earth's ecological biocapacity. Both these factors are expressed in gha – global hectares – and allow us to answer the key question: what yield per hectare of fertile land or sea do we use in relation to the maximum amount that a hectare can currently produce? This method has both supporters and opponents, but it at least enables us to make the calculation in a variety of different ways: for the whole world, for a continent, a country, a town or city, or even a company or individual.

Our 'overshooting' started (inevitably) during the third industrial revolution: the age of mass production. Since 1970, we have been consistently using more than one earth per year. It was during that year – now more than half a century ago – that the Earth Day initiative was first launched to heighten awareness of the depletion of the planet's finite resources. Understandably, there is a huge difference between the dates of the Earth Day of different countries: Qatar has its Earth Day on 11 February, Luxemburg on 16 February, the US on 14 March, Belgium on 5 April, Brazil on 31 July and Indonesia on 18 December.

I recently calculated my personal Earth Day and was alarmed to discover that it falls on 31 March. In other words, I use up four earths each year, mainly because I commute to work each day (even though my car is fully electric), fly regularly, have a large house (by Western standards), regularly eat meat, regularly buy pre-packed products and therefore create a large amount of waste. Critics of this kind of calculation argue that it is a fairly rough-and-ready method that takes little account of recycling, alternative sources of energy and other ameliorating factors. Even so, it gives a striking and easily visualised impression of the impact that each of our lives has on the planet. Innovation encourages the greater consumption of products and services, which demands the use of more energy and resources, resulting in the use of more and more earths. Today, the innovativeness of a population is directly related to its use of scarce resources.

The fact that we are becoming increasingly aware of our overuse has given rise to different expectations, both for society and for companies. We now demand that each company or government focuses greater attention on its social and

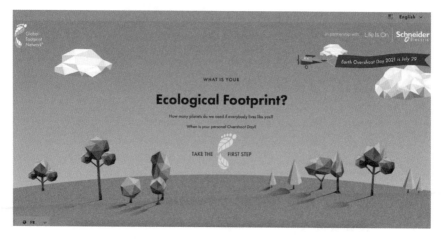

Figure 10 – *Do you want to calculate your own Earth Day?*
You can do so on https://www.footprintcalculator.org or by scanning the QR code.

environmental roles and makes greater efforts to promote sustainability – and certainly more than the minimum imposed by regulations or the principles of CSR (corporate social responsibility). Everyone now knows that densely packed groups of people and animals can lead to zoonoses, outbreaks that allow viruses like Covid-19 to be transferred between different species. Everyone now also knows that there are problems with mobility, poor air quality, diminishing food and resources, mountains of waste, global warming, etc. Innovation has helped to create these problems and it will take innovation – and a great deal of perseverance – to deal with them. This rescue operation needs to start with each of us as individuals. Just as importantly (if not more so), it also needs to be made a priority by our legislators and by companies.

This will actually work to the benefit of companies. Research has shown that when companies set objectives that go beyond standard sustainability obligations in order to achieve additional economic, social and environmental progress, this also stimulates their innovation potential and yields them a greater competitive advantage.

This is where innovation has failed in the past. Each time a new innovation revolution emerges, the dominant companies fail to recognise the changes that this implies quickly enough, so that they are insufficiently able to adjust to the new reality and the new needs of consumers/users. They try to defend themselves by clinging on to their existing practices, but these cost increasing amounts of energy just to maintain the status quo. In short, they fall back on what they know, but this prevents them from making the progress they need to make. They are surprised and overtaken by the speed of their creative new rivals. As a result, change is something that happens to them rather than being something they can shape and control. Instead of embracing creative destruction, they fall victim to the specific phase of the S-curve of innovation.

The current debate is therefore primarily concerned with the question of whether or not organisations, in light of the sixth wave of innovation, can be made to incorporate sustainability objectives as a core element of their vision and mission for the future.

To make sustainability the core of innovation, it will be necessary for companies to pass through five phases of transition, in keeping with research first published in the Harvard Business Review:
1. It is first necessary to see sustainability as an obligation. The faster companies adjust to this, the greater the chance that they will benefit from it.
2. More sustainable value chains need to be introduced, starting with the supply chain. Are we working with sustainable suppliers? Do we use environmentally friendly materials? Do we limit waste creation to an absolute minimum?
3. The design of products and services must be improved, with sustainability and circularity as the prime movers. This is the phase that many of today's companies wish to implement.
4. Current business models must also be redesigned and replaced by more sustainable alternatives.
5. The final phase involves constructing a platform for the systematic development of sustainability initiatives.

It should come as no surprise that in each of these phases technology can be the solution that will make possible the improvements required. For this reason, I am convinced that the further evolution of the third IT sub-wave will pave the way for the sixth wave of innovation: the age of technological revolution. Creating new, sustainable and human-oriented technology will be the challenge for every company that hopes to become the new dominate design. In this way, sustainability will stop being something philanthropic or purely CSR-related and will instead become the core of the innovation that is necessary to remain relevant in the future.

In a nutshell

I began this chapter by making clear that innovation is much more than being creative, inventive or bookishly wise.

I described the innovation cycle of a company, using the three phases of the S-curve: the fluid, transient and specific phases. Finally, I examined the six waves of innovation and explained why the sixth wave, which is currently in progress, was the outcome of the three IT sub-waves of the preceding fifth wave.

Now that I have clarified what I mean by innovation, I want to look at the cost of failing to innovate.

3

KODAK: THE COST OF MAKING THE WRONG INNOVATION CHOICES

I intend to use the Kodak case to highlight the cost of failing to innovate properly. A number of opinions have been expressed in the past about the reasons for Kodak's demise: they missed the train, they failed to see what was coming, they stuck their heads in the sand, they shot themselves in the foot, etc. In my opinion, however, their failure was more complex and more nuanced than these simple assessments. There are very few people who know what really happened and how the situation developed from year to year. The truth is that Kodak did invest in the future and did attempt to diversify. In fact, at one point the company was even the market leader in digital cameras and they even started the first online sharing service for photos. So how did things still manage to go so badly wrong?

I believe that it is important to give the history of Kodak a central position in this book, so that the full story in all its details can be told for the first time. Blow by blow, as it were, almost as if you were there. As a result, this analysis will go further than other comparable analyses in the past. It will continue where they stop. The general consensus of these past analyses can perhaps be summarised as: 'Uber yourself before you get Kodaked'. Following my research, I no longer agree with this over-simplistic advice. My alternative?

You cannot change a super-tanker into a speedboat.
So get off the tanker, buy a speedboat, and sail away.

I realise that this opinion might be controversial for some and it is not the kind of advice that you would usually expect to find in a management book. And it would, indeed, be more logical for me to also accept that Kodak was just a dinosaur that failed to listen enough to the tech gurus of the day and ended up causing its own downfall. But I just can't do it. Because it isn't true. That is not what happened. Kodak did innovate, but they went about it in the wrong way. It is not because you try to do things properly that you always succeed. This was Kodak's tragedy and it proved to be fatal. They were the victim of what I call 'the cost of not innovating', in the sense of not innovating in the right way. They failed to ask the questions that needed to be asked: What will we miss out on if we fail to start this innovation trajectory? What might we save now, but lose later? Should we think about selling our company while it is still lucrative? Or should we just carry on as before? These are questions that all entrepreneurs need to ask at some point in their business career and most would pay a lot of money to know the answers. But you can get them for free by simply reading to the end of this book...

As an entrepreneur, you will usually try to calculate in advance the NPV (Net Present Value) of your investment in innovation. If the NPV does not look promising, you will probably do nothing and carry on as before. With an eye to the future, however, I would formulate the question that needs to be asked in a different way:

Is it worthwhile trying to innovate in the same market or should we be seeking to diversify into a completely different market, where we can still use the skills we possess? In this process, should we be following the technology or should we be listening to what our service skills (CX, customer experience) tell us?

This is a better question, don't you think? And the Kodak case provides a surprising answer. So read on – because it is going to get interesting!

A story full of controversy

In 1881, George Eastman founded the Eastman Dry Plate Company. He sold cameras that made use of a dry gelatine plate instead of a glass plate, and the result was better photographs. At that time, developing photographs was still a fairly complex matter. To take a photograph, you needed to insert a new plate (of whatever kind) into your camera each time. In other words, 1 photo = 1 plate.

Figure 11 – *Eastman's first dry plate cameras and photos.*

In that same year, a Scottish immigrant to America, David Henderson Houston, registered a patent for a camera that would make use of a roll of film to take a series of photographs. The film roll would be made from a celluloid material that was flexible and did not need to be replaced after each shot. There was just one problem: Henderson had not yet perfected the film. Even so, the idea of a camera with a film roll was born. He decided to call his idea 'Nodak', an abbreviation of the state of North Dakota, where he lived. Because the Scot was not able to create a suitable film himself, he agreed to sell his patent to George Eastman, whose skill with gelatine offered better prospects for a solution. This involved a considerable risk for George: leaving the lucrative gelatine plate business for the more complex and uncertain world of film.

Apparently, George was a great lover of anagrams and legend says that he devised the name 'Kodak' by using an anagram set, replacing the 'N' in 'Nodak' with a second 'K', so that the new name could not be associated with anything but his new company. The first Kodak camera was developed in 1888. It was essentially a wooden box with a lens opening that was closed by a shutter and a simple rolling mechanism that made use of a film roll capable of taking a hundred photographs. It was sold with a leather case for the price of 25 dollars (equivalent to 692 dollars today). Once you had taken your hundred photos, you needed to send your camera to the Kodak factory, where the roll was developed into a hundred round prints (with a diameter of 2 ⅝ inches). For 10 dollars (now 270 dollars) you could have your camera loaded with a new film, before it was sent back to you with your prints.

This was a lucrative business, based on what is today known as the 'razor blade' business model: a relatively cheap device making use of expensive consumables. Modern equivalents include Senseo, Nespresso, jet printers and even Gillette, the pioneer of the original disposable razor blade in 1904 – some 15 years after Kodak launched their first camara.

The Kodak concept soon caught on with the public, because it totally revolutionised the way photographs were made. The entire process became more spontaneous, since there was no longer any need to pose. What had been a formal 'event' became an everyday activity. Kodak's marketing made sure to stress this ease of use, with their legendary slogan: "You press the button, we do the rest". And for once, this was a marketing boast that was 100% true! Internally, the company referred to this as their 'silver halide strategy', after one of the chemical substances that was a basic component of their film technology.

Consumers quickly fell in love with the Kodak camera and the company became a generic household name. People began to talk of a 'kodak moment', a moment that you wanted to preserve for ever. Before long, an extensive Kodak retail network of photographers and photographic stores came into being, all able to make a profit and all thanks to Kodak. In time, the company became a giant: mass production, falling costs, internationalisation, extensive marketing, constant investment in R&D and – most importantly – constant listening to its customers. In particular, it was necessary to continue investing in the core manufacturing technology, because the production process was complex and expensive: the smallest flaw had the potential to decimate the company's high margins.

One of the biggest risks taken by the company in the first half of the 20th century was the transition from monochrome to colour film, not in the least because the coloured variant was initially inferior and even more complex to make. Nevertheless, the company's constant focus on R&D ensured that Kodak kept its technological lead, resulting in what was effectively a duopoly (with Fuji in Japan). In essence, Kodak set the bar so high that it was very hard for newcomers to break into the market. It was a successful strategy and in 1930 the company was added to the Dow Jones Industrial index, where it was destined to remain for a further 74 years, until 2004.

Kodak's position seemed impregnable, but appearances can be deceptive. As the 20th century progressed, storm clouds started to gather on the horizon, storm clouds that would eventually see the company threatened from two different directions. The first of these threats was the emergence of serious competitors. The second was the arrival of digitalisation.

Threat 1: Attacks on the core business

In 1934, Fuji Photo Film was founded in Japan. This new company had the same core business in Asia as Kodak in the US. It was not until 1972 that Fuji finally broke into the American market, offering a price advantage of around 20%. At first, Kodak was not unduly worried. Fuji had a market share of just 4% in comparison with Kodak's 90%, and the American company was confident that Americans would continue to buy American-made film. Fuji's first major attack on Kodak occurred in 1984, when the Olympic Games came to Los Angeles. Since 1896, Kodak had sponsored every edition of the Olympic Games, but in 1984 – on home soil! – it lost the franchise to Fuji. Kodak's marketing director at the time, Carl Gustin, now accepts that this was a serious strategic error. It handed Fuji a golden opportunity to get its foot very firmly in the door of the American market. During the period of the 1984 Games, their market share doubled to 12%. They followed this up by building a factory in the United States, so that they could continue to attack Kodak with aggressive marketing and further price reductions. The trend established in 1984 was intensified: between 1990 and 1997 Fuji's market share increased from 10% to 17%, whereas Kodak's share fell by 5% between 1987 and 1992 and by a massive 10% between 1996 and 1997. This debacle represented a corresponding fall in turnover from 16 billion dollars to 14.3 billion dollars, with net profits melting away from 1.29 billion dollars to zero.

To make matters worse, by the mid-1980s a number of other competitors emerged to disrupt the market even further. These included the German-Belgian Agfa-Gevaert and the Japanese Konika. In general, however, the high threshold initially set by Kodak continued to do its work.

Kodak tried to counter these developments by attempting to make its own breakthrough into Fuji's domestic market, but the results were disappointing. Kodak's market share in Japan never rose above 10%, whereas Fuji remained unchallenged on more than 70%, and this in a film market that was almost as large as the American one (2 billion dollars in Japan versus 2.7 billion dollars in the US). According to Kodak, one of the reasons for their Japanese failure was the fact that countless barriers were erected to hinder the sale of their products in a country where people were already very attached to their 'national' film brand: Fuji. In 1996, Kodak initiated a procedure through the US Government at the WTO, arguing that Fuji were engaging in unfair market practices, but the claim was dismissed. Undeterred, the company decided to give its Japanese rival a taste of its own 1984 medicine by buying the exclusive sponsorship rights for the 1998 winter Olympic Games in Nagano. For this privilege, Kodak paid a staggering 44 million dollars and probably a multiple of that amount for the television rights. In addition, all 650 accredited photographers were provided with free Kodak film. More than 1.2 million people were expected to visit the Games, half of them Japanese. It was a make-or-break moment of truth for Kodak. At first, things seemed to be going well. There was an initial growth in the sale of Kodak film, but to a large extent this was due to the company now making its own deliveries to Japanese outlets, deliveries that Fuji was unable to hinder. But once the Games were over this temporary interest quickly ebbed away. Fuji closely followed all its competitor's price reductions and the Japanese company's annual reports for this period show that it was already prepared to invest in cost reduction as a response to what it saw as the likely decline of the film market in the future. The scene was set for a clash of the film titans.

Threat 2: Digitalisation

Whereas the first threat was primarily market-related and created an opening for an energetic fast follower (Fuji), the second threat was of a totally different order. This threat was the result of a technological breakthrough in a completely different domain: this time not in silver, but in silicon. To understand why Kodak's response to the new threat was so unsuccessful, it is interesting to take a wider look at the management and culture of the company, and at the actions that it took or – more crucially – did not take.

A prototype

Walter Fallon (1972-1983) was Kodak's CEO in 1973 when a young 23-year-old electronics engineer named Steven Sasson first joined the company. Steven was something of an odd-man-out among his colleagues, who were mainly mechanical or chemical engineers. Not really sure what to do with him, his manager put him in charge of a project to investigate a new device that had recently been invented by Bell Laboratories: a CCD-chip (charge coupled de-

Figure 12 – *The first digital camera invented by Steven Sasson at Kodak.*

vice). This device was capable of converting light that fell onto a checkerboard of pixels into electronic signals that could be stored and manipulated. Was this the technology that was necessary to make digital photography possible? Steven set to work and eventually developed a first prototype that was the size of a toaster. The electrical impulses were stored on a cassette tape, before being projected as grainy images onto a screen. It took Steven almost two years to get this far, but by 1975 he was ready to show his prototype to everyone at Kodak.

Diversification as the answer
Under the following two CEOs – Colby Chandler (1983-1990) and Kay Whitmore (1990-1993) – Kodak entered a period of unbridled diversification. Following the launch of the digital Sony Mavica in 1981, the company felt it had no choice. It had to do something! It was Colby Chandler who took the initial decision to diversify and I am personally convinced that he was right. Kodak bought the photocopier business from IBM, moved into the field of medical imaging and started the production of floppy discs, as well as engaging in a number of other new activities that were close to its core business. Managers felt comfortable with all this, because it did not require them to move too far from their own comfort zone. The company also explored the possibilities that digital photography might offer, but always from the standpoint of their own

knowledge and skills in relation to chemical film. Thanks to Steven Sasson, they had actually invented the first digital CCD-sensor camera, but they were not prepared to invest in its development. The photographic film business was still far too lucrative to consider any major withdrawal. In collaboration with Philips, Kodak did, however, offer its customers the possibility to transfer their digital photos to a photo-CD via their usual business channels. This is a classic example of a company that wishes at all costs to transfer its core knowledge and skills to a new medium; in Kodak's case, a digital medium.

> *Unfortunately for them, digital photography (the silicon business) was very different from analogue photography (the silver halide business).*

The next CEO, Kay Whitmore, also had no great affection for the new generation of tech wizards, such as Steve Jobs and Bill Gates. There is a story that during a meeting with the Microsoft boss to discuss making the photo-CD compatible with the more popular CD-ROM for use on a PC, he actually fell asleep!

> *Mr. Whitmore said he would make sure Kodak stayed closer to its core businesses in film and photographic chemicals.* VIA THE NEW YORK TIMES (12/9/1989)

Belatedly, the next CEO, George Fisher (1993-1999), realised that digital photography would eventually eliminate Kodak's core business. The former Motorola top man made contact with Microsoft and Apple to set up a collaboration for the further development of digital photography. Fisher pumped more than 2 billion dollars into digital imaging R&D. The result was the QuickTake, a revolutionary but expensive camera that was made by Apple using Kodak technology. Kodak also launched its own alternatives: the DC20 and DC25 digital cameras. Unfortunately, all these ventures were little more than a knee-jerk reaction, an overhasty response to the digital threat that was based on no clear, long-term version for how the digital world would evolve. Kodak's only ambition was to become the market leader in digital cameras, but they looked no further than that. At first, it seemed as though this limited ambition might be achieved. Dozens of new products were launched and many of them were popular, but the cost of production was so high that Kodak's section of the digital market offered almost no scope for profit. At the same time, the company's market share in the photographic film sector was also coming under pressure as a consequence of the growing competition from Fuji and their spate of price reductions, which threatened the income stream that Kodak used to finance its digital innovation efforts. Unfortunately, none of the company's new digital initiatives came even close to producing the same margins that film had produced in the past.

Faced with this pressure, Fisher sold most of the company's hardware business. This was effectively putting all Kodak's eggs back in one basket and relying on the old 'razor blade' business model to get the company out of the hole it had dug for itself. Fisher believed in what he was doing and famously declared: "Electronic business will not cannibalise film". Hastily, he installed more than 10,000 digital Kodak print kiosks in retail stores, because he was convinced that people would still want to print off all their photos. It was yet another (and equally futile) attempt to keep the old silver halide philosophy alive at all costs in the new digital world, because Fisher and others thought that it was the only way to get the funding needed for further innovation. This was a case of 'cognitive inertia', another classic example to be added to Kodak's growing list of classic errors. Of course, it failed to turn the tide. The company's business results for 1998 were catastrophic, leading to a massive cost-cutting exercise that saw 20% of all Kodak jobs disappear.

The company badly needed a new external CEO with experience of the digital world, but in 2000 decided to appoint a Kodak insider, Daniel Carp (2000-2005), to the job. After the drama of the Fisher years, Carp tried to pick up the pieces and move forward again. The sale of Kodak film rolls continued to decline, a process that was accelerated by the advent of the Sony CyberShot digital camera, the ever-increasing speed of the internet, and the rise of social media. People now shared their photographs digitally; printing them off belonged to the past. Kodak now tried to blame the company's plummeting results on the world crisis that followed the 9/11 attacks, but succeeded in deceiving no one but themselves. By now, the digital writing was so very clearly on the wall that not even the Kodak management team could fail to ignore it. In 2001, the company changed emphasis again and launched a new and large-scale digital offensive. Dan Carp led a new 'digital division' that had been set up specially to seize digital opportunities. This new division operated separately from the classic divisions and one of its first actions was to purchase the photo-sharing website Ofoto in 2001. But old habits die hard and once again – as with its print kiosks – the company used its new acquisition to encourage people not only to share their digital photographs, but also to print them off. Although there was a recognition that digital was the future, there was still a reluctance to accept that the age of printed photographs was dead. This confused logic saw things go from bad to worse. Kodak's EasyShare was the second-best digital camera on the market behind Sony and in 2005 even managed to topple its Japanese rival from the number one position. However, this obsession to become market leader had only been achieved by a willingness to lose 60 dollars on each camera it sold. Not surprisingly, this created huge tension between the Kodak Digital and the Kodak Film divisions. The former generated twice as much turnover as the latter, but was still making a huge loss.

Kodak underestimated the speed with which digital cameras would become a commodity.

Prices collapsed and profits continued to be elusive, but money was still needed for the non-stop R&D that was essential to stay ahead in the technological race. But Kodak was fighting a losing battle. By 2007, the company had slipped down to fourth position in the market. By 2010, it had slumped to number ten. The digital modular world had bankrupted the Kodak business model. All the major players had focused on specific modules of that world, such as chips, lenses, hard drives, processors, screen or modems. Modularisation of this kind turns consumer products into commodities. This explains, for example, how a Californian surf fanatic like Nick Woodman was able to found GoPro in a matter of months, get it noted on the Nasdaq index with equal speed, and conquer the consumer video camera market in record time, before himself being undermined by cheaper Chinese manufacturers. As Woodman proved, you no longer needed much experience or knowledge to become an active player in the digital world. That is why in these rapidly changing times I decided to include 'speed' as a numerator in my Future Fitness Formula!

In the meantime, yet another new challenger arrived on the market: the smartphone with camera.

When Steve Jobs launched the Apple iPhone in 2007, the floodgates of disaster opened once again for Kodak. The growth of smartphone cams exploded and the market for digital cameras collapsed. Old-fashioned film cameras ceased to exist entirely. The ease of use of the iPhone, which allowed people to see and store photos instantly via iTunes and iPhoto, was unparalleled. The following graphic shows just how dramatically the iPhone turned the camera market on its head.

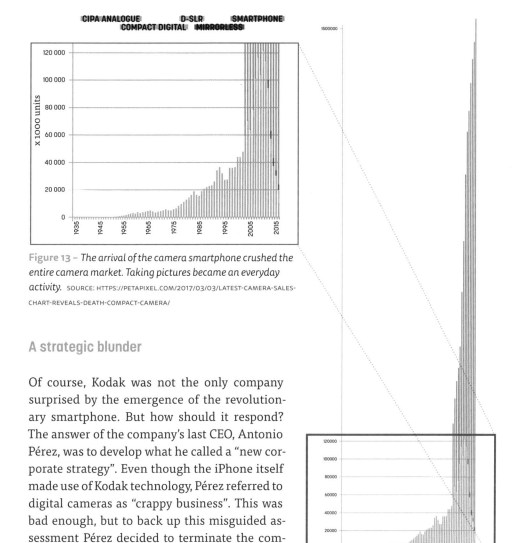

Figure 13 – *The arrival of the camera smartphone crushed the entire camera market. Taking pictures became an everyday activity.* SOURCE: HTTPS://PETAPIXEL.COM/2017/03/03/LATEST-CAMERA-SALES-CHART-REVEALS-DEATH-COMPACT-CAMERA/

A strategic blunder

Of course, Kodak was not the only company surprised by the emergence of the revolutionary smartphone. But how should it respond? The answer of the company's last CEO, Antonio Pérez, was to develop what he called a "new corporate strategy". Even though the iPhone itself made use of Kodak technology, Pérez referred to digital cameras as "crappy business". This was bad enough, but to back up this misguided assessment Pérez decided to terminate the company's manufacture of its own digital cameras and to rely instead on OEMs (original equipment manufacturers). This meant that Kodak would henceforth no longer have its own technology and its own knowledge base in matters relating to sensors and image processing. It was a move that even Shigetaka Komori, who was then the CEO of Fuji, said was a "serious strategic blunder". Kodak likewise turned its back on film production, sold all its film production factories, and made 27,000 of its employees redundant.

To compound the situation still further, Kodak immediately made a second crucial strategic error: in spite of shutting down its own production of digital cameras, it continued to invest in the digital cameras produced by the OEMs. And to make possible this further investment in "crappy business", the company even sold its profit-making health-care and pharmaceutical activities! Some of the capital was also used to diversify into the high-quality ink-jet printer market. These printers would allow consumers to print off top quality photographs in their own home, but instead of following the 'razor blade' business model of market leader HP, based on cheap printers and expensive ink, Kodak opted for a different approach, based on expensive printers and cheap ink. It was another addition to the company's long list of bad decisions. Within a couple of years, the printer division was sold off at a knock-down price. By now, the end was in sight. Kodak largely spent its final years engaged in litigation. The company felt that it had been deceived and cheated for decades and now wished to make use of its rich portfolio of patents to claw back some of its losses. In 2010, a successful action was brought against LG, which was forced to pay 838 million dollars in compensation, and efforts were made to instigate similar actions against Apple and Research in Motion (BlackBerry). This was the final nail in Kodak's coffin. The outcome of Pérez's "new corporate strategy" was a crippling rise in costs, while turnover fell to 8 billion dollars and cash reserves were down to just 1 billion dollars. A cash burn rate at this level was no longer sustainable. On 19 January 2011, the company filed for bankruptcy under Chapter 11 of the US Bankruptcy Code. The long history of Kodak was finally at an end.

THE INSIDE STORY OF STEVEN SASSON

Steven Sasson is the inventor of the first digital photo camera and I was fortunate enough to have a long and frank conversation with him. Is it true, I asked him, that Kodak simply failed to see the inevitability of the digital revolution in photography? Or was there another reason why they ultimately missed the boat? And what can we learn from what happened?

Innovation provokes resistance

Steven's story begins in the mid-1970s. As a recently qualified graduate engineer, he started work in the applied research lab at Kodak. One day, his supervisor, Gareth Lloyd, handed him a new piece of technology: the charge-coupled device (CCD), which had been developed by Fairchild. Lloyd asked him to investigate the possible potential that this new technology might have for making digital images and then left his new junior researcher to get on with it. With the help of other colleagues from different departments, Steven succeeded in integrating the CCD into a portable camera that was able to capture images, although the image quality was far from brilliant. When he demonstrated what he had achieved to senior management, he was disappointed by their sceptical response. He was more or less told that everyone was quite happy with the current use of 35mm film. How, he was asked, did he think the photo developers would respond to his invention? Why would they give up their successful businesses for the sake of this new-fangled 'toy'? In short, the top brass at Kodak were unable to see any way in which Steven's prototype could be integrated into a successful business model, particularly because the image quality was far below what Kodak customers usually expected.

Kodak had worked very hard for more than a hundred years to build up its reputation for quality, and the company was not prepared to throw that overboard for something which at first sight seemed to be inferior. In other words, Steven was not told "It will never work" but was asked "Why should we ever want it to work?" Or as Steven himself puts it: "When you show people something new, at first they are enthusiastic, until they realise that the things they currently like to do will have to be done differently in future."

"Everyone is in favour of innovation, until it happens to them."

Notwithstanding their initial reaction, Kodak was still smart enough to patent Steven's invention, but without giving too much publicity to the matter. Moreover, the episode as a whole demonstrates the three forms of resistance that innovation usually has to face: the technological barriers that need to be overcome; the lack of an immediately obvious business model; and the possible reaction of the public.

In large organisations, it is quite common for managers to be afraid to show innovations to their bosses, if they do not yet have all the answers to all the questions that might be asked. When Steven's supervisor approached Walter Fallon, who was then CEO of Kodak, for instructions about whether to pursue Steven's brainchild any further, Fallon answered: "Yes, let him carry on, but let's hope that he fails." By contrast, Steven was optimistic. He thought that Moore's Law – which states that the speed and capacity of microchips will double every 18 months – would also apply to the CCD. Yet while no one any longer doubted Moore, everybody – or at least everybody at Kodak – seemed to be doubting Steven.

External pressure accelerates the process

Later, it became known that Sony was also experimenting with digital photography, in the form of its Mavica camera. However, Sony approached the problem on the basis of a completely different technology; namely, its expertise in video technology. Steven told his bosses that in his opinion this was the wrong approach, but the mere fact that a possible external threat now existed was enough to heighten Kodak's interest and boosted their willingness to innovate, particularly as the Sony experiment had also awakened public interest. As a result, Kodak began investing heavily to build more powerful CCDs, but did so in secret, for fear of undermining its existing film roll business. Before long, the ability to compress images without loss of quality dramatically improved and it even became possible to transmit good quality images via a telephone line, an application that was potentially very useful for news agencies. Steven and his team built a relatively compact camera with a memory card and asked the Kodak marketing department whether or not they would be able to sell it. "Of course," was the reply. "But why should we want to do anything that will harm the market for classic cameras with film?"

By selling digital cameras, the existing lucrative business in rolls of film would be put in jeopardy.

This is another important reason why innovations so often fail. Key figures in the business lines are evaluated on the basis of targets that relate to past sales and present sales, but not future sales. For this reason, they are less inclined to test new products on 'their' public. In their eyes, this only brings them extra headaches, not extra turnover. As a result, they protect their sales channels with an almost fanatical determination, in order to prevent innovations working their way through the system at their expense. This is an important bottleneck that you need to address if you wish to market new products successfully: make your most successful channels available to promising innovations.

But let's return to Kodak. Steven's new digital approach, which would result in (unnecessary) information being filtered out during the compression process, went against the company's traditional culture – a culture that continued to believe firmly in the value of the film negative as the repository of all the original information. During the previous hundred years, Kodak had invested huge amounts of time and energy to optimise this process. Why should it now throw away all that hard work? To reach a compromise, it was agreed that the camera would be fitted with a button that would allow the image compression function to be deactivated, so that people could still make 'real' photos. Once again, this product was never brought to market, but a patent was taken out on the technology that would have made it possible. Even so, it was inevitable that what Kodak could do, Canon or Sony would soon also be able to do, even if they had to take a different route to get there.

Steven eventually left the camera department and transferred to the printing department. But he continued to be confronted by the same kinds of mistakes. The development of thermal printing made it possible to print off hard copies of digital photographs. But the idea of building kiosks that customers could use to print off their own photos was held back for the same reason that the development of the initial digital camera had been held back: fear of angering the photographic developers. If, for example, people were allowed to print off their own wedding photographs, an entire branch of the film business would collapse almost overnight – or so the marketing people claimed. Once more, innovation failed because the company was not prepared to upset the apple cart: the existing situation had to be protected at all costs. In other words, the objections were no longer based on quality, but on potential harm to the business model. As a result, Kodak was more inclined to place its faith in the photo-CD, which it had co-developed with Philips in Eindhoven. This meant that the photographic developers would now have an extra product to sell to their customers, which, it was thought, strengthened rather than weakened the business model. Apart from the addition of this extra product, nothing needed to be changed. Less risk, everybody happy. Except, of course, the customer, who needed to pay an extra 400 dollars to be able to print off his own photos. Not surprisingly, the market failed to follow.

In the early 1990s, Apple was keen to collaborate with Kodak. The new CEO George Fisher – the first person to hold the position who indicated that he was willing to break with the past – introduced a number of 'digital guys' into the company, although most of the senior management continued to be convinced 'film guys'. Kodak technology was used to build a new Apple camera, the QuickTake. At the insistence of the 'film guys', this new device was not allowed to look like a traditional camera and it had to be positioned in the market as a computer input device. What's more, under no circumstances should the name Kodak appear! Even so, the same camera was later marketed as the Kodak DC40. Fisher believed that Kodak should offer every form of image making and in this context Steven Sasson argued that the company should be more active in the photo finishing-printing business. The idea was that part of the photo-finishing process should always be digital, so that people with digital cameras could get high-quality photographs quickly and easily. Although Steven was only (in his words) "a nobody", just one of Kodak's many middle managers, CEO Fisher was prepared to listen to him. As a result, Steven continued his work to develop an effective digital photo thermal printer, eventually producing a device that was reliable, high-quality and had a profit margin of 70%! Yet when Fisher was later replaced as CEO by Daniel Carp, Steven was amazed when he discovered that his new boss had negotiated a collaboration with Phogenix for the development of a less performant ink-jet technology. A separate unit was set up for this purpose in Silicon Valley – far away from Kodak's headquarters in Rochester NY – where the company set about making new ink-jet printers that it made no serious effort to market. Sasson was later told that this was a purely strategic move to prevent Phogenix from building ink-jet printers that they would then seek to market through Kodak channels. In other words, it was the application of the 'keep your enemy close' principle, so that Phogenix could be kept away from one of the most lucrative parts of Kodak's business.

A final domain in which Kodak failed was pharmaceuticals. The development of the classic roll of film is essentially a chemical activity, so that Kodak actually had more experience in chemical technology than in digital technology. The high margins that are also common in pharmaceuticals made the move into this sector doubly interesting. With this in mind Kodak bought Sterling Drug Inc., but then quickly sold it again to Sanofi and SmithKline. The new CEO, George Fisher, was openly sceptical from the start: "We are an imaging company, but you all think that we are going to earn more money in pharmaceuticals. Okay, so first tell me how." No one was able to give him a cogent answer.

According to Steven Sasson, the fundamental question that every industry needs to ask itself when confronted with innovation is the following: do you stay with the technology you know or with the market you know?

When I asked Steven how he now looked back at this period, he answered: "I overestimated how fast we were going initially, but even I underestimated how fast it would go after that." According to him, Kodak could have and should have taken a gamble on the chemical industry, as it attempted to do with one of its spin-offs, the Eastman Chemical Company. But to achieve real success in chemicals it would have been necessary to get rid of all the 'imaging guys' and the company was too proud to do this. Another promising venture was the idea of perhaps buying into Apple (during the CEO-ship of John Sculley), but in the end the senior management was not really interested enough in computers. Even if they had been, Steven doubts if this would have been a good move for Apple, which was soon destined to find its second wind following the return of Steve Jobs. It is certain, he feels, that the culture of the Kodak management at that time would never have been reconcilable with the cultural vision of Steve Jobs! The top people at Kodak were all much too concerned about how the company could make a few more dollars during the next quarter than with the development of a long-term mission or strategy. This kind of short-term market thinking is still a recognisable danger, and one that can be seen in many of today's stock-listed companies.

In contrast to what many people now think, Kodak was ahead of the field in terms of research and development, and did foresee the potential digital disruption that seemed to be heading their way. But the senior management was convinced that during 'their time' this disruption would remain within limits. And because they were all judged on the basis of turnover from the company's traditional lines of business and not on the prospect of future business, they were not prepared to contemplate the company earning a red cent less. It was a recipe for disaster – and a salutary lesson for us all.

Dare to cannibalise your own business, before someone else does it for you.

Steven also thinks that companies generally like innovators, but they are often not prepared to empower them by giving them the resources they need and access to the most successful sales channels, so that their ideas can be properly tested.

In addition, he says that innovators need to be given total freedom and not be burdened with overheads and the complex decision-making and financial reporting procedures that are common in mother companies. "It's not just because you inherit the well-known brand name that you must pay in all costs. That is how you kill new business." This is something that you see quite often: an innovative new product or service is launched but it is immediately expected to pay its 'fair share' in the costs of the 'old' system. This leads to the collapse of the innovation in question, even though in reality it often has no need of the old system. This means that companies must be prepared, even after a hundred or more years, to change the rules that made them successful in the past.

Like Steven, I can still see the same problems today in sectors as diverse as car manufacturing, banking, retail and oil.

These sectors will soon be facing the same problems that Kodak faced, only they will be facing them more quickly. The transition cycle that took 40 years in the case of Kodak nowadays only takes about 10 years to complete. Even the mighty Apple is currently undergoing a rapid evolution, so that it is becoming more and more of a service company and less and less of a computer company. Nobody can escape these evolutions. Do you remember what I wrote earlier about Tesla and the electric vehicle industry? For businesses, the real future lies not in EVs themselves, but in everything that surrounds them: mobility services for autonomous driving, online and hybrid shopping, experience services and so much more.

The initial question is always the same: where is the money? Kodak saw that it could earn money with its patents, but failed to see how it could market the technology itself. This was a missed opportunity, because no company in history was ever better placed, better prepared and better provided with the right marketing channels and customers to make a success of the digital imaging revolution.

"Half of the people in big companies are 'no' factories; they say 'no' to everything." STEVEN SASSON

This is yet further confirmation of my Future Fitness Formula. The numerator consists of speed, flexibility and vision, and Kodak had all three of these. Almost all the components for a high level of future fitness were present, but the final component – experience – let it down. And by experience, I mean the old Kodak culture. This was the denominator, the determining factor that was greater than the combined strength of the numerator. In fact, it was insidiously present within the components of the numerator. As a result, the company's future fitness was eroded by an excess of experience, the suffocating effects of a hundred years of heritage. Its future was snatched from it by the cognitive inertia of its management, which was ingrained in the company's culture. It was this that finally brought Kodak crashing down.

What I remember most about my conversation with Steven is this: if you work in a large company, it is difficult to see how you can make a difference as an individual, especially if you work in R&D. This is why innovation needs to be marketed both internally and externally. Companies need to put their innovation in the spotlight. You need to show your own developers exactly what changes for the better they can bring about in people's lives. Unless you do this for them, it will pass them by. Steven never received that kind of recognition at Kodak. Fortunately, however, he did later receive a medal from President Obama for his contribution towards the development of digital image forming, a development that changed all our lives for good.

A strategic analysis

The million – or even billion – dollar question is this: should Kodak have invested heavily in the digital camera when Steven presented them with his prototype in 1975?

Before I give you my answer, I first want to say something about the photography market at that time. Let's begin by looking at the following chart.

On the left, you can see the number of analogue and digital cameras that were sold. On the right, you can see the number of rolls of film that were sold. This data allows us to draw a number of interesting conclusions:

- The market share for digital cameras was initially very small. The period from the launch of the Sony Mavica in 1981 until the turn of the century was primarily a period of experimentation by Sony and Fuji but also by Kodak, producing relatively expensive models. During this period, the Kodak en-

THE TIDAL WAVE OF DIGITAL PHOTOGRAPHY

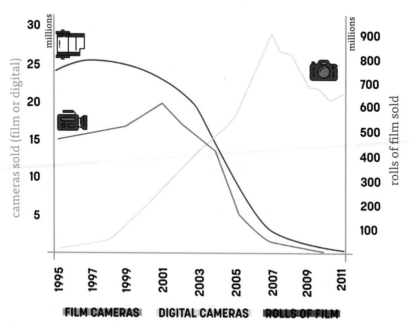

Figure 14 – From 2000, the digitisation of photography accelerated to completely replace analogue devices and films from 2007. Then the digital camera was in turn supplanted by smartphones with increasingly better cameras.

gineers and their managers laughed at the poor quality and high price of these models, which offered an unrealistic business model in comparison with classic film.

- After 1999, the market share for digital began to grow, thanks to the availability of fast and cheap internet, which made it possible to send photos easily. 1998 saw the arrival of Google and the option for searching for images. The first social networks, like SixDegrees, and chats, like Microsoft Live Messenger and ICQ, all started in 1999. Similarly, there was an explosion of news websites. Journalists but also consumers wanted to see photos posted online in double-quick time, even if the quality was not perfect: "I want it all and I want it now!" Where have we heard that before?

- From 2000 onwards, Sony made the big breakthrough with its CyberShot cameras, the price of which fell significantly each year. 1999 was the high-water mark for the sale of analogue cameras, followed in 2000 by the first (small) downward turn. This seemingly minor kink was actually the canary in the coalmine: disaster was approaching, and approaching fast. From then on, the sale of rolls of film fell dramatically. Kodak accelerated to become market leader and the company seemed to have all the trump cards in its hand.

- By 2003, as many digital camaras were being sold as their analogue counterparts. This meant a fast rise in sales for the former and a fast drop in sales for the latter. It was a perfect replacement market. Kodak was still market leader, but was starting to lose money to the digital camera business.
- From 2007 onwards, the sale of digital cameras also started to fall, largely as a result of the success of the iPhone, which introduced the concept of the smartphone as camera. From this point on, the fate of digital cameras was sealed.

Economic differences in the business models of analogue and digital

It is interesting to look at the different economic motivations that underpin the photography market. The price per analogue photograph was based on a number of components: the price of the camera, film roll, developing and printing. Around 1999, when the Kodak empire was at its height, it was possible to buy disposable cameras. You took your snaps with a cardboard camera, took it to a shop and paid for the development of perfectly printed photos. For this kind of camera – the Kodak Fling, which took 24 photos – you paid 10 euros. The development in supermarkets or at special photography stores, which were equipped with a special high-end Kodak photo printer, cost around 5 euros, a price that was regularly and heavily subsidised by promotional campaigns. This resulted in a cost of roughly 0.60 euro per photo.

Alternatively, you could buy a decent analogue camera for around 500 euros. Imagine that over a period of time you use 200 rolls of film, each with 24 photos per roll, which amounts to a depreciation of 2.5 euros per roll. In 1999, such a roll cost 7 euros. The development of the roll cost 5 euros. Adding this all up results in a total cost of 14.50 euros for 24 photos, which (again) is also equivalent to 0.60 euro per photo. This business model was therefore based on 80% income from consumables and 20% income from hardware.

In contrast, the digital camera was based on a totally different concept. The early digital cameras were expensive. The first model we had in Living Tomorrow

Figure 15 – *The Minolta RD175, the first digital camera that we started using at Living Tomorrow in 1995. The cost then was about $10,000.*

back in 1995 was the Minolta RD175. This was a portable SLR camera with a CCD of 1.75 megapixels and it cost 9,995 dollars or roughly 8,500 euros. The camera was profiled in the market as a consumer camera, but its high price meant that it was largely purchased by photographic journalists. The growth of digital newspapers, websites and social media made necessary the faster provision and distribution of news-related visual material. Speed was the key; quality was less important. The digital camera fit the bill perfectly: it was quick and easy to use, allowing press photographers to save time and deliver faster. Prices soon began to fall, so that by the year 2000 you could buy a Canon Digital Ixus S100 for 815 euros. From this point onwards, the process of commoditisation gathered pace and prices fell further, until a price of a just a few hundred euros was reached: in 2007, you could get a Sony CyberShot for 250 euros. But worse was still to come. The 'price' continued to plummet as the market collapsed, ending with a value of around 10 euros, based on an estimate of the cost of the camera components in an iPhone.

Digital photographs were stored on the hard disc of a PC, which by this time were commonplace. The storage price was negligible and there was no longer any development/printing cost. All that remained was the depreciation of the camera per photo.

How does this all compare with our analogue example? Again assuming that we take 4,800 photos, the cost per photo makes interesting reading:

- Minolta RD175: 8,500 euros / 4,800 photos = 1.70 euros per photo
- Canon Digital Ixus: 815 euros / 4,800 photos = 0.16 euro per photo
- CyberShot: 250 euros / 4,800 photo = 0.05 euro per photo
- iPhone 1: 10 euros / 4,800 photos = 0.02 euro per photo

For the RD175, the case is clear. It could not compete with its analogue rivals, unless speed was an important factor. It was only the journalists who were willing to pay 1.70 euros per digital photo instead of 0.60 euro per photo with a decent analogue camera. Moreover, with a good quality scanner it was possible to convert analogue photos into high resolution images for transmission. In other words, end of case. This is a scenario that must often have been discussed at Kodak management meetings.

After the year 2000, the story changed dramatically. The 0.16 euro cost per photo with the IXUS made it four times cheaper than the analogue cost of 0.60

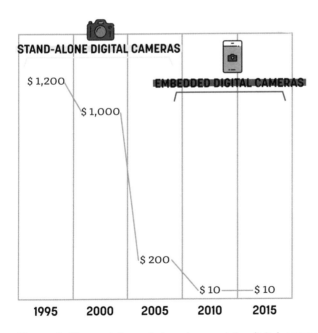

DIGITAL CAMERA PRICES IN 2014 DOLLARS

Figure 16 – *The smartphones destroyed every existing digital camera and photography business model, if any generated profit at all.*

euro. Happy days! But then came the iPhone and ruined everything. The price per photo became minimal. After all, nobody buys a smartphone for the quality of its camera alone; that is simply a 'nice to have'. As a result, the price per photo is virtually zero. As is the marginal cost. This was the kiss of death for Kodak.

The disruptive effect is clear: it brought about reduced quality at a reduced price reaching an increasingly larger target group. The speed with which the quality subsequently improved simply served to further accelerate the growth of this target group. So, should Kodak have played the digital card back in 1975? Should they have 'done an Uber'? What would you have done?

What if Kodak had applied scenario thinking in 1975?

What else might it have been possible to do with the skills that Kodak possessed in 1975, in light of their knowledge that digital technology would boom in the coming decades? Here is one possible scenario... At that time, the sending of telegrams was still common and in 1964 Xerox had launched the fax machine, which largely served the same purpose. Kodak already had an instant camera – the famous Instamatic – on the market. Put all these things together and you

Figure 17 – Kevin Systrom and Mike Krieger in the early days of Instagram. A year after founding Instagram, the founders sold the company to Facebook for $1 billion.

end up with an instant photograph that you can send quickly to your family, friends, work, etc. In other words, an instant camera + telegram = Instagram!

Fast-forward to March 2010. The iPhone has been on the market for three years and is a huge success. The combination of the smartphone, location-based services and social media is skyrocketing. Apps such as Foursquare, which allows you to check in at stores and earn virtual points, are in the lift. This was the moment when Kevin Systrom and Mike Krieger developed a similar app and were able to secure 500,000 dollars of seed capital from Baseline Ventures and Andreessen Horowitz. Systrom and Krieger realised that their app was just a bit too much like Foursquare and so they decided to reposition it as a photo-sharing app, which they called Instagram.

Systrom posted the first photograph of his girlfriend and his dog on 16 July 2010 – and the rest is history. Scarcely six months later, in February 2011, they secured an additional 7 million dollars of funding, which saw the value of their young company shoot up to 20 million dollars. A further funding round in April 2012 brought in another 50 million dollars, with the company's value now estimated at 500 million. At the same time, they launched their Android app, which became the most downloaded app the world had ever seen up to that point: one million downloads in just a single day. Six days later, Instagram was purchased by Facebook for 1 billion dollars in cash and Facebook shares, with a guarantee that the app would remain independent. It was a golden move for all concerned.

It is interesting to compare the situation of Kodak in 1999 with Instagram in 2013. Both companies had the same objective: instant photography and sharing. The only (but hugely important) difference was that Kodak wanted to make and share memories using analogue technology (a traditional camera), whereas Instagram wanted to do it digitally (with a camera-equipped smartphone). Given this difference, a comparison of the key figures of both companies makes fascinating reading.

Table 1 – *Comparison Kodak and Instagram.*

KODAK 1999	INSTAGRAM 2013
800 million rolls of film sold, with an average of 27 photos per roll.	60 million photos per day. 30 million users
21.6 billion photos per year.	21.9 billion photos per year.
50 cents per photo (see above, without camera cost).	Free.
10.8 billion euros turnover.	No turnover.
Market capitalisation 1999 = 20.9 billion dollars.	Value 2013 = 1 billion dollars (Facebook purchase price)
Employees: 83,000	Employees: 12

This remarkable comparison makes clear the scale of the Kodak market that was replaced by digital services. An evaporation of 21 billion dollars of value and the redundancy of 83,000 employees has a massive impact. If they had been armed with this foresight, might it have been a smart idea for Kodak to take the plunge into the digital photo business and try to become Instagram? The answer to this question has to be 'no'. It is simply not realistic to turn a super-tanker like Kodak, with hundreds of factories, an extensive value chain, a network of photo dealers and tens of thousands of employees, into a fully digital company with a workforce of just twelve people and a value of a billion dollars. Facebook's core business initially also had little to do with the sharing of images, but the company made a very shrewd move when it decided to buy out Instagram. Instagram's turnover is now estimated at 24 billion dollars, which is equivalent to 36% of Facebook's total turnover. Its value is estimated at a massive 100 billion dollars or more, which is one-tenth of Facebook's total value. There are now 1.4 billion Instagram users worldwide, 70% of whom are younger than 35 years of age. Ka-ching, ka-ching.

There is an interesting postscript to this story. Do you remember Dan Carp, the Kodak CEO who set up a digital disruption team, whose main 'weapons' were EasyShare and Ofoto? The strategy was focused on the sharing of photographs in much the same manner as Instagram would do ten years later. When Kodak went to the wall, Ofoto was sold off for 25 billion dollars as part of the bankruptcy plan, at the same moment that Facebook was prepared to pay 1 billion dollars for the baby Instagram.

It is clear that in the case of Kodak digitalisation caused an entire business to evaporate, and to a much greater extent and at a much greater loss of value than we saw with later examples, such Blockbuster versus Netflix or EMI versus iTunes and Spotify. In these cases, there was simply no more money left to earn. All the turnover had been squeezed out, except perhaps for the internet bytes or digital cloud storage for photo books, although even this was already being offered free of charge by Yahoo and later by Flickr and Google.

What if Kodak had applied scenario thinking?

Develop foresight skills and, if necessary, leave the market.

What happened on that evening in 1975, when Steven Sasson first presented his digital camara to the Kodak management? Rebecca Henderson, MIT Sloan Professor, has described a fictional conversation between Steven and a Kodak executive:

"I see. You're suggesting that we invest millions of dollars in a market that may or may not exist but that is certainly smaller than our existing market, to develop a product that customers may or may not want, using a business model that will almost certainly give us lower margins than our existing product lines. You're warning us that we will run into serious organisational problems as we make this investment, while our current business is screaming for resources. Tell me again just why we should make this investment?"

It is a conversation that is still no doubt taking place in boardrooms today. When they are looking to the future, it is understandable that leaders look for new certainties and in Kodak's case they simply did not exist. The idea of a digital camera confronted them with something completely unknown. As a result, they preferred to fall back on what they already knew, on what they were good at. Kodak should have realised that the company was living on borrowed time, unless they could implement a radical change in skills and strategy, and even then success was by no means guaranteed. In interviews many years later, the top men at the time admitted that secretly they did indeed fear that "film is dead". This was the point at which they should have set up a foresight team to search for possible future scenarios that could save the company.

This is a situation you can learn from. Have the courage
to look uncertainty in the face. Dare to experiment.

Spend a proportion of your budget exploring the future. Try to estimate the impact of likely developments in the years ahead and assess how you can protect yourself against any harmful consequences. If you conclude that protection is not possible, dare to accept that your company is end-of-life and try to get out while you can. A sale of Kodak in 1980 would still have been worth billions.

Embrace the digitalisation challenge by setting up a separate team

Steven Sasson took his digital camera to the Kodak board in 1975. Their reaction was dismissive: "Just a toy"; "It will never catch on"; "Not worthy of the Kodak name". All the senior management wanted to do was get back to 'business as usual' as soon as possible. They felt they had more important matters to consider. At that time, operational excellence was a key priority. Every process error had the potential to cost millions, which could be crucial in the battle with an emerging new competitor, Fuji. It was this battle that dominated Kodak's thinking. If you have a 90% market share with a decent profit margin, surely that is something worth defending, isn't it?

Yes, it is, and that is what Kodak rightly did. But at the same time they should have set up a separate team, even one with limited resources, to explore the possibilities of digital photography. Not only from a technological perspective, but also with a view to developing a viable business model. It is clear that Kodak was asking the right questions in 1975. Will people be interested in seeing photographs on a screen? Will they be prepared to pay for it? What will a digital photo book look like? But asking the right questions is one thing; doing something to find out the answers is something else. Kodak should have dug deeper into these matters, experimented, found solutions. The splitting off of a separate division as a start-up would almost certainly have led to an Apple, Instagram or Sony. Whilst at the same time the rest of the company could have concentrated on milking what was left to be milked out of the 'old' film market. It was a massive missed opportunity.

It is wrong to think that people who do not believe in innovation and renewal, as was clearly the case at Kodak, will instantly do worthwhile things if they suddenly have access to large amounts of time and money.

Today, I still see many companies reacting in this same short-sighted way. They are shown something new, but view it narrowly from the familiar perspective of their existing business model. They think: "This can't touch us; the product is inferior; and the earning potential is lower than our current situation". How wrong they so often are!

The cost of not innovating: at least 150 billion dollars

It should be clear by now that failing to innovate cost Kodak a lot of money. But how much exactly? To begin with, there was the cost of the impossible 'catch-up' operation that the company launched after first sitting on its hands for six years. This belated investment in digital R&D was budgeted at 5 billion dollars a year for ten years. And although this operation did result in some new products, their market focus was completely wrong. Conclusion: 50 billion dollars thrown away.

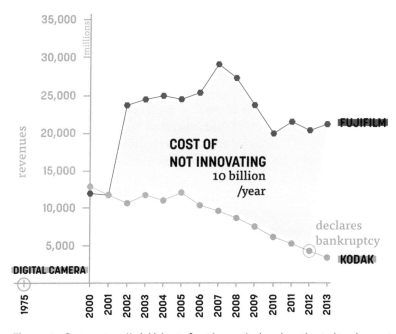

A TALE OF TWO FILM MANUFACTURERS

Figure 18 – Post-mortem, Kodak's 'cost-of-not-innovating' can be estimated to a large extent when we compare the turnovers against the successfully diversified Fuji.

But we also need to take account of the turnover difference between Fuji and Kodak. Over a ten-year period, Kodak lost half of its previous turnover, whereas Fuji gained half, thanks mainly to the Japanese company's carefully focused diversification in certain niche sectors, and this in contrast to Kodak's broader approach in too many domains. This resulted in an estimated loss in revenue for Kodak of 100 billion dollars during those ten years. Taken together: at least 150 billion dollars lost or wasted.

Why is this case still so important today?

As a result of the rapid pace of technological development, digital transformation and the sustainability revolution, I am convinced that many companies today find themselves in exactly the same situation as Kodak in 1975. It is too easy just to say that they should take the innovation plunge and plough forward full steam ahead. As the Kodak case shows, the challenge is much more complex than that. You need to be alert to many different developments, and even if you invest heavily and are recognised as an innovation leader, there are still many other aspects that you need to manage with skill, if you want your innovation to be successful. In particular, this success is based on a combination of three critical factors: the right technology, the right business model and the right organisational culture (people).

You would be surprised how often history repeats itself. You can compare Tesla's history with the development of the first digital camera by Sony in the 1980s. Today's market leading car manufacturers in both East and West are much like Kodak and Fuji used to be, each competing furiously with its rivals in terms of market and price, but failing to invest sufficiently in the radical digital transformation of mobility.

Do you recognise the following scenario? You see a new technological breakthrough that opens up new possibilities in your market. But as far as the future of your company is concerned, you think it is not feasible, your customers won't want it, it is too complex in comparison with your existing refined processes, its profit margins are too low (because the investment costs are too high), etc. In short, you find reason after reason... for doing nothing!

Use the insights yielded by the Kodak case
to avoid making the same mistakes.

So, what should you do? Start today by asking the right questions and by setting up a strategic foresight team to find the right answers. Depending on what you find, are there areas where you can diversify in a smart and focused manner? Are there areas of your current activities that you need to shut down or sell off? Who will be your customers in this new future? Who will be your competitors, bearing in mind that the competitive landscape is not dependent on your history but on your strategy? Should you think about participating in a start-up to boost the R&D capacity of your (currently thriving) business? Do you have the right talent in the company to survive in the medium term? Is the digitalisation of your business and product enough to ensure survival? Are you getting the most out of the long-term benefits of investing in sustainability and digitalisation? Will you stick with the customer experience you know or back the technology that is strange to you? At the very least, foresight will give you more plausible future scenarios and solutions, so that you can develop a dynamic action plan; a kind of rolling strategy that you can implement and explore step by step, making adjustments along the way, as and when they are necessary.

You don't think that any of this applies to you? Your situation is completely different? And much safer? Really? I would suggest that you read on, if you want to discover just how future-proof your company and your teams truly are.

4

BRINGING YOUR INNOVATION SUCCESSFULLY TO MARKET

When Living Tomorrow Amsterdam was opened in 2004, I invited the CEOs of Philips, Unilever and CMG for a debate about innovation. During this debate, the Philips top man said:

"Innovation is bringing something new successfully to market."

His words have always stayed with me; in part, I think, because at that time Philips was finding it difficult to market its own inventions successfully. Back then, Philips was largely a company for engineers (my apologies, but I am also an engineer!). Engineers are often good inventors, but not always good innovators. Because they have little or no contact with their end-users, the customers, they frequently lack market insight. With this in mind, in 2007 Philips Research launched a new initiative known as the Creative Conversion Factory. At the request of Professor Dr Emile Aarts, who was then the Chief Scientific Officer at Philips, I served as a member of the 'founding father board' for a number of years. The CCF was an excellent example of open innovation, a specifically chosen team from Philips Research and Design, supplemented by external advisers, some of whom even came from rival companies like TomTom and Siemens. Together, we formed a multi-disciplinary unit whose purpose was to translate the rich intellectual property of Philips into market-ripe concepts and products. To give you some idea of our approach, I have reproduced below the text of the vision document we drew up in May 2008.

CASE: CREATIVE CONVERSION FACTORY: AN INNOVATION SUPERMARKET

"As was the case with the first industrial revolution in the 18th century, we believe that we are now standing on the threshold of a new age of technological and knowledge-based revolution. A revolution which, in addition to the use of new techniques, systems and ideas, will be initiated and dominated to a significant degree by creativity.

But if creativity, inventiveness and innovation are the drivers of new products and services, whatever became of all the good ideas from the past and what were the reasons for their failure to come to maturity in larger organisations?

There are seven possible explanations:
1. A lack of the right knowledge: looking at the idea exclusively on the basis of your own competencies and discipline.
2. A lack of the right technical solutions: overdependence on traditional production processes, too little capacity and insufficiently radical digitalisation.
3. Economic circumstances, which necessitate a falling back on core activities.
4. Not having or not daring to use the right distribution and sales channels.
5. Reliance on traditional sales channels, so that no new markets can be developed.
6. Timing: some ideas arrive before their time; others too late.
7. Distance or lack of access to new markets.

If we can link a solution to these obstacles with the concept of Open Innovation, it must be possible to improve the creation of new businesses and/or new business activities within existing companies. This conclusion forms the basis for the CCF (Creative Conversion Factory). The CCF distinguishes itself from other incubator organisations as they currently exist in larger companies by the fact that:
- A radical choice has been made to employ an open innovation structure, in which several parties (universities, institutions, SME organisations and large industrial concerns = triple helix) work together on an equal footing.
- The focus will be placed on 'ambient experience', the combination of design and intelligent technology. [Today, we would call this human-centred artificial intelligence.]

- The focus will not be placed on mass volume, fast-moving (consumer) goods, but on smaller series of special products and services."

The CCF was set up in Philips as an open innovation initiative in which companies, designers, technological institutes, knowledge and education institutions and market partners could meet to exchange intelligent, promising ideas and convert them into brilliant concepts. It was intended to be a project management and service organisation that extended wider than Philips alone, with the aim of embracing, facilitating, cherishing, coaching, directing and guiding ideas, in order to bring them to maturity and make them market-ripe. Market-ripe meant that the new concept must have demonstrated the effectiveness of its working principle by means of completing phase 1 of a POC (proof-of-concept), also described as 'from knowledge to know-how to ka-ching' or, if you prefer, K3 (which is also the name of a popular children's pop group in the Low Countries).

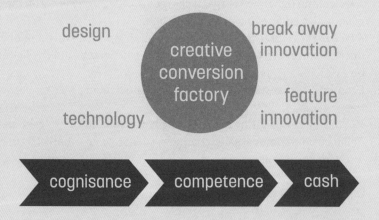

Figure 19 – *The concept note for the CCF at Philips, a first successful step towards systemic open innovation.* SOURCE: CCF, PHILIPS

From knowledge, through know-how to ka-ching – the concept of the innovation supermarket

Various IP (intellectual property) discoveries were examined in the CCF and a number of pilots were set up. The Factory operated almost like a start-up, with multi-disciplinary input from different teams (but teams that were already well-established and respected in their different market fields), supplemented by new skills and go-to-market ideas. One of the successful pilots was 'ambient wayfinding', developed in collaboration with NH Hotels, which made it possible for an intelligent and light-emitting carpet (with the aid of a smartphone) to show hotel guests the way to their room. (In March 2021, Google announced the launch of something similar, with an extension to Google Maps – Google Indoor Maps – that works with augmented reality.)

Other successes? The 'intelligent playgrounds' project, developed with the Korein childcare centre in Eindhoven, made use of intelligent mats linked to each other, in order to create interactive concepts that will allow growing children to become familiar with the idea of smart structures. (At the start of 2019, Tinkamo launched a similar 'smart building blocks' project via Kickstarter.)

In a similar vein, the 'interactive street furniture' project developed a range of urban furnishings for the 21st century, making use of features such as sensors, wifi, intelligent lighting, smart touchscreens and battery charging points. These elements will form – are already forming – the basis of the smart cities of the future.

The 'ambient garden' was developed with Alnwick Gardens in the United Kingdom, where it is possible, when skating on the castle lake in the winter, to leave behind a trail of coloured light with your skates, so that you can create works of art on the ice in real time.

'Photonic textiles' was one of the projects I worked on. This pilot involved collaboration with Lufthansa Technics and Brussels Airlines/Airport and aimed to develop intelligent seats that would light up with the relevant passenger's name when he/she entered the plane or, alternatively, show the number of the relevant gate in the departure hall.

The CCF made IP available to Philips Research and other partners, and served as both a catalyst and a broker between the different parties involved, who mainly came from the creative industries sector, the knowledge institutions and the market. The common purpose was to create an open innovation setting that could make a success of the many inventions that could not be implemented through the normal large business units and therefore were never converted from an invention into an innovation (= market winner). This would all be funded by the payment of a commission on the IP that was successfully marketed.

The CCF concept was ground-breaking and can be seen as the forerunner of today's ecosystems and open innovation clusters. Even so, it failed. Not because of a lack of dedication and enthusiasm in the CCF team, nor because of a lack of interesting IP, technology and ideas. No, it failed because of people. The CCF started off as a reasonably independent project with the participation of many external parties, but at each new meeting an extra chair was added to the table for yet another new internal Philips manager. As a result, it gradually became an inside-out project, instead of the outside-in, open innovation project that had been planned. The CCF was no longer a neutral catalyst, but had become an extension of Philips Design and Philips Research. This led first to friction and eventually, just three years later, to the termination of the project.

How did this happen? In the end, the interests at stake were just too high and the level of investment too important to make honest and open collaboration viable in the long term. Members of the Factory innovated, but then along came Philips to see how this could be translated into a practical and profitable application – primarily for them. In other words, the 'outsiders' were allowed to innovate and lead, but were not allowed to claim the fruits of success. That is not how the ecosystems of the future are supposed to work.

Even so, the CCF can still be rightly regarded as one of the first real attempts to institutionalise open innovation and is one of the main reasons why Philips Research survived. This open innovation motor increasingly allowed Philips to become a world leader in health technology. With its 1,200 researchers from 50 different countries, the laboratory generates 1% of Philips turnover (1% of 20 billion euros = 200 million euros). This makes it the largest private research laboratory in the world and is responsible for two-thirds of all the intellectual property within Philips. Without its emphasis on open innovation within a physical ecosystem, involving hundreds of pilots, partners, the academic world and even the European Union, Philips would no longer exist. In this way, it was able to find the perfect answer to the perfect storm created by the start-ups that became scale-ups and even global companies. It searched for and found a new long-term vision in future health, in collaboration with many other partners.

Why can innovation sometimes fail?
Through a faulty balance between internal
collaboration and open innovation.

95

PART 1 – WHY INNOVATION?

Systemic innovation via open innovation

The business world's view on innovation changed fundamentally after the year 2000, to a large extent under the impulse of the insights developed by Berkeley professor Henry Chesbrough. Large companies were starting to notice that it was increasingly difficult to innovate successfully in the race with the new start-ups, which were starting to emerge from Silicon Valley in particular. These start-ups had stacks of money obtained from venture capitalists, the best talents who were willing to experiment and, above all, no Kodak-like baggage from the past that would prevent them from pursuing new ideas for fear of damaging old ones. The time was past when the brilliant new technical innovations were developed in the R&D labs of closed organisations, innovations that the R&D people then 'sold' to the company's business units, which were expected to successfully market the innovation with the aid of an army of marketeers and sales people. Part of the problem was that these labs had simply become too big. Changes in technology were accelerating in almost every field, creating an ever-increasing number of research opportunities. Eventually, the labs were producing new ideas so quickly that they could no longer be absorbed and converted by the business units into successful innovations in the marketplace. In particular, 'experience' (in other words, existing channels and ways of thinking) had a tendency to slow down or even de-rail market introductions, as we saw in the case of Kodak. At the same time, the research was also becoming so complex that even the R&D labs of the major companies realised that they could no longer do it on their own. They simply did not have all the skills; they needed help from outside. Henry Chesbrough called the model he developed to make this possible 'open innovation'.

The Creative Conversion Factory at Philips was an early example of how a large organisation attempted to innovate openly in a systemic way, by continually striving to bring new ideas successfully to market via an ecosystem. And preferably an ecosystem with a physical hub, because this was found to work better than a virtual network for open innovation purposes. Later, the CCF concept was further (and better) developed to become the Philips Research Campus in Eindhoven, which was subsequently (and more neutrally) renamed as the

Eindhoven High Tech Campus. Today, the campus is a magnet for 235 companies (both great and small) and 12,000 international researchers. In contrast to the CCF, it is a neutral environment, a mini-Silicon Valley where open innovation is given free rein. It has sometimes been called "the smartest square kilometre in Europe". To eliminate the spectre of Philips dominance once and for all, the site was bought by an American real estate group in 2020. The campus is already one of the most innovative tech hubs in the world and aims to become the most sustainable by 2025. Its focus areas are health and vitality (a Philips speciality, of course), sustainability, AI, smart environments and connectivity, and software platforms.

Systemic or continuous innovation requires large organisations to think more wide-rangingly and to look beyond the confines of their own market. In other words, they must think and look from the outside to the inside: how can they organise themselves optimally to explore, discover and bring in new external ideas, some of which may be close to what the company already does, whereas others – at first sight – may seem to be radically different? By adopting this outside-in approach, organisations will open themselves up to impulses, knowledge and experiences that will take them out of their comfort zone, allowing them to gain more knowledge and greater insight into the dynamics of innovation in their market and making them better able to pick up signals from their environment that they can translate into internal insights, wisdom and action.

A CONVERSATION WITH PROFESSOR DR EMILE AARTS

For many years, Emile was closely involved with the innovation process at Philips Research and by the end of his 30-year career with the Philips organisation he was both a member of the Research Management Team and Chief Scientific Officer. He was the founder of the Philips HomeLab and the Creative Conversion Factory, as well as being one of the prime movers in the transformation of the Philips Research Campus in Eindhoven. When I first visited the campus, this massive park was dominated by Philips buildings and surrounded by a metres-high fence. The place was full of innovation secrets and they needed to be protected! To enter, you had to pass through an identity check and leave your ID card behind. You only got it back when you left again. You were not allowed to walk freely around the campus, but had to be picked up from reception by the person with whom you had an appointment. Thankfully, all this has now changed. You can drive into and out of the campus freely. No fence, no reception, no identity control. Just 150 companies that all hope in one way or another to change the world. The difference with the past could not be greater. And it is only because of this difference – the switch to openness and open innovation – that Philips Research still survives and has become a world leader in domains that were scarcely developed when the campus first started.

I asked Emile why Philips has succeeded where Kodak failed: "Of course, I am familiar with the innovation problem at Kodak. I often refer to it as the problem of 'ambidextrous innovation'. With this kind of innovation a company is like a body that has two hands, neither of which knows what the other one is doing. Instead of working together, they work independently. The result is two different and opposing streams of thought within the same organisation, which make conversion to successful market innovation much more difficult. The secret of innovation success in these circumstances is that you need to feed both streams in parallel, although it is sometimes necessary to separate them completely, if you want to innovate effectively. The key is to find exactly the right moment of transfer, the moment when you opt to switch from the old ways and try something radically new. I can still remember the furious discussions in defence of the old and bulky Philips CRT (cathode ray tube) televisions when the first flatscreen models emerged from our lab. There were plenty of people in Philips who believed that the flatscreen would never be a commercial success. A CRT television occupied a position of prominence in people's living rooms; it was part of the furniture, often 'displayed' on a sideboard or in a cabinet of its own. Who on earth would want to replace this with a flatscreen hung on a wall? At first, we found it very difficult to sell the new screens through our traditional market channels. The breakthrough came when the large chain stores like Fnac started to give more prominence to the new models, pushing the large CRT TVs to the back of their displays. After some encouragement, their sales staff also began to explain the new screens to customers in a much better way. Suddenly, we were off and running. The market began to swing in our direction. Fortunately for Philips – unlike Kodak in similar circumstances – it was not too late for us to become market leader.

But how do you actually manage this transition to something new? Rick Harwig, one of our former CTOs, once told me: 'You have to think big and act small. Take little steps. If you take big ones, you will end up falling over.' On the one hand, you have the completeness of the vision – the innovation

– you want to realise, the development of which is actually quite cheap. On the other hand, there is the question of whether you are capable of converting this into something marketable, which is very expensive. Not only the realisation, but also the channels, the earning model, and training people. The implementation of 'something new' demands long and consistent investment of a magnitude which is so great that it has the potential to destabilise the entire organisation. We have made these kinds of mistakes in the past. Just think of the V2000 and the DCC player. You have to invest so much in the execution of an idea before you can get it to the market that you need to sell millions of whatever it is before you start getting a return. That is why you have to think big, but act with more restraint. At one time, we used to invest huge resources in intrapreneurship. At its peak, Philips Research had an annual budget of 300 million euros and employed some 2,000 people. The research teams didn't need to worry too much about earning models, because the money came from the company's strategic investment fund, but there was always discussion about the size of the investment and the related scale of the return. Back then, however, the important thing was to generate patents. Patents were measurable output that created revenue and that formed the basis of the business case to justify the scale of the funding for R&D. When things started to go less well with Philips, the banks injected a huge amount of new capital, and the IP portfolio was part of the collateral. Today, that would be unthinkable. But in those days there were lots of industrial labs like our own Philips NatLab (Research) and they all worked in the same way. There were Thompson Research Labs, Nokia Labs, Siemens Forschung Labor, Bell Labs, Xerox PARC and IBM Labs, to name but a few. At Philips, we were jealous of IBM Labs, because they had Nobel Prize winners in their teams! The senior management at Philips didn't think that was necessary. What they wanted was for us to make as many new inventions as possible. And so we tried to find ways to innovate further and more deeply than ever before. But this led to a new problem: the various Philips business units were unable to absorb our huge output of new ideas. They simply didn't have the time or resources to convert them into execution, although part of the reason was also the fact that Philips had shed a number of its units, such as the semi-conductor branch, so that there was less cross-fertilisation.

During the 1990s and at the start of the new century, lots of new ideas were generated by start-ups, who were financed from other sources, including venture capital. This way of working began in Silicon Valley. The start-ups hardly had any rules when it came to innovation. For example, they weren't hampered by the need to work through classical channels. Their organisational approach was lean and they innovated in sprints, with a much shorter time frame than we were used to. As a result, they had less pressure to sell huge volumes of their product or service in order to be successful. Instead, they sold their idea and their company to large organisations. Philips bought many start-ups in this way, because by now it was clear we needed to do things differently. The mother company no longer provided the same level of resources for R&D: the strategic fund had dried up. The name for this new approach was 'shrink to fit'. Many of the company labs disappeared or were obliged to collaborate with external partners. It was the only way to attract resources; both budget and IP. This was the start of open innovation. But it wasn't all plain sailing. Sometimes unused IP from Philips Research was sold for next to nothing to our competitors, as though this was the most normal thing in the world. At first, this provoked heated discussions between the R&D people and the senior management at Philips HQ. How could we more or less give away IP that was financed with company money to our rivals?

The situation became ever more difficult for the major companies. Some of the large labs from the past were able to survive as part of a campus, working in collaboration with numerous external partners in a so-called 'open innovation' concept. It was in this manner that physical ecosystems came into being. One example of this is the High Tech Campus in Eindhoven – the cradle of Philips Research – which has grown into a world-class innovation ecosystem. It works better than the more virtual networks, which have generally been less successful. For many large organisations, these open ecosystems are the answer to the storm created by venture capital and start-ups. The present-day Philips innovation division operates within this kind of ecosystem, with a focus on human artificial intelligence, or ambient intelligence as we used to call it. At one point, the Finnish European Commissioner Erkki Liikanen was a true champion of this unique form of European collaboration. He had witnessed at first hand the downfall of Nokia, a company that was once the pride of Finland. He said: 'Collaboration is the creation of a certain image, an image with allure. You need to attract people, make them want to be a part of it. Together, we are strong. As a major company, you can be the leader of such a collaboration, but you can no longer claim it as your own.'

Thinking of this kind gradually led to the development of a European collaboration mentality as a triple helix: companies, research institutions and the government. Philips Research agreed to lend the name of its Ambient Intelligence programme to this ambitious European collaboration, which eventually be-came known as the Ambient Assisted Living project, in which billions of euros were invested. One of the finest achievements of this project was the fact that for the very first time scenarios were used as part of the innovation process. Working with the Belgian professor in Open Science, Jean-Claude Burgelman, who was then head of the IPTS, we developed various ambient assistance sce-narios. One of the personages we created was 'Marie', who lived in the future and was surrounded in her daily life by human-oriented artificial intelligence. People and users were suddenly placed at the forefront of our plans for a new information society. The scenarios were drawn up by many different stake-holders from all the major industries in Europe. It was an important step to-wards laying the foundations for fundamental human-centric open innova-tion." Dixit Professor Aarts.

And so it was that Europe embarked on a new path, a path that led to open innovation ecosystems. It was a different policy from the heavy investment in the rampant growth of start-ups to scale-ups that had been adopted by other world players, like China and the US. This European decision is now starting to bear fruit. The climate for collaboration, also with new start-ups, is healthier here than it is anywhere else in the world. In America and China huge resourc-es were used to foster the 'winner-takes-all' principle, with the result that the unicorns grew into international super-companies like Facebook, Google, Al-ibaba and Tencent. These companies have become so powerful that they risk losing themselves in unbridled capitalism and imperialism.

China in particular feels threatened by these developments and at the end of 2020 the Chinese government put its foot on the brake and set limits to the activities of Jack Ma. The other Chinese mega-companies were also compelled to fall into line. Even in the United States more and more people are starting to sound the alarm. Mo Gawdat, a former Chief Business Officer at Google, is a Silicon Valley super-geek who is now trying to warn us against the apocalyp-tic dangers posed by artificial intelligence. Brittany Kaiser, ex-director of pro-gramme development at Cambridge Analytica (CA), has blown the whistle on the unethical use of smart systems by the largest companies to influence and mislead electorates. Frances Haugen testified to the US Senate that Facebook consistently puts profit before the public interest. In October 2021, 21 employ-ees of Blue Origin, the space company of Amazon founder and boss Jeff Bezos, published an open letter setting out various 'irregularities' that in their opin-ion would lead to unsafe space travel.

The transformation from Philips Research to Open Innovation was a powerful signal for change. It was the start of a true collaborative process, with all the trial and error that this involves. What have I learned from this experience?

- Make innovation a process.
- Make sure that this process has an owner, who is sufficiently powerful and respected to guarantee the necessary budget. If you cannot find the full budget you need from this owner, you will have to look elsewhere, but this means that you risk bringing in too much from outside, which always has consequences and results in obligations. If you attract external resources and skills, you need to know exactly what you want to achieve in the long term. What is your higher purpose?
- Have the courage to terminate dead-end trajectories. "At Philips, we celebrated the failure and termination of activities with congratulations for the project leader, with the idea of showing that this kind of culture also needs to exist in large companies. In particular, the German engineers found this difficult. They thought we were laughing at them. But I learned that above all you need to create a safe environment for your innovation people. They need to know that if they fail, they won't be sacked on the spot, but can later go on to work on something even more interesting. You can regard it as developing a kind of social plan for innovation with intrapreneurship. In a start-up, you risk everything. In an established organisation, you want certainty – even when things go wrong." Or so says Professor Aarts.

In a nutshell

In this chapter, I shared my experiences at the Philips Creative Conversion Factory to show that no matter how important the success of systemic open innovation might be for our future, achieving it involves serious challenges. It requires organisations to think further and deeper than their own market, so that they can lead – but not claim – an open ecosystem. I also presented a model for an alternative K3: from knowledge to know-how to ka-ching. Remember also the wise advice of Professor Emile Aarts: build a social plan for innovation.

"Let's go invent tomorrow instead of worrying about what happened yesterday." STEVE JOBS

PART 2
HOW TO INNOVATE: THE SEVEN KEYS TO SUCCESS

In the previous part of the book, I described the evolution of innovation and technology through time. From this point onwards, I will take you on a voyage of discovery into the future, a voyage powered by technology, because this will have an increasingly major impact in the decades to come. Not only on our organisations, but also on society and on us as people in our daily lives. To make this voyage a successful one, I will provide you with seven keys that will allow your organisation to innovate to the maximum possible extent and in the best possible way (see opposite).

Throughout my career, I have heard time and again in conversations with companies and government organisations that innovation is best achieved by first searching for a business strategy, before then moving on to find via scouting the right technology that can help to successfully implement that strategy. In my opinion, this approach is fundamentally wrong, for almost every organisation. As we saw in the previous chapters, technology is evolving at lightning speed and offers new opportunities almost every day. In other words, nowadays the technology comes first and only then is it followed by new and innovative services and business models. Some examples? First there was the steam engine and then came the industrial revolution (in transport, production, trade flows, etc.). First there was the jet aeroplane and then came the international commercial aviation industry. First there was the internet and then came e-commerce. First there were reusable rockets and then came space tourism. In other words, it is technology that always starts the ball rolling. This is often disparagingly referred to as 'techno-optimism'. The reality, however, is different: if you let your rigid business model determine the speed at which you adopt new technology, you are already standing on the edge of the precipice. Over the years, I have witnessed this scenario in many organisations, which sooner or later got into difficulties. And it will continue to happen in the future.

KEY 1:

Focusing your tech lenses on the future

KEY 2:

Is your organisation Future Fit?

KEY 3:

Innovation structures

KEY 4:

Putting together a winning innovation team

KEY 5:

Three horizons for building the future

KEY 6:

Scenarios as the core of your innovation

KEY 7:

Develop ecosystems

BONUS KEY:

Stay alert with early warning systems

You need to invest in future thinking. This means you must investigate which of the technologies from the previous chapter will determine how you will deal with your customers in a fundamentally different way in the years to come, and then adjust your activities accordingly. If you fail to do it, you can be certain that someone else will. Someone who is perhaps not even on your radar at the moment. If you want to remain relevant in the future, you will need to take these new possibilities as your starting point and then use them as a basis for changing your business or organisational model – and not the other way around. From now on, looking towards the future will be a necessary new tool for building the right processes.

First and foremost, this will involve examining the needs of your future customer as a person, citizen, patient, traveller, employee, etc. Secondly, you must analyse the new technological possibilities that will be available in the future and will allow you to provide totally different solutions to these customer needs. Thirdly, you need to assess your 'next connectivity' with the consumer, the way in which you will communicate and remain in contact with them. Today, this is often referred to as the digital transformation of service provision, but it actually goes much further than that.

How can an organisation remain resilient and prepare for tomorrow and even the day after tomorrow? This is a question that you hear increasingly in business circles. But is it really necessary to focus so strongly on the future? Yes, it is. Why? Because following the exceptional circumstances created by the Covid-19 pandemic, our companies will find it more challenging to display creativity and resilience during a decade in which new innovations will be brought to market faster than ever before. A crisis like the Covid-19 crisis can be an opportunity to create new value and to see how things can be done differently. The business pack of cards has been reshuffled, so that people now have a different hand to play. Change and innovation are two sides of the same coin. If you are able to take advantage of this change momentum, your organisation will not only be ready for the race to get the world 'back to normal' once the crisis is over, but may even give you a lead over your rivals.

The change I am talking about is happening now and it should be forcing you to innovate. For that reason, it is important to start finding the right people for your team and to set a new point on the horizon for which you wish to aim. There are no ready-made recipes for innovation, but there are many things that you can already do to get your innovation projects off the ground.

But how exactly do you 'look to the future'? How can you know which things will have an impact? How can you integrate innovation into your organisation and anchor it in a future-oriented culture? How do you remain competitive today without forgetting to innovate, so that you can remain relevant tomorrow?

Before you can start, you need to be aware of the context in which your organisation operates. You need to have an understanding of the societal, technological and environmental trends that affect you. In short, you must have the courage to stare the future in the face, to establish the direction in which you wish to travel and then to rethink your business model from the perspective of this new destination in a future world of new possibilities.

Innovation doctrine

Innovation is a long-term effort. I am convinced that you need more than just a good strategy to innovate successfully. You must have an innovation doctrine, a conviction to remain relevant in the new future world that you have mapped out for yourself. I am not talking about a set of rules and procedures. Instead, this doctrine will be a kind of guide as you move forward, outlining the 'how' and the 'why' of the way you do things. In formal business terms, a doctrine is defined as the fundamental principles that direct the actions of an organisation to achieve its mission. Everyone in the organisation needs to be aware of this doctrine; otherwise, it will not work. You already have a strategy? Great! But a doctrine is something different, something more powerful. A doctrine describes how and why you innovate as a company. A strategy merely describes the way in which you will achieve your future-based objectives. A tactic (or roadmap) describes each step of that process in detail.

If you look at the successful military doctrines of the past, which made it possible for people to fight together as a large group to achieve a common future objective, you will see that they answer six crucial questions:
- Who am I and what are my objectives?
- What obstacles do I face? What are my internal strengths and weaknesses?
- What is the nature of my opponent? What opportunities and threats exist?
- How can I prepare to fight my opponent?
- What methods can I use to win?
- How can I remain alert for rapid changes in the situation?

You will find variants of these same crucial steps in the keys that I will offer you for innovating successfully. Before you start, you first need to assess the technology of the future. This is key 1. Together, we will gaze into the crystal ball of that future and make use of the universal technological laws. You are not tech-minded? If you prefer, you can already turn to the conclusions section at the end of the chapter.

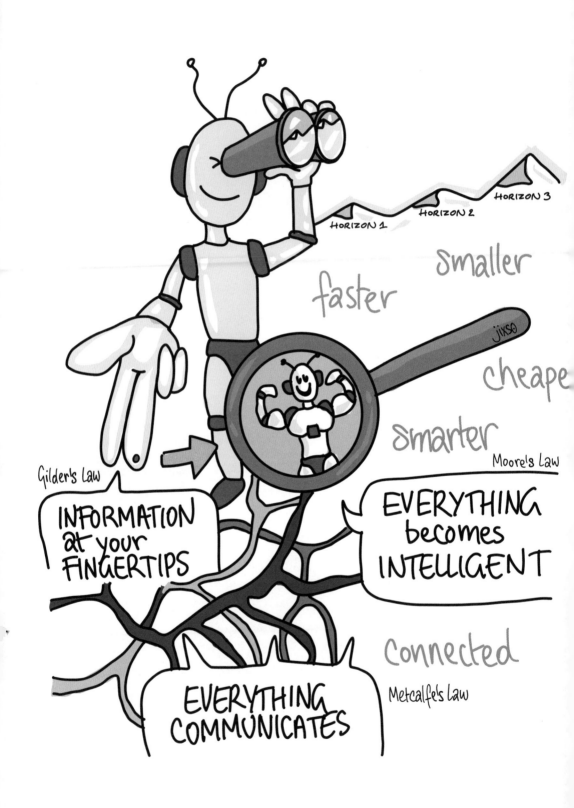

KEY 1
FOCUSING YOUR TECH LENSES ON THE FUTURE

The laws of technology

We are only at the beginning of the new age of digital change. The world wide web (www) started on 6 August 1991, with the appearance of the first public internet page. That is not so very long ago.

Perhaps you were born after 1980, which makes you a millennial? In that case, you might not even know what a fax is and how it works (or worked)? Technologies come and go. Some of the technologies I have described above will no longer exist in 2040. Like the fax, they will be part of history, replaced by something new, different and better, which will open up yet another new age of unprecedented new opportunities. Radical innovations like artificial intelligence (AI), augmented reality and the metaverse as the successor to mobile internet will all be with us by the end of the 2020s. Technology never stands still, but its evolution is getting faster and faster, a trend that will continue in the years ahead.

NO FAX
NO GSM
NO SMARTPHONE
NO WWW

NO FAX
NO GSM
NO SMARTPHONE
NO WWW

1980 ➤ 2030

Figure 20 – *An era of change.*

From my engineering studies, I remembered three laws that have guided me throughout my 25-year career in my search to discover the future. These are Moore's Law, Gilder's Law and Metcalfe's Law.

They have made it possible for me, up to a certain point, to predict the future of technology. They have given me better insight into what is likely to happen in five, ten or twenty years' time. I would like to share these laws with you, because I am convinced that they will continue to be crucial guidelines for the next half century or more to see clearly into the technological future.

THE FIRST TECH LENS - MOORE'S LAW

Smaller, smarter, cheaper, faster...

From Moore to Jen-Hsun Huang

In 1965, when the American engineer Gordon Moore was working as the director of R&D at the chipmaker Fairchild Semiconductor, he sketched a few graphics to depict the cost trend for integrating a number of transistors per integrated circuit (IC). He had noted that between 1959 and 1964 this cost had fallen significantly, while the transistors had become smaller, allowing them to be placed closer together – and therefore more numerously – on the same IC area. At the time Moore made his observation, the chips that he had helped to develop were fairly rudimentary: a circuit board with just a few soldering points and a handful of transistors. Moore drew a curve on his graphic to illustrate how in his opinion the number of transistors that could be fitted onto each board would double every year. He then wrote up his observations in an internal note entitled 'The Future of Integrated Electronics', in which he predicted that by 1975 a chip would contain 65,000 components, followed in 1976 by 130,000 components, and so on. This 15-page document was later published as an article in the *Electronics* journal on 19 April 1965, under the title 'Cramming more components onto integrated circuits'. This was the day on which Moore's Law entered into history.

In plain language, Moore's claim that the number of transistors doubles every twelve months meant that the computing power of smart systems would double every year or, alternatively, that the same level of computing power would become half as expensive during that same year-long period. As a result, everything would eventually become smart, microscopically small and dirt cheap.

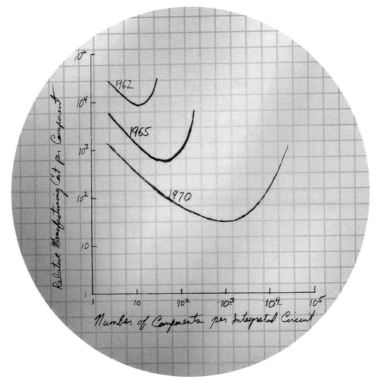

Figure 21 – *The sketch that changed the technological world. Moore's personal notebook contains his first observations. Moore's Law was born.* SOURCE: INTEL, GORDON MOORE

By this stage in his career, Moore was already well known in the American tech industry, but he only secured his place in the history books beyond doubt when he later went on to become a co-founder of the Intel Corporation, one of the technological giants of the 20th century. At the end of the 1970s, Moore was appointed as the company's CEO, a position he held for almost ten years. In 1975, Moore adjusted his initial prediction. He then thought that the doubling of capacity took place every two years, instead of every year, although future experience showed that the doubling took place roughly every 18 months. In essence, a transistor is nothing more than a switching unit that is capable of performing a certain number of calculations. A doubling of the number of transistors every two years (or every 18 months) implies that the computing power of the same surface area of a circuit board would also double during that same period. At the same time, it also implied that the cost of a fixed amount of computing power would be halved every two years (or 18 months). However, there was a further and equally important implication: not only would everything become ever smaller, more powerful and cheaper, but the speed of these evolutions could also be predicted with reasonable accuracy. In other words, Moore's Law offers us an interesting insight for the future: what seems impossible today because of a lack of computing power is certain to become possible tomorrow. This should serve as a constant reminder to design engineers of the need to develop their products with the launch moment in mind; otherwise, they risk their products being outdated before they even reach the market. You think I am exaggerating? Moore's Law shows that I am not. This law works with a logarithmical progression, so that increases in computing power now occur at lightning speed. During the last hour that you have been reading this book, computing power has increased by as much as it did between 1959, when Gordon Moore assembled the first IC, and the year 2000. That is 40 years of evolution compressed into just 60 minutes.

Ever since the 1960s, scientists have constantly been trying to build the fastest computer in the word: the so-called supercomputer. The power of this kind of system is expressed in FLOPS (floating operations per second). The father of supercomputing was Seymour Roger Cray. It was he who first used the brandnew Fairchild Semiconductor silicon chips that Moore had helped to develop. In terms of overheating, they were much better than the germanium chips that had previously been used and they led to the CDC6600, the first of Cray's supercomputers, which had a computing power of 3 MFLOPS. The launch of this new wonder machine was announced in the *Business Week* journal in August 1963, with the comment that "computers should still follow a quadratic law; if the cost price doubles, you should get four times the computing power for your money."

The impact of Seymour Roger Cray on the computer industry cannot be overestimated. It was every bit as great as Thomas Alva Edison's impact on electricity. In 1972, he founded Cray Research, which even today is still a leader in the development of supercomputers (although since 2019 it has been part of Hewlett Packard Enterprise). Under the stimulus of Cray and others, supercomputers continued to get bigger and better, making use of the massive parallelisation of microprocessors with multiple computing cores. They could either be used for general purpose computing or for specific purpose computing. A good example of the latter application is IBM's Deep Blue, which was specifically developed to beat the world chess champion Garry Kasparov in 1997, thanks to its computing power of 11.38 GFLOPS. More typical tasks for supercomputers include cancer research, weather modelling and, more recently, pandemic simulations.

There is always a great temptation to compare the power of supercomputers with the power of the human brain. However, this comparison is pointless, because the brain works in a very different way to a computer. That being said, it is not pointless to ask how many FLOPS would be required before a computer can acquire a level of performance that can be broadly compared with that of the human mind. In 2007, IBM built the Blue Gene/P supercomputer, which attempted to artificially replicate roughly 1% of the neurons in the human brain. This was equivalent to 1.9 billion neurons with 9 trillion connections. An artificial network to replicate the brain power of a mouse was also developed and for the first time exceeded the barrier of 1 petaFLOPS (= 1,000 trillion FLOPS).

According to Moore's Law, it should have taken 15 years – in other words, until 2022 – to increase this massive computing power by a factor of 1,000. However, the even more magical barrier of 1 exaFLOPS was already broken on 25 March 2020 by folding@home,* a distributed supercomputing model or cloud-supercomputing project. This initiative makes it possible for ordinary consumers to make their laptop or PC available for other computing tasks when they are not being used. This power has been harnessed, for example, to study the misfolds in proteins and the manner in which illnesses can develop there. At the start of the Covid-19 pandemic, the project also received considerable media attention when its computing capacity was largely put at the disposal of scientists working to gain insight into the Covid-19 virus, with the aim of developing possible remedies to combat it. Many ordinary people wanted to make a contribution to meeting the greatest medical and societal challenge of the century so far and made their home computers available for this purpose. This led to a doubling of the project's computing power in just one week, smashing the 1 exaFLOP barrier and achieving a maximum capacity of 2.4 exaFLOPS. This was more than the combined capacity of the world's top 500 supercomputers at that time.

On 22 June 2020, again stimulated by the impetus of Covid-19 research, the Japanese supercomputer Fugaku,** named after Mount Fuji, established a new record score of 1.4 exaFLOPS. In November 2021, the system pushed its record

---

* https://www.sciencealert.com/so-many-people-are-running-folding-home-that-it-s-created-the-world-s-biggest-supercomputer
** https://www.nytimes.com/2020/06/22/technology/japanese-supercomputer-fugaku-tops-american-chinese-machines.html

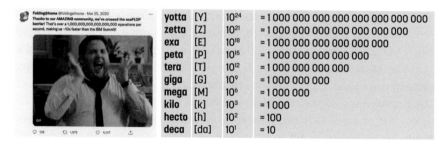

yotta	[Y]	10^{24}	= 1 000 000 000 000 000 000 000 000
zetta	[Z]	10^{21}	= 1 000 000 000 000 000 000 000
exa	[E]	10^{18}	= 1 000 000 000 000 000 000
peta	[P]	10^{15}	= 1 000 000 000 000 000
tera	[T]	10^{12}	= 1 000 000 000 000
giga	[G]	10^{9}	= 1 000 000 000
mega	[M]	10^{6}	= 1 000 000
kilo	[k]	10^{3}	= 1 000
hecto	[h]	10^{2}	= 100
deca	[da]	10^{1}	= 10

Figure 22 – *The folding@home project was the first to break the exaFLOP barrier.*

up to 2.0 exaFLOPS on the HPC-AI benchmark.* This is the equivalent of 5 million top-of-the-range smartphones in a single room and is starting to approach
what some people believe is the basic computing power of our human brain. Of
course, we know it will not stop there. Within the next two years, it is almost
certain that the 10 exaFLOP mark will be reached and passed, continuing inexorably and exponentially upwards towards the zetta scale of 1,000 exaFLOPS,
which, according to Moore, should happen sometime around 2030. This will
represent the start of a totally new computer paradigm.

What, as a society, are we going to do with this massive computing power? In
the past, supercomputers have been used to put the first man on the moon, to
crack super-codes, and to develop both ground-breaking medicines and potentially super-destructive military systems. And in the future? Digital neuromor-
phic hardware (supercomputers that are specially made to simulate the human
brain) like SpiNNaker 1 and 2 will continue to get bigger, better and more powerful, and will play an important role in decision-making and thought processes that have not as yet been humanly possible.

At the present time, the power of supercomputers is also helping neuroscientists to better understand the mysteries of our human brain. And it is inevitable that future supercomputers, with the help of AI, will be used to create
faithful and increasingly functional replicas of that brain. This is likely to provoke serious ethical discussions, which may take generations to settle. What is
the perception of consciousness? What is the definition of thinking? For what
purposes can, should and must the artificial super-brain be used?

---

* https://www.fujitsu.com/global/about/resources/news/press-releases/2021/1116-01.html

The essential question is not whether we will ever succeed in creating a super-computer that is powerful enough to simulate human thought, because one day that will certainly be possible. The question is whether we should be try-ing to create such an artificial brain. Until now, 1 exaFLOP has generally been regarded as the minimum computing power of the human mind. As we have seen, this barrier has already been reached and passed. So does this mean that supercomputers are already as smart as human beings? It is a bit more com-plicated than that. In fact, the answer is both 'yes' and 'no' – for now. In terms of computing power, the answer is 'yes'. But intelligence is more than a mat-ter of straightforward computing power. The human brain is superb when it comes to making connections and acquiring insights and knowledge based on experience. That being said, neural networks that simulate the workings of the brain have been making huge progress in that direction and the moment of

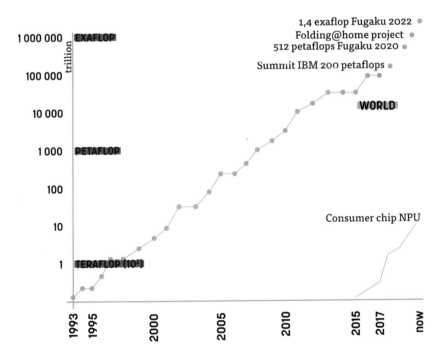

Figure 23 – *The race for the most powerful supercomputers is accelerating. And your new home computer is as powerful as a supercomputer in 2005.* SOURCE: TOP500 SUPERCOMPUTER DATABA

singularity – the moment when artificial cognitive skills reach the same level as human skills – is now estimated to occur at some point between 2040 and 2050. After that, in keeping with Moore's Law, this effect will continue to snow-ball, so that by 2070 a virtual assistant will have a level of cognitive skill that is equivalent to all the human brains on earth... Of course, this is still some distance in the future, so let us return for the moment to the present.

The main challenge currently facing supercomputing is the concentration of the necessary computing power into a single system at a single location. To keep an exaFLOP computer in operation requires around 40MW of electricity. This is a massive amount of energy and requires an equally massive cooling capacity. This in turn leads to significant stabilisation and reliability problems. For these reasons, it seems likely that for the time being the shortest route to exa-computing and zetta-computing will continue to be through the further development of distributed supercomputing. It is possible that in the not-too-distant future the chips in our smartphones, cars and smart homes will all form part of a super-intelligent network that can make available several exaFLOPS of computing power, whilst at the same time avoiding the energy, cooling and reliability problems that are hampering today's generation of central systems. For now, a collective supercomputer is smarter and more powerful than any of the 'independent' alternatives.

Moore's Law in practice

In my opinion, the importance of Moore's Law – and, in particular, its predictive power – is difficult to underestimate, although not everyone agrees. For some, it is too theoretical. For others, it is only relevant for engineers and computer scientists. Really? Let us return to that moment in December 1975 when Steve Sasson showed his prototype of the first digital camera to his bosses at Kodak. One of those bosses, who could see the potential danger of the new technology for the existing Kodak business model, asked Sasson how long it would take before the company's analogue empire would be replaced by its new dig-ital rival. Sasson was prepared for this and on this occasion Moore's Law was his ally. Sasson's camera made use of the light-sensitive MV-100 chip, the very first CCD that contained a total of 10,000 transistors (100 transistors on each of 100 CCDs). Sasson had already asked the optical engineers at Kodak a very concrete question: how many transistors would he need to place on a chip to make a camera with sufficient image quality to rival the Kodak cameras that were then on the market? The boffins replied that 2 million pixels ought to be enough, which sounded a ridiculously large amount at that time. But not to

Sasson. Using Moore's Law, he calculated how long it would take to get from a CCD with 10,000 transistors to a CCD with 2 million transistors. His conclusion was that it would take just twelve years. In fact, his estimate turned out to be too cautious. In 1981, only six years later, Sony launched the Mavica, the first commercially viable digital camera. What if the Kodak management had listened to Sasson's prediction? The fate of the company could have been very different.

This is just one example of the business value of Moore's Law when looking at the future. Since 1970, the law has also formed the core of the silicon industry in one of the most innovative regions in the world: Silicon Valley. The near-perfect progression of its predictive curve has helped to create a multi-billion dollar sector, generating smart technologies that today play an important role in all our lives.

Since 2015, however, there has been a noticeable (temporary?) slowing down of the curve. This has led some commentators to claim that Moore's Law is finite and may be approaching its end. And indeed, even though microprocessors

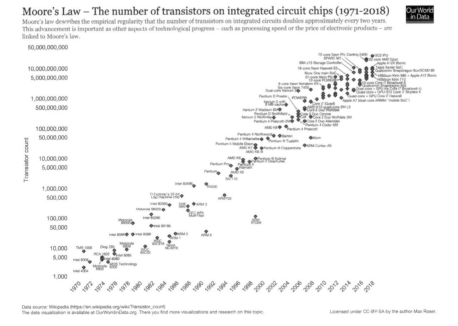

Figure 24 – *Moore's Law from the start to today in chart. A constant acceleration.* SOURCE: WIKIPEDIA, OURWORLDINDATA.ORG – LICENSED BY CC-BY, MAX ROSER

continue to get smaller and smaller, at some point even the most sophisticated forms of nanotechnology will find themselves confronted by the boundaries of physics. The most recent chips from TSMC – anno 2021 the largest chip maker in the world – are now just 5 nanometres big (or small). However, IBM has recently launched a 2 nm chip that is half as fast again and also – just as importantly – 75% more energy-efficient. These developments mean that it is now possible to put billions of chips on a single standard circuit board. In theory, it should still be possible to go even smaller, but the cost of building the factory to manufacture such miniscule chips is likely to be too high to make their production commercially viable. In other words, viewed from a purely technical perspective Moore's Law is probably approaching its limits. Be that as it may, following the age of 'ordinary' circuit boards and graphic processors we are now standing on the threshold of a new technological revolution, where the law's precepts may still be of great importance: quantum computing and neural systems-on-a-chip. I would like to take a closer look at the second of these.

Huang's Law: the revival of Moore's Law

The fundamental working of the 'classic' chip (CPU) in which Intel specialised hardly changed for 65 years. These chips were ideally suited for performing general tasks and serial operations at very high speed. However, for graphic operations with a highly complex structure, the use of more powerful graphic processors (GPU) – a field in which NVIDIA leads the way – is more appropriate. A GPU is constructed in a completely different way to a CPU, primarily because it houses many different parallel processing units that all compute at the same time. For this same reason, the training of neural networks (machine learning) is also ideally suited for these GPUs – far more so than for the classic CPUs – due to the similarity between mathematical processing and image processing. On the downside, GPUs continue to be less efficient for dealing with serial tasks than CPUs.

The newest form of processing power is now the NPU (neural processing unit), which has been specifically developed to carry out ML/AI (machine learnings / artificial intelligence) tasks. As a result, NPUs are not suitable for general tasks. To this we should add the DSP (digital signal processing unit), which has also been specially designed, but this time for the processing of digital signals. Like the NPU, it is not suitable for general tasks. The NPU is no longer exclusively a piece of hardware, as was the case with the silicon CPU. It is a combination of a hardware structure developed for AI purposes with modified software. The resulting computing power is very impressive. So impressive, in fact, that it looks set to significantly accelerate the rate of increase predicted by Moore's Law, so that the computing power that is necessary to train neural networks and apply what they have learned will skyrocket dramatically in the years ahead.

In this context, one increasingly hears the name Jen-Hsun Huang, an electro-technical engineer of Taiwanese-American origin who in 1993 founded the NVIDIA Corporation. Thanks in part to his amazing entrepreneurial spirit and technical genius, the gaming industry has grown to become the most important branch of the global entertainment business. Today, NVIDIA develops the most powerful AI chips in the world, the capacity of which (for certain AI operations) increased by a factor of 317 between 2012 and 2020. The NVIDIA chief executive described recently how the speed of the new NPU chips, with their combination of hardware and software, more than doubles every two years, a

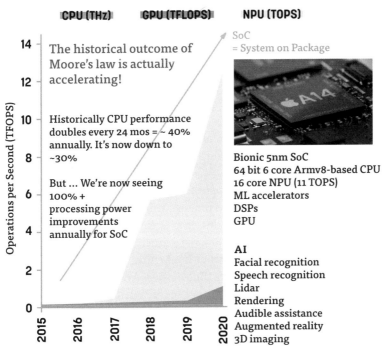

THE EXPLOSION OF ALTERNATIVE PROCESSING POWER (EX. A9 - A14)

CPU (THz)   **GPU (TFLOPS)**   **NPU (TOPS)**

The historical outcome of Moore's law is actually accelerating!

Historically CPU performance doubles every 24 mos = ~ 40% annually. It's now down to ~30%

But ... We're now seeing 100% + processing power improvements annually for SoC

SoC = System on Package

(A14 chip image)

Bionic 5nm SoC
64 bit 6 core Armv8-based CPU
16 core NPU (11 TOPS)
ML accelerators
DSPs
GPU

AI
Facial recognition
Speech recognition
Lidar
Rendering
Audible assistance
Augmented reality
3D imaging

(y-axis: Operations per Second (TFOPS), values 0, 2, 4, 6, 8, 10, 12, 14; x-axis years: 2015, 2016, 2017, 2018, 2019, 2020)

Figure 25 – *The neural processing units of the latest chips accelerate computing power in two domains simultaneously: hardware and software.* SOURCE: SILICON ANGLE – DAVE VELLANTE, DAVID FLOYER [8]

phenomenon that is now sometimes referred to as Huang's Law. In other words, by expanding the scope of the 'old' Moore's Law from the number of transistors or gross CPU capacity to cover total computing power instead, a 'new' Moore's Law will continue to do service during the coming decades. This is important, because it will allow us to continue making reasonably reliable estimates about the further development of computer chips, a process in which the lightning-fast evolution of the new NPU technology will be a real game-changer. This further exponential growth will have an impact on all aspects of our day-to-day life, from self-driving cars, hyperloops and autonomous diagnostic systems on our wrists to the far-reaching application of super-intelligent facial, voice and object recognition in everyday products,

In addition, great progress is also currently being made in the attempt to integrate all the different silicon chips (CPU, GPU, NPU, DSP) into a single system. In this way, it should be possible to eliminate the unnecessary connective links between the different chips, resulting in greater speed and efficiency, combined with reduced energy use. The above graphic illustrates the evolution of the various types of processors. The CPU is measured on the basis of its frequency (THz), which is one serial operation per clock cycle, sometime simultaneously in different cores, which can be eight or sixteen in number. There is little scope for increasing this significantly. The GPU is measured in trillion floating point operations per second or TFLOPS. Here a degree of progress has been (and continues to be) booked. The NPU is measured in trillion operations per second or TOPS. This is represented by the grey area in the curve, which makes clear that the NPU is responsible for by far the largest proportion of computing power growth in the system as a whole.

The major efforts being made by Apple to develop its own Ax/Mx chip are also part of this process. They refer to the resulting technology as the 'System on a Chip' (SoC), because their new M1 chip is capable of integrating different components. As a result, these SoCs are much quicker and much more efficient than the previous generation of Intel chips. The memory in an SOC is not upgradable, but it works many times faster. An M1 contains 16 billion transistors and in October 2021 the company launched the M1-Max, which has increased this number to 57 billion. This is the largest number of transistors that Apple has ever been able to cram onto a single chip, making it (so far) the fastest ever chip built for consumer use, as well as achieving good scores for performance-per-watt. Although the chips were designed by Apple, they are manufactured by TSMC (Taiwan Semiconductor Manufacturing Company).

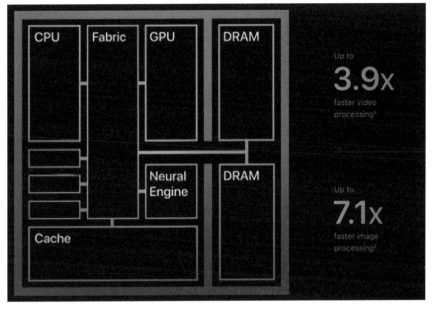

Figure 26 – *Apple's System on a Chip ensures that computing power continues to grow exponentially.* SOURCE: APPLE COMPUTER 2021 – THE M1 SOC

The newest M1-Max GPU has an output of 10.4 TFLOPS, while the NPU variant generates 11 TOPS. If we apply Moore to these figures, this means that within 17 years Apple's MacBook Pro chip will be capable of producing an exaflop of computing power. In other words, as much computing power as the human brain by 2039. Singularity reached? Check!

What can we learn from all this? The main conclusion would seem to be that Moore's Law is alive and well, albeit in a slightly different form. As a result, it will still be able to show us the way towards the creation of a new generation of multi-billion dollar companies, for those who are smart enough and brave enough to engage in the chip wars of the future.

A chip war in the making?
The need to protect the economy of the future against new monopolies became clear in 2021. Production shortfalls at TSMC meant that the company could no longer keep up with worldwide demand, resulting in a scarcity in all the sectors that build chips into their products. Not only PCs and game consoles, but also 'edge' devices that are connected with the cloud, such as smartphones

and sensors. The car industry was likewise hard hit, and production lines were closed for lack of chips.

This is a worrying development. Over the years, TSMC – whose production units are concentrated exclusively in Taiwan, a country prone to earthquakes – has built up what is effectively a quasi-monopoly for the manufacture of the world's most powerful microchips. They currently hold around 80% of the world market. If one adds to this Taiwan's geographical location and the political threat posed by neighbouring China, which regards Taiwan as a rebellious province, it becomes clear that the future supply of chips is a highly contentious issue, whose outcome is far from certain. Pat Gelsinger, the new and ambitious CEO of Intel, is concerned by the implications of this situation and wants to set his company on a new course. Following an announcement that the current shortage of chips may last as long as five years, which looks set to cost the automobile sector billions, Gelsinger promised to invest 20 billion dollars in new production capacity in the US. At the same time, he is asking the EU for a 10 billion dollar subsidy to do the same in Europe, and has invested a further 200 million dollars in a brand-new R&D facility in Israel.

Under President Joe Biden, Intel wants to return America to its former position as the world leader in chip design and manufacture, with an emphasis

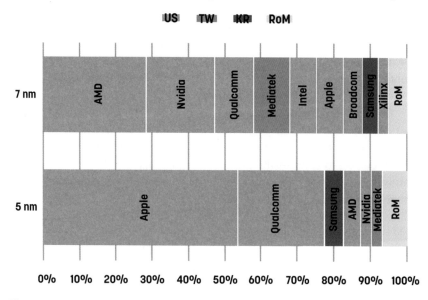

Figure 27 – No European players in 7nm and 5nm chips, especially Apple is dominant.

SOURCE: STIFTUNG NEUE VERANTWORTUNG VIA EENEWSEUROPE

on local production. In similar vein, the European Commission has launched its Digital Compass 2030, which makes a priority of boosting the chip design and production capacity that Europe currently lacks. In the Belgian IMEC it does at least have an excellent R&D facility of world class. But if the West is uneasy, China is nervous as well. During the past decade, China has tripled its own production of chips and is now ahead of the EU and the US. In this way, Peking wishes to make itself less reliant on its Taiwanese competitor TSMC, which, thanks to Apple, in the undisputed world leader in chip manufacture. TSMC – which was originally founded by the Dutch Philips group and the Taiwanese state – responded to this challenge by announcing new investments amounting to 100 billion dollars, which is five times what Intel is planning in the US. And so the moves and counter-moves continue. The seriousness of this situation should not be underestimated. If a country finds itself starved of its supply of semi-conductors, the resulting crisis will be far worse than when countries were starved of oil in the 1970s.

Although currently lagging behind in the chip race, Europe nevertheless plays a role of some importance through ASML. During the 1990s, Philips sold its interest in TSMC and concentrated all its chip activities in ASML. This high-tech company is a monopolist for the manufacture of EUV (extreme ultra-violet) lithographic machines for the production of the world's smallest semi-conductors. Using laser beams, these machines (each costing 100 million dollars) apply nanometre circuits to a silicon wafer on which a total of 1,000 chips can be 'soldered'. According to its CEO, Peter Wennick, ASML is currently capable of producing 50 machines a year. It could theoretically produce more, but is hampered by the long delivery times – often more than a year – for some of its key components, such as ultra-powerful lenses.

It is clear that the chip sector is in a precarious situation, pressured by the twin forces of globalisation and the need for greater cost efficiency. The key question is whether the current worldwide shortage of chips and the perceived need for greater independence of supply will lead to over-investment, which in turn will inevitably result in over-production and price collapse.
The race for minimal energy use and ultra-smart miniature devices Chip architect NVIDIA recently acquired ARM Holdings for over 40 billion dollars. ARM is famed for its production of energy-efficient chips, which is one of the greatest challenges for the successful visualisation of AI applications. Consider, for example, self-driving cars. To reduce the number of accidents to zero, every car needs to be fitted with top-notch AI neural networks and chips, which re-

quire huge amounts of energy before their computing power can be used to its fullest extent. For this reason, in years to come a chip's operations per second watt (OPS/W) may become even more important that its operations per second (OPS).

How much energy does a chip need to perform a single operation? There is very little energy present in, for example, smart glasses or a brain-computer interface, so that every operation that can be performed with the same Watt represents a significant gain. This message is also clear from the NVIDIA graphic reproduced below. The computing power of their NPUs has increased 317 fold during the past five years, but their energy efficiency has also increased 200-fold – and that is just the start. "Over the last three to five years, machine-learning networks have been increasing by orders of magnitude in efficiency," says Dennis Laudick, vice-president of marketing in ARM's ML group. "Now it's now more about making things work in a smaller and smaller environment. ARM's smallest chips are tiny enough to be powered by a watch battery and can now enable cameras to recognise objects in real time."

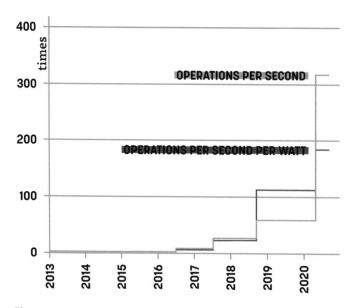

SPEED AND ENERGY EFFICIENCY OF NVIDIA'S CHIPS AS A MULTIPLE OF PERFORMANCE IN 2012

Figure 28 – *NVIDIA chips accelerated 317x in 5 years.* SOURCE: NVIDIA

This is important in light of the switch from the cloud to the edge, but to understand it properly we first need to look at Gilder's Law.

THE SECOND TECH LENS - GILDER'S LAW

Some things become infinite

If we want to try to accurately estimate the speed of technological innovation, we all owe a debt of gratitude to George Gilder. Gilder is an American investor, futurologist and author. He achieved worldwide fame for his insights into the speed of communication and has generally created a furore with his boundless and optimistic belief in future progress. In his futuristic book *Telecosm: The World After Bandwidth Abundance*, Gilder argues that the growth of bandwidth for the transmission of data increases at a speed greater than predicted by Moore's Law. According to Gilder, this bandwidth trebles each year. Is he right? He certainly seems to be, at least in a laboratory environment. But what about in the real world?

> *In plain language, Gilder's claim that the broadband increases by a factor of three every 12 months means that in years to come information will be more than ever 'at your fingertips', thanks to the elimination of all bottlenecks in data flow and transfer.*

The promise of fibre-optics

As early as the 1960s, the first tentative experiments with fibre-optic cables were being carried out as a possible solution to the limitations of classic copper cables. Back then, it almost seemed like a crazy idea, but has since proved its worth. Even a very thin layer of glass absorbs nearly all the light that passes through it. The most transparent glass in the world, of the kind used in endoscopes, is 200 times better in this respect than standard glass, but already loses 20% of its light over a distance of one metre. After 20 metres, nearly all the absorbed light is dissipated. It was Charles Kao, a researcher at STL, a British telecom company, who first raised the bar to a significantly higher level in 1966, with his objective of 99% loss over one kilometre. In other words, 50 times better than endoscopic glass. Five years later, Donald Keck, a researcher at Corning Glass, developed the first optical fibre with optical losses low enough for wide use in telecommunications: 96% over one kilometre. These developments were by no means easy, because they required two totally different worlds to interact with each other: the telecom world that understood nothing about glass and the glass world that understood nothing about communication. Even so, people continued to believe that fibre-optics were the future of data transmission.

The break-up of AT&T in 1982 suddenly created a competitive market in long-distance telephony and the newcomers focused heavily on fibre-optics instead of relying on traditional – but less future-proof – copper wiring. The development of a successful optical amplifier by the University of Southampton gave a boost to the transmission of optical signals, while the doping of optical fi bres with erbium – a rare-earth element that has optical fluorescent properties – further enhanced the strength and clarity of transmission and made possible the manufacture of the first optical cable that was capable of spanning an ocean. This was the TAT-8, which was installed in 1988 and connected North America and Europe across the Atlantic. In the first instance, this was primarily intended to link the CERN particle physics laboratory in Europe with a hub of the early American internet system – the NSFnet – at Cornell University in New York. It was via this link that Tim Berners-Lee, a researcher at CERN, was able to show his first HTML-page to his American colleagues and TAT-8 went on to form the physical basis for the world wide web, which went public for the first time on 6 August 1991. The capacity of the TAT-8 was 280 Mbps, which was roughly ten times more than the previous trans-Atlantic link, which was a combination of radio waves and a coaxial cable. It was thought that it would be possible to work with the TAT-8 for a decade, but after barely 18 months its maximum capacity had been reached.

Even so, it was a historic breakthrough. From that moment on, fibre-optic capacity and the internet grew at a rate that exceeded Moore's Law. This new rate of growth was sometimes referred to as Keck's Law, after the fibre-optics pioneer at Corning Glass, but it was ultimately George Gilder who took the honours in 2000 when he predicted the impact that this would have on the explosive expansion of the internet.

MOORE'S LAW VS. KECK'S LAW, LOG SCALE

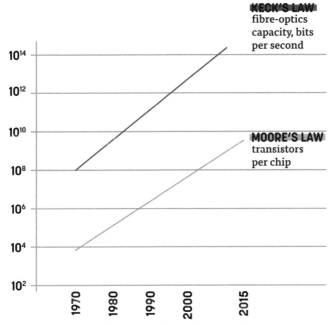

Figure 29 – *The capacity of fibre optics is faster than Moore's law.* SOURCE: THE ECONOMIST, FROM THE
UNIVERSE TO THE DATAVERSE

Anno 2021, fibre-optics are now more or less standard and in laboratory conditions can achieve a maximum speed of 319 terabits per second (1 terabit =
1,000 gigabits) in a single core optical fibre.* In theory, this should be sufficient
to transmit the entire Netflix library from one side of the world to the other in
just one second. Moreover, this transmission speed looks set to increase still
further, in keeping with the provisions of Gilder's Law.

The impact of these developments on our world and our way of life has been
seismic. Think back to how we used to look for information before 1998. That
was the year in which Google became the search engine market leader for
the very first time. Before Google, we had to plough through encyclopaedias

---

* https://www.vice.com/en/article/bvz5kd/japan-transfers-319-terabits-per-second-setting-internet-
  speed-record?utm_source=motherboardtv_facebook&utm_medium=social

or ask others to find out what we wanted to know. After Google, we simply looked it up for ourselves online. Since then, things have now progressed so far that children nowadays are increasingly asking their parents and teachers why they still need to learn anything by heart. Why not just ask Alexa! "Alexa, what is the distance between the earth and the moon?" Answer (in a matter of seconds): "384,400 kilometres." That is what Bill Gates meant when he talked about "information at your fingertips" in his Comdex keynote speech in 1994: everything you ever need to know, just a mouse click away.

What about my home connection?

What will all this mean for the internet connection in your home, your office and your mobile applications? These all work at a much lower speed than the systems we have just been talking about. And also improve in speed more slowly. Which is precisely what Jakob Nielsen of the Nielsen Norma Group realised. He now refers to this as the Law of Internet User Experience, which states that the speed of use for a high-end internet user doubles every two years or, to put it another way, increases by 50% each year. This is slower than Moore's Law and six times slower than Gilder's Law. So how can this be justified? In essence, there are three reasons to explain why the commercial roll-out of broadband by telecom companies does not comply with Gilder's principles for theoretical broadband.

Firstly, it would require a massive investment to continually update and install each newest and fastest internet connection. Streets would need to be broken open to lay better cables to people' homes and the new and better performing end-devices are always expensive, the cost of which all needs to be earned back in one way or another.

Secondly, a faster rate improvement would not always make a significant difference to the end-user. When you invest in a computer that works twice as fast, your software also works twice as fast. When you buy a hard disc that is twice as large or pay for twice as much cloud storage capacity, you can save twice as much data. But paying for a home internet connection that is twice as fast does not necessarily mean that you will gain access to the internet twice as quicky. This will depend on your servers and the network in your vicinity and on every point in between. The weakest link in this chain will form a bottleneck that will slow down your fast internet connection.

Thirdly, there is also the question of internet adoption. Major users have been on the internet for years. But people who are only now coming online often have no real need of a huge broadband solution. As a result, the internet providers know all too well that in practice the demand for internet download speed is not as great as it theoretically should be.

If we step back thirty years in time and compare the speed of the very first modems at the start of the 1990s with the speeds that the average cable connection offers us today, it soon becomes clear that Nielsen's amended version of Gilder's Law is reliably accurate.

In 1990, my first modem had a speed of 14.4 kbps. Two years later that had already doubled and in 1995 my first ISDN-modem boosted that still further to 64 kbps. Around 2002, I switched to cable, which took me through the magic barrier of 1 Mbps. By 2010, that was 10 Mbps. According to Nielsen's commercial version of Gilder's Law, I should have reached 1 Gbps in 2022, but I actually reached it at the end of 2020. In other words, a year earlier than foreseen, but still close to expectation. If we extrapolate this law to the future, we should be looking at 1 Tbps by 2040 and a gigantic 32 Tbps by 2050. This is a clear road map for the years ahead.

Wireless has evolved in a similar way or even at a slightly faster rate than Nielsen predicts. 1990 saw the introduction of GSM (global system for mobile communications), with a maximum speed of 14.4 kbps. This was followed circa 2000 by GPRS/EDGE (2.5G) with speeds up to 512 Mbps and in 2003 by UMTS (3G) with theoretical speeds of up to 42 Mbps. LTE (4G) arrived on the scene in 2010 and achieved peak speeds of 1 Gbps. We are now entering the 5G era, where peak speeds of 10 Gbps are likely to become normal and Samsung has already launched a vision paper for 6G, in which it sets targets for peak speeds of 1 Tbps.*

Because mobile networks supply multiple users, you should probably divide the theoretical network values by ten to get a good idea of your actual download speeds (depending on the available reach at your given location). Speed performance is noticeably better with a fixed cable. At non-peak moments a cable will generally be able to provide you with speeds of up to 1 Gbps. 5G will also make download speeds of 1 Gbps available for mobile networks, which will make it possible for them to compete with the existing commercial cable network. For 6G, it seems (theoretically, at least) that the sky is the limit, with anticipated speeds of around 100 Gbps.

---

* https://cdn.codeground.org/nsr/downloads/researchareas/6G%20Vision.pdf

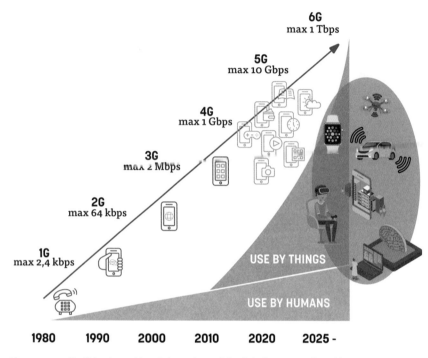

Figure 30 – 6G will be the real breakthrough to a fully digital, connected world.

6G will offer far more additional benefits than speed alone, such as spectacular energy efficiency (1 nanojoule per bit), latency (1 µs delay), and connection reliability, even if you are moving at a speed of 1,000 kilometres per hour in a location with a concentration of 10 million connected devices per square kilometre. Is this all just so much jargon to you? If so, the following practical example will make it clearer. Imagine that you want to download all 50,000 films on Netflix in HD-quality. At 4.5 Gbps per film, this means a total of 220 Tbps. How long do you think this would take, both now and in the future?

Table 2 – *The bandwidth evolution follows Gilder's Law (Nielsen).*

FIXED DOMESTIC INTERNET CONNECTION (PRACTICALLY ACHIEVABLE SPEEDS)		MOBILE DATA CONNECTION (PRACTICALLY ACHIEVABLE SPEEDS)	
Today (1Gbps)	3 weeks	3G (2003, 500 kbps)	119 years
In 2030 (25 Gbps)	1 day	4G (2013, 100 Mbps)	6 months
In 2040 (1 Tbps)	half an hour	5G (2020, 1 Gbps)	3 weeks
In 2050 (32 Tbps)	1 minute	6G (2030, 100 Gbps)	5 hours

Enough said.

From cloud to edge computing

Speeds of this kind mean that in the foreseeable future information will be available to us everywhere and at all times. This is a promise that the internet has already been making for a number of years, but until now it has only been a theoretical promise: so far, low speeds and limited capacity have created insurmountable bottlenecks. Moreover, as more and more devices come onto the market that wish to send and receive huge amounts of data to and from the cloud, this problem is only going to get worse. This is not just because we all want to watch hours of YouTube or Netflix in 8K resolution, but also because Covid-19 has brought about the irrevocable breakthrough of the video meeting. At the same time, an exponential increase in machine learning for AI applications has created a further mass of data that needs to be uploaded to the cloud, so that we are approaching saturation. The commercial roll-out of networks can no longer meet the demand for more broadband. Satya Nadella, the top man at Microsoft, said in March 2021 that the computer industry had already reached peak centralisation and suggested that it was perhaps not necessary to send everything to the cloud for processing.

This is where Moore's Law comes back into the picture. When the systems we use become more intelligent and perform more energy-efficient operations, neural networks will be better able to separate relevant information from superficial data at the local level. This is what edge computing is slowly starting to achieve. Smart local processing units increasingly have the ability to process everything locally, before only sending the important conclusions to the neural network. This is another reason why NVIDIA wanted to buy ARM. In 2019, Nexar – an app that converts your smartphone into an AI traffic monitoring system – still did 40% of its work in the cloud. Today, that has fallen to just 15%, thanks to the use of the more powerful ARM processors. A growing number of AI vision applications, such as smart parking with cameras, will not be possible without edge computing. In this way, the cloud will be relieved of a massive part of its burden and future growth will be found less and less in data centres the size of a football field and more and more on the 'edge'. In addition, this will also lead to huge savings in terms of broadband. This implies a paradigm shift for the business world. Companies will need to abandon the current dogma, which says that it will be impossible for them to get all their information pumped through, as well as the stubborn idea that this will be so expensive that it becomes economically unviable.

Anyone who is developing new products and services in the future should not allow themselves to be misled by the current limitations of our systems today, but must take full account of the impact of Moore's Law and Gilder's Law, and take full advantage of the developments that this will make possible; for example, in the field of edge computing. Within the foreseeable future, we will be surrounded at all times and in all places by super-smart new systems that will have all possible information available to them. This will be a huge game-changer.

THE THIRD TECH LENS – METCALFE'S LAW

An exponential force boosts the metaverse

Fifteen billion, worldwide: that, according to a study carried out by IOT Analytics Research, is the total number of smart devices that currently – anno 2022 – are connected with each other in one way or another. This ranges from waste bins that can be monitored at distance (and can therefore be emptied before they get full), through sensors in gas and water pipes (and can therefore give early warning of leaks), to fully-fledged IoT applications (that can, for example, make huge industrial complexes safer and more efficient). In 2021, there was an average of ten connected devices per household. By 2030, it is expected that each of us will be wearing fifteen or so connected devices, pushing up their global total to around 50 billion worldwide. In fact, this is probably a serious underestimation, although the Covid-19 pandemic in 2020 and the resulting chip shortage in 2021 has temporarily slowed down this process. Given these statistics, it is hardly surprising that the expectation pattern for the Internet of Things has shot through the roof in recent years. With this in mind, it is crucial to make an assessment of the likely speed of technological innovation in the decades ahead. And to do this, we need to look no further than Metcalfe's Law.

In plain language, Metcalfe's contention that the value of a network is proportional to the square of its number of users means that in years to come everything will be increasingly connected with everything else, resulting in super-smart systems.

For many years, Robert Metcalfe worked at Xerox's Palo Alto Research Center (PARC), where he invented the ethernet, before starting his own 3Com (computers, communication, compatibility) company in 1979. This company played a key role in the creation and development of the internet, and even at that early stage Metcalfe was already attempting to formulate an answer to the key question of why people worldwide should want to link an increasing number of their devices to each other. He expressed his answer to this question in terms of value and predicted that the value of a communications network for its users would be directly linked to the number of devices that were connected to that network. He decided to add a coefficient to this conclusion, resulting in the equation that the value of a network will increase quadratically in relation to the number of devices or users connected to it. Put simply: more users = more value per user. This became known as Metcalfe's Law, a term first coined by none other than our old friend... George Gilder.

Metcalfe derived his insights from his experience in the world of telecommunications. Imagine that you are setting up a telephone network. If you have two phones, you have just one connection. If you add a third phone, you now have three connections. A fourth phone gives you six connections, and so on. Each new phone you add creates greater additional value than the previous one. This is referred to as the 'network effect' and can be seen in many different domains, such as the use of a language between people or the emergence of currency. These were among the very earliest networks, where the powerful effect of the added value generated by each incremental user first made itself felt.

A network effect of this kind consists of two components: the direct added value (every extra user = extra value per user) and the indirect added value, which manifests itself as an additional strengthening effect when there is a supply-and-demand aspect to the network, whereby each user on one side of the equation gives extra added value to the user on the other side. Consider, for example, Wikipedia or TripAdvisor: the users who place content on these sites do so for the benefit of the readers of that content. The greater the number of content providers, the greater the value of the network and the greater the degree of choice. Looking at it from the other side, the more people who access the information, the more that information is used, as a result of which even more people will want to become users or even the providers of new content. This is the principle used by Uber, Booking.com, Alibaba, Amazon, Facebook, Twitter, Netflix, LinkedIn, WhatsApp, TikTok, Bitcoin and, more recently, Clubhouse. The value of their networks increases quadratically each time a new user is added: Metcalfe's Law.

There are two interesting additional insights derived from this law that are worth noting:

1. The law of diminishing marginal utility no longer applies.

   Thinking back to your days as an economics student, do you remember the law of diminishing marginal utility, expounded by Hermann Heinrich Gossen? This law states that when a consumer acquires an extra product, the marginal utility of that product decreases. And indeed, the premises of the law are valid for 'classic' products. But Metcalfe showed that they are no longer valid in smart network environments, where each additional and connected smart device increases the value of the network exponentially. In Gossen's day, economists still had no notion of what the connected world of the future would be like.

2. Every connected person is only separated from every other person in the world by three intermediaries.

   In 1990, the American dramatist John Guare wrote a play entitled *Six Degrees of Separation*. This was a reference to an older theory that everyone in the world was separated from everyone else by a maximum of just six contacts. Thanks to the mechanisms of Metcalfe's Law, by 2016 the number of contacts had dropped to three and a half and has almost certainly fallen further since then. Test it for yourself on LinkedIn. This site shows the degree of connection alongside the name of the person you are looking for. With the first degree, you are directly connected. With the second degree, you have a common contact. With the third degree (3rd+), the person is connected via your second-degree network. From the fourth level onwards, no further degree information is shown. Why? Because every known person in the network will never be separated from you by more than three degrees of separation. You don't believe me? Just give it a try! This is the power of Metcalfe's Law. You can send the whole world an InMail and make contact with everyone.

Our brains are a network

When the first social networks began to appear, it became clear that Metcalfe's Law had been prophetic. And it is inevitable that these networks will become ever more important as the IoT continues to grow. You can even see the law at work in nature; in particular, in the way that our own super-computer – the human brain – is constructed. We know that our brain works as a result of the interactivity of more than 100 billion brains cells, each of which is like a microchip. They collect, process and transmit data in the form of electric signals. The cells in the parts of the brain (the frontal and temporal lobes) that are responsible for processing different kinds of information have larger dendrites. These are large offshoots that are specialised in the collection of information signals. Large dendrites therefore help brain cells to analyse and transmit electrical signals more quickly. Through the use of brain tissue derived from brain operations for the treatment of medical conditions such as epilepsy, it has been discovered that people with a high IQ also have larger dendrites and therefore also a faster action potential, especially during periods of increased activity. Or to put it in more simple terms: neuroscientists have discovered that the brains of smart people contain larger and faster brain cells. They can process information more rapidly and store it more abundantly, because their brains have more connections and, consequently, are 'more networked'.

The same evolution can be seen today in the development of intelligent computer networks. Smart networks exchange information with each other, as a result of which the combination of their different data stores has a greater combined added value. The system is smarter than would otherwise be the case if there was no networking.

If these observations are translated into a business context, your customers – and the information they provide you – are your greatest and most exploitable resource over time. The more insights you can gain into your customers – how they behave and deal with products – the better you will be able as a company to hyper-personalise your products and services. So make sure that your company's 'brain cells' are bigger than anyone else's!

Tesla perfectly illustrates the added value of this approach. The company launched an innovative product into the market, but then had to watch with dismay as the old dinosaurs of the car industry also started to manufacture electric cars. Viewed in purely technological terms, these cars are possibly now even better than those of Tesla, but that is not the point. From a very early stage, Elon Musk understood the importance of creating a learning network, based on a constant real-life and real-time data stream. All his cars transmit a constant flow of information from the users back to the company and its developers, as a result of which Tesla can continually add improvements and launch radical new products, such as self-learning windscreen wipers or headlights, smart battery loading cycles, autonomous 'auto-pilot' software, etc. At the same time, the company – armed with the massive amount of information it now has about its vehicles and their drivers – can also start moving into other markets, because they have the necessary data, knowledge and know-how to do so successfully. Take, for example, car insurance.* Tesla knows exactly how many kilometres per year their customers drive, on which trajectories, how many of them are 'accident-prone', etc. This is priceless information for any insurer.

What would happen if a retailer made his network as intelligent as Tesla's and used the information he collected in a comparable way? That is why Amazon is investing so heavily in Alexa, its voice control system. Even after a product has been bought, Alexa continues to send back information to Amazon: when and how often does the customer use a particular product, what is it used for, etc. This information will make it possible for Amazon to continually update, optimise and automate its business in a way that its rivals will not be able to match.

The moral of the story?

New technology develops at exponential speed, while people are still thinking linearly.

Companies that persist in clinging to a linear vision of the future will sooner or later – and probably sooner – find themselves overtaken by exponential technological innovation. The laws of Moore, Gilder and Metcalfe can help them

---

* https://www.forbes.com/sites/enriquedans/2019/08/30/what-does-teslas-tentative-move-into-car-insurance-mean-for-thesector/?sh=9f192cc148c3

to defend themselves against this doom scenario, by giving them some idea of the speed at which this technological tidal-wave of change is approaching. Of course, in each sector a degree of uncertainty will remain about the direction in which this new technology will develop and about the possible interesting opportunities that the rapid growth of neural networks will create for companies. This uncertainty will be heightened still further by the fact that these developments will be influenced by other – and often unpredictable – factors, from legislation reflecting new societal trends to greenhouse gases and the warming of the planet. But with Moore, Gilder and Metcalfe, you will always have a better chance of finding your way to success.

In a nutshell

The three technology laws formulated in recent decades will give you a clear view of how the future of technology is likely to progress. Moore: computing power will become cheap and minutely small, so that everything will become intelligent. Gilder: information will always be available whenever you need it. Metcalfe: platforms will become ever more powerful and surpass all other process forms in terms of intelligence and value.

> *"Any sufficiently advanced technology is indistinguishable from magic!"* ARTHUR C. CLARKE

These three laws perfectly predicted the rise of the multi-billion dollar industries that became Silicon Valley, the internet, social media and network platforms, industries that have changed the face of our world forever. Even our day-to-day lives and social interactions are influenced by these laws. Moreover, in this chapter I have shown that all three laws are still as relevant today as they have ever been and that in the century ahead they will form the basis for a series of innovations and social changes of seminal importance. It is for each of us to consider what this means, what role we can play, and how we can prepare our organisations to face the future.

KEY 2
IS YOUR ORGANISATION FUTURE FIT?

Do you find it difficult to get innovation projects off the ground in your company? If so, you are not alone. Former Harvard Business professor Clayton Christensen concluded that roughly 95% of all newly introduced products are failures. So, how can you avoid this prospect and ensure that your innovation does become a success?

Rethinking innovation: failing is not a failure

The following is a list of comments that I often hear during evaluation reviews of unsuccessful innovation efforts.

- We tried to innovate, but it didn't work.
- Our customers weren't interested.
- We can't take a risk on new ideas, because our margins are too low.
- We don't have the resources to attempt innovation.
- If the economy changes, then we will…
- We got rid of our idea box; people were suggesting the craziest things.
- Our business is analytical; we can't be innovative.
- We prefer to focus exclusively on operational improvements.
- Every time we try to innovate, something urgent happens that causes us to shift our focus.
- We are not used to dealing with change and uncertainty.
- It is difficult to demonstrate the ROI on investment.
- There is no clear difference in approach between innovation & project management and R&D.
- Innovation in our organisation is like an island, limited to the efforts of individuals.

- We have too few new ideas and/or are too small to be disruptive.
- We have no clear definition of innovation for our organisation.
- As an organisation, we are not agile enough to innovate.
- Our daily operations don't leave us enough time to question things.

Sadly, too many companies today regard innovation solely from the perspective of a tangible end result, such as a market-ready product or service. Innovation projects bring with them greater risk and uncertainty than many other business projects. For this reason, it is not logical to try and view them in the same way as your other activities. Companies that expect direct and tangible results from their innovation projects are therefore likely to be disappointed. In contrast, companies that see innovation – including the occasional failure – as part of a long-term strategy will reap the rewards of their foresight and patience.

> *The question 'what is the result?' must be replaced by 'what can we learn from this?'*

Future Fitness Formula

Self-knowledge begins with having a good insight into your own organisation: to what extent are you ready to meet the challenges of a turbulent future? The health of your organisation is determined by more than just your employees and your culture. You also need to have a vision, a point on the horizon for which you can aim. What's more, you need to be capable of moving in the direction that will lead you there. Often, it takes some time to notice when you are moving in the wrong direction, but with the necessary innovation, creativity and the right partnerships in your ecosystem, you will soon get back on the right track.

With this in mind, I have developed my Future Fitness Formula. Following interviews with an organisation's leadership team, I use this formula to get a picture of the main challenges they are facing. But as we shall see later, you can also use the formula yourself:

$$\text{Future Fitness Formula} = \frac{Vision \times Speed \times Agility}{Experience}$$

"It is not the strongest of the species that survives, nor the most intelligent, but the one most responsive to change." This famous quotation by Charles Darwin also applies to organisations that want to remain fit for the future. We already saw in the first part of the book that the average life expectancy of companies is falling fast, because too many of them fail to react with sufficient speed to the accelerated pace of change, which is increasingly driven by technological innovation. The business environment has become so turbulent that only agile organisations will be able to remain successful. That being said, turbulence is not always negative. Nor is it something new. As our historical survey in Part One made clear, uncertainty comes in waves, roughly once every ten years. Change is something that will never go away. And there is no reason why it should, because it actually creates plenty of new opportunities. Many organisations go to the wall during turbulent times, but many others take their place. If you don't want to be one of the losers, you need to keep a close eye on your future fitness parameters.

So, how does this translate in terms of innovation? To understand this, we need to take a closer look at the different component elements of the Future Fitness Formula.

Do we have a vision of the future that makes innovation meaningful?

Saying that you need a clear vision might sound like stating the obvious, but you would be surprised how many organisations do not have one. They know what they are going to do in terms of activities, but they do not know what they want to achieve. In other words, they only formulate a mission, not a vision. There is a big difference.

A vision is the reason why your organisation exists. What do you want to achieve in the future? What are your dreams?

You know where you are today and you know all your strengths and weaknesses. It is with these strengths and weaknesses that you will seek to achieve those dreams. Along the way, you will be confronted by many threats and opportunities from outside your organisation. You need to be aware of and understand these threats and opportunities, or at least map them as well as you can. Because they are on the outside, in the first instance you will be able to do little to immediately change them. There is also a possibility that you will

INNOVATION JOURNEY

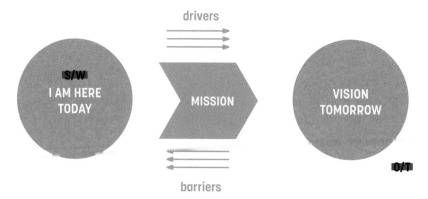

Figure 31 – *Where do we want to go? Mission and vision, internal weaknesses and strengths, external opportunities and threats. The basis of any innovation strategy. It sounds simple but it is all too often forgotten.*

confuse these external threats and opportunities with internal strengths and weaknesses.

If you want to realise your vision based on what you have today, you need to make a plan. This will be your mission. It will inevitably be a step-by-step plan, because you will not be able to realise your mission all at once. Implementing your mission is something that you do every day. It is the basis of your activities. You will encounter some elements that move you forward (drivers) and other elements that hold you back (barriers). Managing these elements will take up a good part of your focus.

Does this all sound too abstract? Let's take a remarkable organisation as an example: SpaceX. The reason for SpaceX's existence – its vision – is to conquer Mars. This is not something that will happen overnight. It will, however, offer a number of opportunities along the way, such as making space travel more attractive and more feasible for an increasingly larger group of people and organisations. But what is the best way to exploit these opportunities, without losing focus on the main vision? One possibility was collaboration with the American space agency, NASA. NASA has been unable to innovate sufficiently for years, as a result of lack of budget, skills and political will. For this reason, they were interested in collaboration with partners from the private sector.

SpaceX was also interested, but at this stage had little more to offer than the brains of a few brilliant scientists. On this basis, a mission was drawn up: the step-by-step development of rockets that can be built as cheaply as possible and can preferably be reused.

Everyone will be familiar with the images of the initial failed test flights and exploding rockets. In order to improve the quality of the test programme and increase the number of test flights, a new mission was developed and vested in a new organisation: Starlink. Starlink's objective is the development of dependable rockets that will make possible the mass production of flights, so that the price per flight can be cut dramatically, with the aim of putting into orbit 12,000 (and in phase II, 30,000) satellites to provide the world with fast, affordable and reliable internet.

As you can see, developing and implementing your mission can be full of ups and downs, and may require adjustment as you move forward. But you must never lose sight of your vision: the experience and expertise gained by Starlink will be invaluable for the Mars mission.

How good is your organisation at defining its vision and implementing its strategic mission? By answering the following questions, you will discover how well you currently score.

Which of the following comments fits your organisation?

VISION:
- 1 point = We have no clear written vision or strategy.
- 2 points = We have a vision and a strategy, but it is locked inside the heads of a few of our top people.
- 3 points = Managers and experts are involved in our strategy/mission process. We document what we agree and take action afterwards. Even so, a part of the organisation still feels no connection with the strategy.
- 4 points = We regularly invite external partners to challenge our strategic vision. Afterwards, we discuss internally how we can fine tune this vision to take better account of the future.
- 5 points = Our vision and strategy are known and supported throughout our entire organisation, so that it has become a part of our culture.

Are we agile?

An organisation is strategically agile if it is capable of changing its strategic course quickly and effectively in response to threats and opportunities in its environment.

In his book *The Upside of Turbulence*, Donald Sull of the London Business School describes three levels of agility: strategic, portfolio and operational.

Strategic agility relates to seizing opportunities that present themselves. Many companies have done this in recent years. Think, for example, of Apple that embraced the i-age with such success: digital media in which 'I' (me) is central. The result was the iPod, iMac and iPhone, followed by the AppleWatch and Apple TV.

Portfolio agility relates to the flexible transfer of the organisation's resources from failing markets to new product and market combinations with high potential. Microsoft is a good example of this kind of agility. There was a time not so long ago when Microsoft seemed dead in the water. Satya Nadella put new life into the company by investing heavily in the cloud, thereby making Microsoft's operation programmes available on all platforms. Similarly, Philips also managed to work its way through difficult years to become world leader in the booming sector of health technology.

Operational agility relates to the way in which an organisation does things that make it different or better than the rest, often with ground-breaking results. Think of Spotify, which launched streaming music in a world where everyone was in the process of switching from CD to MP3. Or Ryanair, which made air travel cheap by getting tourism subsidies from its destination countries and injections of capital through the stock market rather than through expensive ticket prices.

In which state of agility does your company currently find itself? Once again, give yourself a score.

AGILITY:
- 1 point = We do not look towards the future. Everyone is too busy with today.

- 2 points = We measure the things that are subject to change in our company. Where necessary, we adjust the budget accordingly (target budget versus year-to-date) and we try to anticipate what will happen in the following quarter.
- 3 points = We have an active approach to strategy, which is regularly discussed in internal groups and coordinated with senior management. The aim is to give the best possible guidance to our divisions, with due attention to future growth possibilities.
- 4 points = We are engaged in a process of constant strategic evolution. We also connect outside-in with experts and soundboard groups, whilst at the same time our internal specialists scan and document our sector, with an emphasis on the most important technological developments.
- 5 points = We have a foresight team with both internal and external participants. We look at the future in a structured manner and map our observations and options. We have systems for detecting early signals of change and for knowledge exchange.

Are we moving fast enough?

In addition to being agile, a successful company also needs to be able to adjust its strategy quickly. Nowadays, long-term plans often become outdated before the ink on them has even dried. To survive, you need to evolve towards a continuous and flexible strategic process, which is generally referred to as a 'rolling strategy'. It is crucial to find the right reaction speed, but that is easier said than done.

If you react too slowly, you are in danger of being overtaken by others, which will compel you to calculate the 'cost of not innovating' before deciding whether or not it is worth attempting to make up your lost ground. Look, for example, how Netflix and the ever-inventive Disney have eaten into the 'classic' television market, so that traditional broadcasters are now being forced to invest heavily in their own streaming services. This requires everyone involved to make difficult choices. Even Disney had to make the difficult decision to launch new productions on their platform at the same time as (or even earlier than) they were launched in cinemas. The effect of the Covid-19 pandemic on cinema attendance helped to sugar this pill, but the organisation's relationship with the cinema sector has been fundamentally changed forever.

At the opposite end of the spectrum, reacting too quickly may mean that you get to market with your new product or service ahead of everyone else, but this still involves a high degree of risk and takes an awful lot of money to make it work. Tesla is a case in point. Tesla's electric cars were on the market for a decade before the models of the traditional car manufacturers arrived, and although Elon Musk's brainchild is now the undisputed market leader, it took a long, hard and expensive fight to get them into this position. People tend to forget now that Tesla was on the edge of bankruptcy on more than one occasion. It was only thanks to the drive and determination of their CEO and an exceptional future fit team that they were able to pull through.

> How quickly can your organisation change direction? Give yourself a score, but have the courage to be brutally honest, if you want to get a true idea of your future fitness.
>
> **SPEED:**
> - 1 point = We seldom take new decisions and, if we do, we take them slowly.
> - 2 points = Management are quick to pick up on new ideas, but our internal organisation cannot follow at the same pace.
> - 3 points = We innovate continuously, but the market is often not ready for our ideas.
> - 4 points = Our decision-making is based on an iterative process that guarantees us speed. We dare to leave the well-trodden paths and test out new ones. We frequently boost and stop projects, as appropriate.
> - 5 points = We have developed a structure to optimise the speed of our decision-making and the necessary follow-up. We stress-test ourselves regularly.

What is the value of experience?

Experience is an advantage in a stable environment, but can hold you back when you need to innovate in rapidly changing circumstances. In turbulent and complex times, attempting to rely on your experience can slow you down. Companies want to protect what they know and have achieved, so that they remain on familiar pathways that now risk leading them even deeper into the jungle, which makes the next step to the future even more difficult and dangerous.

Many organisations have a 'no' mentality towards new developments, as we saw in the Kodak case. You need to guard against this kind of knee-jerk reaction. Almost by definition, past experience is not always necessary or even possible when you are launching something completely new. In fact, experience might even slow down your way of thinking and acting. Without the illegality of Napster, shops would still be selling records, CDs and other data carriers. Without Napster, there would be no iPod or iTunes, and without iTunes there would be no Spotify. Without Uber, the taxi sector would still be where it was 30 years ago. Without Airbnb, hotels would still be able to dictate their own terms. Without Netflix, cinemas would still be full and we would all still be watching linear television. In other words, there are examples enough of people who have revolutionised sectors of which they had no experience.

You can assign experience a score between 1 and 5. You assign a low experience score if there are many new people with a different and fresh view of new challenges. The other extreme scores 5 when there is a lot of experience present and this often leads to resistance to change. Then you can calculate your final Future Fitness Formula with all the scoring. That will vary between 0.20 (very low) and 125 (very high). A higher Future Fitness gives you an indication of the future robustness of your organization.

> *"Vision without action is daydreaming. Action without vision is random activity. But action and vision together can change the world".* NELSON MANDELA

In a nutshell

How do you make an organisation ready to innovate? It starts with a serious dose of self-knowledge. This is where the Future Fitness Formula can help you. Do you have a clear vision of the future? Are you agile? Can you move quickly enough? Is your experience working in your favour or is it a hindrance?

how do we structure innovation?

culture
metrics
ecosystem outside in
idea management
DRIVE BREAK
people
tools & data
digital
process
training
facilities
strategy
leadership

KEY 3
STRUCTURAL INNOVATION

Obstacles on the innovation road

We can still learn a thing or two from a research project that I started during my MBA studies in Belgium (Flanders Business School) and at Kellogg University in Chicago. My thesis dealt with the setting up of innovation support services, which later grew into the TomorrowLab. One of the main concerns with innovation is recognising and understanding the dissatisfaction that many business leaders often feel when they innovate. I asked all the companies (more than 250) that we were working with at that time and were investing heavily in innovation why they were not always satisfied with the results of their innovation efforts. I have repeated the same study on various occasions in recent years and, surprisingly, the answers have always remained broadly the same.

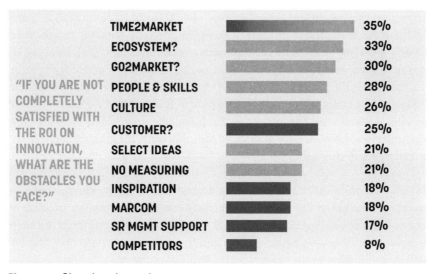

Figure 32 – *Obstacles to innovation success.*

The results given teach us the importance of checking properly whether or not we are able to innovate successfully and how we can avoid failing in areas where others before us have failed.

Obstacle: length of time to market

This is the most common complaint: it simply takes too long to bring something new successfully to market. In part, this is explained by the importance that organisations attach to short-term (quarterly) results. They want to see progress and want to see it quickly. Surprisingly, this is also the case with government authorities at all levels. Even though they are not 'competitive' in a business sense, they also – like everyone else – want to see 'quick wins'. The life expectancy of a business manager or an elected official is getting shorter and shorter, so that they need to score faster and faster. A quick win gives immediate success, media attention, recognition, a bonus and re-election!

This is also the reason why in recent decades the large R&D centres in major organisations (Bell Labs, NatLab, PARC, etc.) have been systematically decommissioned. From the short-term management perspective, it was no longer possible to defend the long and costly process of basic research that would only lead to major leaps forward at some undefinable point in the future.

Of course, there were also other reasons, such as the inability to market many of the inventions or the increasing complexity of the domains in which research is taking place. As a result, much of the important work in research has now been switched to the universities and to specific knowledge centres, such as the world-renowned IMEC for nanotechnology or the CERN for particle physics. That being said, it is still often hard to find 'believers' who are willing to fund research over the long term. Even major sponsors, like the European Commission or NASA, have shortened their horizons for making and marketing their break-throughs.

Making progress quickly is obviously a good thing, but it remains open to question whether or not we are also missing crucial opportunities because of the need for speed. For this reason, it is wise for organisations to spread their innovation efforts over both the short and the long term – something that we will look at further in the chapter on the three horizons of innovation.

Obstacle: inadequate external collaboration and open innovation

When we first conducted this survey some years ago, the answer 'there was too little external collaboration' hardly featured. Back then, organisations wanted to do everything for themselves, so that they often ended up re-inventing the wheel. As we saw in the section earlier in the book on the Creative Conversion Factory at Philips, a change in this 'do-it-yourself' way of thinking kicked in around the turn of the century. It was no longer possible for larger companies to match the innovation speed of the small-scale start-ups in the Valley, above all in the fields of digital services, internet and connectivity. These larger companies realised that they could no longer innovate alone. Too many research domains had become so complex that it was now necessary to have dozens of different teams, whose numbers of researchers ran into thousands or even tens of thousands at large companies like IBM. This was not only phenomenally costly but also generated so much IP that it could not all be absorbed by the business units, so that future research funding was put at risk through a lack of sufficient profits. It therefore became necessary to search for other sources of research income, combined with the creative reduction of costs.

The sea change in this respect was brought about by... a group of students. In 1991, Linus Torvalds, a student at the University of Helsinki, posted his hobby project on the internet: the 'Linux' operating system. It was by no means a finished product, but it at least had a stable core. Torvalds released the source code for Linux, so that other programmers could gain access to the core and give feedback. He thought that maybe a dozen or so people might be interested. He was wrong. Less than two years later, in 1993, hundreds of programmers, many of them from IBM, were working on the development of Linux. At work, they were paid to perform fairly basic programming tasks; now they were working unpaid with others to create something new. The result of all this passion was a remarkable end-product that resulted in the formation of several companies, including SuSE and Red, which marketed Linux-based software. By the end of the 1990s, Linux had become so stable that it could be used on major servers and had the added plus of being free. The big software companies like IBM and Microsoft, who had invested billions in the same field, watched what was happening with dismay but could do nothing about it – except draw the right conclusions for the future. IBM was the first to fully embrace this new method of innovating and the publication on their website in 1999 of a document entitled 'Linux – the era of open innovation' laid the foundations for the most successful open-source project in history. Linux was developed still further to become a completely free and professionally supported open-source platform that went on to form the basis for Google's Android and even for Tesla's operating system.

From the year 2000 onwards, it became clear that there was another way of innovating other than trying to create your own products, developed in closed campuses and strongly protected by international property rights. Henceforth, there would be greater sharing of expertise and collaboration on innovative ideas. The era of open innovation was born. Professor Henry Chesbrough was the pioneer of this new innovation paradigm. Sharing resources, exchanging knowledge and working with others, sometimes even with your competitors, became the new norm.

Not everyone was happy and many companies had difficulty accepting this new way of working. It was not just a question of the insourcing and outsourcing of intellectual property. It was the fact that they had to pool all their other resources as well and work with others with whom they had never worked before. Earlier in the book, we saw how the Creative Conversion Factory at Philips Research in Eindhoven attempted to structurally anchor open innovation in the company's R&D operations. "We are creative enough – that is not the problem," Theun Baller, who was then the global COO at Philips and general manager at Philips Research, once told me. "It is much more complex than that. We need all kinds of different competencies in all kinds of different areas. Today, more than ever, we need to cooperate in groups in domains where we do not have enough of the right expertise." A few years later, the same kind of system was built up around Johnson & Johnson Pharmaceutical Research & Development in Turnhout. But these transformations, as the story of the CCF again shows, did not always run smoothly.

In 2015, Cargill in Brussels approached our team with the request to help them to speed up their innovation processes. Cargill is one of the largest agro-industrial players in the world. Brussels is the location of their European R&D innovation centre, where roughly 250 top engineers are employed to develop new products for the foodstuffs sector. However, they were being increasingly confronted by the fact that they needed to recruit even more people with a growing number of different profiles to keep on top of ever more complex development projects. But this expertise was becoming harder and harder to find, and they couldn't even 'steal' it from their competitors, because they didn't have it 'full time' either! Cargill's question to us was therefore this: how can we reduce our innovation costs and improve/accelerate our go-to-market strategy. Our answer? Open innovation.

It was an interesting and ultimately fruitful operation. Nils Sips, the R&D and go-to-market director for Europe, the Middle East and Africa, put it so: "The markets in which Cargill operates are changing fast. This means that we need to get to those markets more quickly. We need to be more alert and must have more different options and ideas. In the past, we always looked at innovation with an internal focus. Now, with open innovation, we are trying to turn it into a more all-embracing external process. We often still have very close and traditional relationships with our suppliers, but there is more to it than that. Now we can also turn to the suppliers of our suppliers, to the manufacturers of our apparatus, to universities and even to start-ups. In this way, we can supplement our existing knowledge or tap into a new source of knowledge that we do not yet have. The skill that you need today might already have become outdated in three years' time. As a result, you need to be able to build up the competencies in your teams very fast. This makes it necessary to look further than you might have looked before. But how do you come into contact with these external parties? If you want to succeed, you need to have a well-balanced process."

To help develop this process, we introduced a highly pragmatic project plan. This first involved the alignment of the internal organisation, the collection of information, the organisation of interviews, workshops, and brainstorming sessions, and the analysis of open business models to see which ones had the best fit for Cargill. This took quite some time: not because of the models themselves, but to get everyone's nose pointing in the right direction and to open up the Cargill culture to the new way of thinking. Although everyone could see the benefits of sharing knowledge, the organisational culture up to this point had been a very closed one, in keeping with the custom in the sector at that time. At the end of our analysis, two possible business models were still under consideration. These were subjected to a 'pressure test' judged by a group of ten important external stakeholders, one of whom was actually an important competitor. My team acted as the neutral catalyst.

Of course, the Cargill management could not talk with other companies about the exact nature of the things they were innovating, but they could at least communicate about how they were doing it. This is a non-competitive process, and if you do it properly everyone stands to gain. In this way, it is possible that your competitor of today may become your partner in the years ahead. More-over, many of Cargill's best customers are very forward-thinking, which lends itself to open collaboration. And in terms of our initial project, it was with one such customer that a first open innovation project was launched. A year earlier, this would have been unthinkable. Cargill's mindset, or at least the mindset of their European R&D team, had become much more open.

This interesting and successful project soon came to the attention of Cargill's HQ in the United States. As a result, the company subsequently put together a worldwide open innovation team to search for new opportunities outside Car-gill's usual sphere of activities, which connected on a much wider scale than ever before. In the words of Nils Sips: "A spin-off of all the ideas we looked at is the growing and accelerating trend towards bio-industrial applications. Companies are searching for sustainable solutions for the products they use. Instead of sticking to petrochemical-based products, they are switching to bio-industrial products. That idea already existed, but this open process has speeded up the trend. Moreover, it is a trend around which we have developed our new strategy, which is clear from our new name: Cargill Food and Bio-in-dustrial Ingredients. This shows that we are now looking wider than foodstuffs alone. Of course, a name doesn't say everything, but it certainly helps to con-tribute towards cultural and behavioural change."

Today, Cargill is reaping the rewards of this open innovation culture in their market. At the start of 2021, the company even took the lead in an open-source innovation project for the entire sector, which also includes their competitors. This 'blockchain-like' platform, known as Splinter, is designed in such a way that every organisation involved in the movement of agri-food items from one place to another is able to coordinate its logistics and resolve potential prob-lems with and through the platform's other users. Covid-19 exposed the vul-nerability of the worldwide food supply chain and many organisations in the sector are making their own large-scale but also largely individual efforts to address this weakness. This is well-meant, but in view of the large number of different actors involved in the process of bringing food from farm to fork, the key to the more efficient and more reliable transport and distribution of food is probably to be found in something that this hyper-competitive and over-pat-ented sector has long viewed with mistrust: collaboration. In light of the inno-vation culture that is now embedded at Cargill, it is perhaps no surprise that they took the initiative to make the Splinter project an open one. I am also proud to have contributed in my own small way to making this possible. Perhaps this uplifting story will help to convince you to start open innovation in your organisation? I hope so.

Obstacle: lack of coordination

Another obstacle in the innovation efforts of many organisations is the lack of coordination. By this, I do not mean that there are no resources available for coordination, but rather that the right skills are lacking to make this possible. Because innovation is becoming increasingly broad, open and complex in scope, a different kind of mentality is required. The typical project-based approach of the past no longer suffices. Many organisations use software that reduces a project to a series of actions, responsibilities and milestones. This can still work well for short-term projects that need to be brought to market very quickly: the so-called downstream projects. The majority of companies still have this type of project well under control and the best of them succeed in developing a real innovation go-to-market machine. Procter & Gamble is one of the best-known examples.

However, the challenges for upstream innovation are more testing. The funnel of new ideas, products and services soon becomes empty, precisely because you need to be better connected to work in this cross-disciplinary way. You need to look further ahead to the needs that customers might not have today but may well have tomorrow, as well as assessing possible approaching trends and the possible impact of new technologies, both of which nowadays evolve at lightning speed. How you can best deal with this is something that I will discuss in the chapter covering the six levels of innovation maturity.

Obstacle: no innovation culture

A culture that inhibits innovation is the main cause of one out of every three failed innovations. To make matters worse, this number is still rising. When I first surveyed this matter in 2007, the figure was under 25%. Today, it is just over 35%, notwithstanding the major efforts made in recent years to make organisations and their employees more aware of the need for innovation. The reason for this rise is probably the ever-increasing pace of change and the persistent determination to focus on today rather than tomorrow. In these circumstances, perhaps it is not surprising that some people have had enough and simply turn their back on innovation. These are the ones who you sometimes hear say: "The way we are doing things now will see me through to the end of my time."

I did not invent the saying "Culture eats strategy for breakfast", but I certainly agree with it. If the development and maintenance of the right facilitating culture is not permanently on your company's agenda, you will never be able to innovate successfully. But there is good news! My experience with our own companies suggests that creating an innovation culture does not always have to be difficult. In fact, it can even be fun. In 2016, we decided (under the impulse of the 'Future of Work' project) to give our offices a new look and feel. We discussed at length what the future of work might look like and, in particular, whether or not we would still need to come into the office, given the fact that in recent years we have been working with increasing frequency from home or on site with customers. Even without the pressure of Covid, we decided that in future our teams should be able to work together on their projects both physically and virtually. We still occupy the same amount of space as before, but the workplace now consists of different environments in which people feel good and which they can occupy depending on what is expected of them. Everyone has a high-performance laptop with a free choice of operating system (Mac or Windows) and everything is stored in the cloud.

The spaces for focused work are furnished with high-low desks and ergonomic chairs, all of which are sufficiently distanced from each other. The consultation spaces are hybrid and equipped with super-large interactive boards, which allows consultation and collaboration with colleagues working from home. Boxes offer a quiet space for individual work or online meetings. High tables with stools and a custom-made 'grandstand' – which can be reconfigured with the help of giant Lego blocks and has a large interactive screen at the front – provide a dynamic and hybrid team work space, where it is also possible to eat and chat over lunch in a pleasant setting. People can work from home as much as they want, with the exception of a single weekly team meeting, which we prefer to hold physically, as far as possible. Of course, even this was not possible during the height of the pandemic, but I noticed that people soon began to miss the physical proximity of colleagues and that small teams in particular now prefer once again to meet face to face for certain tasks.

It has to be admitted, of course, that our building is something special, containing as it does the House, Hotel and Care Room of the Future, which are visited each year by hundreds of thousands of people. Meeting these people and seeing that they are fascinated and inspired by our building gives us energy. So too do the works of art that grace each room, all created by artists who in one way or another have distinguished themselves through the innovative nature of their work. These factors, combined with the new organisation of the office space as a home environment, have unquestionably given a real boost to our innovation culture.

Your people will never be able to innovate unless they can associate themselves with an innovative environment – even if that environment is becoming ever more virtual all the time. So make sure that you give it to them.

Obstacle: limited insight into the customers and market of the future

Companies frequently spend huge amounts of money on market research. The typical questions are primarily *hic et nunc*. What do you think of our products? What services do you want from us? What expectations do you have of us? And so on. It is all about the market of today and perhaps of tomorrow, but no further. For decades, it has been claimed that customer-driven innovation is the best way to ensure continued success: listen to the customer. In this way, it seemed that innovation was no longer the work of creative specialists. Instead, you just commissioned an online survey or invited people to take part in customer panels, asking them what they would like to change about your product. On the basis of their answers, you made the necessary changes and launched a new and improved version. Simple! This process works incrementally and companies that apply it repeatedly often fail to see the tidal wave of more disruptive change when it is approaching. A customer who is asked how her smartphone can be improved to better meet her expectations may perhaps answer that the cover could be of a better quality, or that the home button is poorly positioned, or that the facial recognition does not always work, or that the sound could be louder, etc. In other words, feature innovation – but not real, ground-breaking innovation. It is this 'trial and error' method, which collects thousands of ideas through brainstorming and crowdsourcing, that has led to the 90% innovation failure rate referred to by Christensen. Companies hope in this way to stumble more or less by chance onto the revolutionary idea that will take the market by storm. But this is like looking for a needle in a haystack. And it is very expensive, very difficult and, worst of all, gives you no real insight into the consumer and the market of the future. It is often a recipe for total innovation disaster.

I can still remember an innovation scan that we did back in 2006 for an airport, which had proudly announced the introduction of the very first digital check-in system. You booked your flight online, and at the airport you could check in your luggage at a kiosk, where you could also confirm your boarding and, if so desired, print off a paper boarding ticket. These kiosks were the result of a research project in which different prototypes were used by test customers, whose actions were carefully observed and noted by the research team. On the basis of this customer feedback, the machines were further optimised. The airport told us that so far the new check-in system was causing longer delays, because each kiosk needed a 'mentor' to actually show people how to use it. They referred to this process as 'educating the customer' and they were confident that it would only take a short while. After that, everything would be quicker and better than before. We took our first look at the machines and saw that there were six of them, all neatly lined up in a row. Shiny, attractive-looking machines, each with a large screen and a banner that read 'superfast express check-in'. But apart from the mentor twiddling his thumbs, there was not a customer to be seen! I approached one of the kiosks with my electronic identity card in my hand, assuming that I would need it for the check-in. I was right, but into which of the seven (!) card slots should I insert it? What had happened here? The customer survey had shown that when checking in some people not only wanted to use their identity card, but also their bank card, their loyalty card, etc. (Back in 2006, there was no such thing as a QR-scan via your smartphone). The designers had thought of nothing better than to add a separate slot for each of the cards that people wanted to use! Result: total customer confusion.

I am a big fan of the Lean Start-up and MVP (Minimum Viable Product) thinking. You take your product to the market when it is just about good enough and you listen to the feedback of real customers as the basis for making it better. Often, as was the case with the check-in kiosks, the MVP is changed into a worse rather than a better version, because there are always a few people who find this, that or the other 'interesting'. Typically, these 'mediocre viable products' are the result of focus groups working with design studios. Sadly, not much has changed in 15 years. I recently returned from Dubai Expo 2020. All

Figure 33 – *Innovation is not always user-friendly. The seven slots confuse the customer.*
SOURCE: LIVING TOMORROW, BRUSSELS AIRLINES

our group had checked in online but at the airport we were obliged to deposit our luggage in a... bag drop kiosk! We lost more than an hour because none of us succeeded in making the complex process work first time. And in case you were wondering... yes, the mentor was still there!

You probably also know of innovations that failed because companies listened blindly to what customers thought they wanted. Thinking that your customers are the 'innovation specialists' is wrong. You, the designer, are the specialist. You are the one who needs to see the big picture through the mass of suggestions your customers provide. It is you who has to ditch the irrelevant, keep the essential and think a few steps ahead. That is how design thinking and outcome-driven innovation is supposed to work, but it still happens far too infrequently.

You should never focus on features and details, but must concentrate instead on what people want to achieve. In our example, people want to get on their plane as quicky as possible, so that they can reach their destination with minimum fuss and delay. And they don't care how it happens – as long as it happens. As HBS professor Theodore Levitt once said: "People don't want to buy a quarter-inch drill; they want a quarter-inch hole!" For this reason, you need have no qualms when you say to your innovation team: "Don't listen to the customer!" (You know what I mean.)

So MVPs, although not a bad idea, often go too far. I am more in favour of RATs. RAT stands for 'riskiest assumption test'. You launch something new and you draw up a list of the riskiest assumptions that you have made about your product. You then try to find the cheapest way to test these assumptions. An example? Brian Chesky and Joe Gebbia, like many others, did not have enough money to rent a house in San Francisco. Their hypothesis was that perhaps people would be prepared to pay 80 dollars a night for a room with an inflatable bed and a breakfast. They tested this idea on a minimal website and it turned out that their hypothesis was correct. And so Airbnb was born, a company that is now larger than the biggest hotel chain in the world.

Where will we be heading the day after tomorrow? What will be the changes in our customers' needs? How do they really want to use our product and what can we do to make it happen? These are questions that are all too often overlooked. Earlier in the book, I described the emergence of the third IT wave, which made it possible to bring products that are only partially finished to market. Technology makes it possible to fill products with different kinds of sensors that can send data back to us as the designer. On the one hand, this provides you with lots of valuable user information that allows you to optimise your products and services, often automatically (think of learning algorithms). On the other hand (and just as importantly), this information not only offers you insights into the product of today, but also new insights and ideas for the products of tomorrow.

Obstacle: picking the wrong idea or having too many ideas

Brainstorming and stimulating creativity are now standard practice in the business world. The main problem is often selecting the right idea from the mass of suggestions this produces. Even after you have made your selection, there are few effective ways to measure whether or not your innovation is a success. Often, companies restrict themselves to calculating the revenue that the new MVP generates, but this increases the pressure to upgrade the product and make it even more 'successful' – in other words, generate more cash flow. If that does not work within the next couple of years, the product will usually be ditched. In my opinion, however, there are better tools that you can use to see whether you have picked a winner or a loser. Later in the book, we will look at scenarios that can be used for stress testing and idea selection.

Obstacle: marketing innovation and senior management support

I often see that companies – even highly successful companies – are reluctant to communicate about their innovations, for fear that their customers might get the wrong idea and set their expectations too high. Or else that they might later be forced to admit that the innovation has not been a success. This is the wrong attitude to take. Promoting innovation and making it widely known, even when things go wrong, is a much smarter strategy.

It all started with Google, when they began to develop the first self-driving cars. They put these cars on the road as quickly as they could and communicated about it massively. The car immediately became a mega-hype and everyone thought that the era of self-driving vehicles had arrived. This did Google nothing but good.

Figure 34 – *Google, Boston Dynamics and SpaceX communicate openly about their innovations. Right from the very beginning. Even when they fail they show it.* SOURCES: ALPHABET, BOSTON DYNAMICS, SPACE X

Not only had they created a totally new sector, but they already had a big lead in the technology that over time would make that sector boom. The fact that they gave massive exposure to what they were doing also enabled them to attract even more of the world's top talents.

It was a similar story at Boston Dynamics, which made their robots 'dance' and even showed one of them being attacked by a member of the BD team with an ice hockey stick! This provoked lots of different emotions, but in the meantime everyone had seen that Boston Dynamics was a world leader in robot development. There were probably other companies that had even more advanced prototypes, but none of them had communicated so sexily about the progress they were making.

This is something that Elon Musk also understands. In March 2021, he had no problem to show the explosion of the test version of his Starship in slow-motion on Twitter. He even added a touch of self-mocking humour: "The SN10 is in Valhalla now". This is in huge contrast to the way that most other companies seek to hide their failures. So which approach do you think is best? Which approach brings more benefit to the company? Are you prepared to see failure as an inevitable part of the innovation process? And do you have the courage to show these failures to the outside world? If you do, it will improve your reputation far more than simply posting a pretty photo of a perfectly finished product that is shelf-ready.

Below you can find a summary of the most important reasons why innovations fail and the nature of the underserved needs that companies need to address in order to find the right solution.

Anchoring innovation in your organisation

It is not only vitally important that innovation should originate at the bottom of your organisation; it is also necessary that the top levels must be permeated with the innovation ideal, investing in a culture that stimulates innovation or at the very least makes it possible to explore and improve the possibilities in yourself and others. As a senior manager, the first question you need to ask yourself is this: What is my current innovation status? Am I prepared to integrate innovation into our activities? How far have I got with this process? Do I have the experience required? Am I equipped to make innovation possible and keep it alive in our organisation?

Table 3 – *Every obstacle has a cause and a solution.*

OBSTACLE	UNDERSERVED NEED	SOLUTION
Time to market too long	Skills, capacity, knowledge, tools for faster development	Open innovation, design thinking, agile testing, RAT
External collaboration	Ecosystem, partners	Build your ecosystem
Lack of coordination	T-skills, neutral catalyst	Talent and tool management
Risk-averse culture	Change	Cases, outer box, long term vision, scenarios
Limited customer insight (future)	Future market/consumer/data insight	Increase outside-in foresight intelligence. Decrease traditional market research!
Selecting the right ideas	Knowledge, support	Scoring tools, stress testing
No good way to measure	Innovation metrics	Support, tools, knowledge, data strategy
Not enough great ideas	Inspiration, creativity, guidance, cross fertilisation	Synergy management, inspiration, motivation, culture, scenario thinking
Marketing/ communication	Sensitise and inform	Celebrate steps and failures, use easy platform models to entertain, inform and sensitise
Competitors more innovative	Innovation readiness and level	Structures for innovation
Insufficient senior management support	Top management buy in	Change of KPIs, lighthouse, make it tangible, part of culture

Measuring the effectiveness of innovation efforts and innovation systems is becoming increasingly important, not only because it determines the competitive position of your organisation in the market landscape, but also – and often – because it determines your chances of ultimate survival in a rapidly changing ecosystem. This measuring helps you to monitor and optimise your innovation, allowing you to channel it into the right processes and even, where possible, to automate it, if only in part. The measuring must be done regularly and it must always use the same method. If you fail to measure properly, the whole thing risks becoming nothing more than window-dressing. Perhaps you score well for the first couple of times you do it and respond to what the figures tell you. But after that it becomes just another part of your daily business routine, eventually resulting in the institutionalisation of the associated processes, so that all creativity is lost. Quantifying innovation results and innovation efficiency is not easy. If that were the case, it would have been made a standard part of every management training course years ago.

You often hear comments like: "We invest x% of our turnover in innovation." Or: "We measure innovation results by monitoring the percentage that new products – the products that did not exist five years ago – contribute to our turnover." Or: "We measure the number of new patent submissions we make." Or: "We measure the increase in turnover." For example, a company like Procter & Gamble recalculates its NPV (net present value) retrospectively every few years. This is feasible in a sector where it is possible to go from an idea to a marketable product in just a few years, but it is less feasible in, say, the car sector or the energy sector. In passing, it is also worth noting that P&G's results show that open innovation projects (projects with an external contribution of more than 60%) achieve up to 70% higher NPVs than purely internal, closed projects.

Each of the above-mentioned measuring methods will indeed give a numerical picture of how your innovation efforts seem to be progressing, but this will say very little about the health (or otherwise) of your innovation system, your culture and the manner in which the leadership gives oxygen to the development of bright new ideas for the future, so that knowledge can be turned into know-how and, ultimately, into ka-ching.

This is the theme that has dominated my thoughts and activities throughout my working career. Since the early years of the new century, I have been developing a table based on all the conversations, evaluations and studies I have had or made on this fascinating and important subject. The insights of our own innovation teams, active in many different sectors, further increased our experience and understanding. The end result was my Innovation Maturity Model, which I would now like to share with you. It is a model that will give you an indication of the extent to which your organisation is innovating in a structured way. You can see it as a kind of self-assessment tool, rather than as a metric system. Self-assessment is a good way to measure maturity and to institutionalise innovation processes via policies, structures and standards. As I have already said, you will need to remain alert about your level of creativity: institutionalisation must not lead to tunnel vision that may cause your creativity to ebb away. This is the difference between measuring maturity in, for example, quality processes – which tend to be fairly static – and measuring maturity in innovation, which is constantly in motion. Or as Professor Henry Chesbrough once said during a visit to our Living Tomorrow project:

> *"Innovation is a river that never stops. The flow of knowledge just keeps on going. So, if someone claims to you that they have written the final word in innovation, you know there is something wrong."*

The basic idea for my model first developed during discussions I had with companies as part of my MBA studies. During these discussions, the case of P&G repeatedly came to the fore. They were regarded as the ultimate innovation machine and even had a separate division – Connect & Develop – to hone these skills yet further. It was hardly surprising, then, that I wanted to talk to them. My model was based on six levels of innovation, with the sixth level being the highest. To expand my theories, I wanted to talk to a company in each of the six levels. And for the sixth level, I wanted to talk to Procter & Gamble!

One evening, I received a call from Chris Thoen, who was then the head of P&G Connect & Develop. The division had been set up by the company's charismatic CEO, AG Lafley, who had mapped out a powerful and externally focused innovation vision for the organisation as a whole. In just five years, P&G was able to reach a situation where more than 50% of its innovations were realised through external collaboration. It was a huge success. More than 3 billion dollars in turnover growth was generated each year by the new structure, which supported all the business units with external innovation ideas that could be brought quickly to market. By the time I visited P&G to discuss my model, its total turnover had shot up to 80 billion dollars per annum.

As we talked through my ideas, Chris asked me: "Joachim, where do you think we are in your model?" "In Level 6, of course," I replied. "Wrong!" said Chris. "We are only just in Level 3. We have succeeded in allowing our teams to innovate, but we still have a long way to go with the structure." To embed innovation more firmly in the P&G culture, they launched (among other things) the Synergy Software platform, which subsequently grew into the worldwide SAAS platform for open innovation. My company worked for many years with P&G on open innovation projects and many of the technologies that were only just coming onto the radar back then, like the 'waterless kitchen' and 'waterless cleaning', are now highly relevant today.

His answer set me thinking about whether an organisation needs to try to get to Level 6 per se. From a cost-benefit perspective, a lower level can sometimes better match an organisation's vision and strategic planning. So keep this thought in mind as we now look in detail at my maturity model.

I distinguish six levels of innovation maturity through which an organisation must pass, if it wishes to become an innovation superstar. You can apply the model to a single division or to operations in a single country, but for the time being we will look at it from the perspective of the company level. The six levels are a kind of spectrum, starting at one end with an organisation where innovation is wholly absent and working across to the other end with an organisation where innovation is not only part of the culture, but is also constantly being improved to even higher standards of excellence.

Twelve dimensions

In order to be able to measure innovation effectively, I further distinguish between twelve dimensions that help to make innovation possible. These twelve dimensions are grouped into four major domains. First, there is the innovation

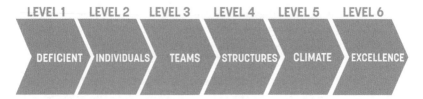

Figure 35 – *Six levels of innovation maturity.*

process itself, where we identify and examine the organisation's installed procedures, practices and activities. The second domain is knowledge and competencies, which deals with available skills, human capital, education and training, and the way in which the digital transformation has (or has not) been integrated. Next comes what I call organisational support, which relates to the structures and strategy implemented by the organisation and the way in which the leadership seeks to build on and strengthen the innovation process by displaying the necessary foresight. Last but not least, there is the cultural domain. Does the organisation have an open or a closed culture? How does it define innovation? What is its approach to taking risks? Which horizons does it have in its sights?

You can give your organisation a score for each of these domains and dimensions. To help you on your way, you will find a number of tables in the following pages. There is a description for each domain, which will allow you determine

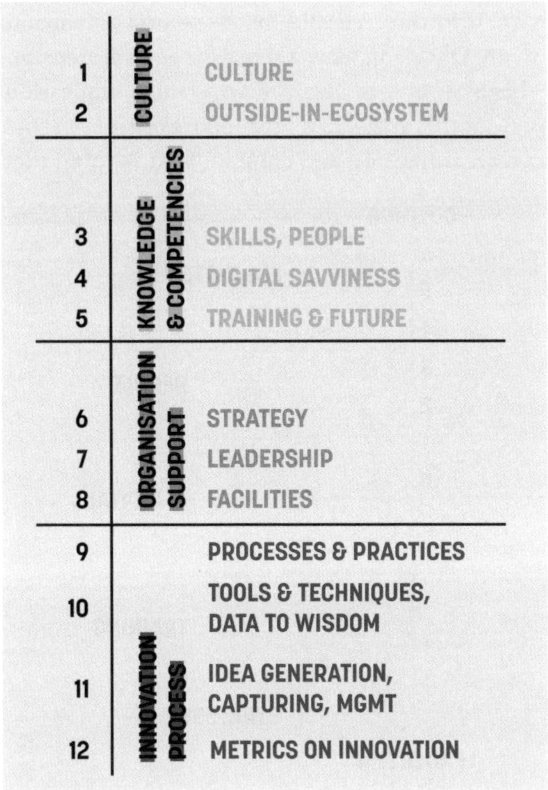

1	CULTURE	CULTURE
2		OUTSIDE-IN-ECOSYSTEM
3	KNOWLEDGE & COMPETENCIES	SKILLS, PEOPLE
4		DIGITAL SAVVINESS
5		TRAINING & FUTURE
6	ORGANISATION SUPPORT	STRATEGY
7		LEADERSHIP
8		FACILITIES
9	INNOVATION PROCESS	PROCESSES & PRACTICES
10		TOOLS & TECHNIQUES, DATA TO WISDOM
11		IDEA GENERATION, CAPTURING, MGMT
12		METRICS ON INNOVATION

Figure 36 – *The 12 dimensions of innovation.*

in which level of innovation maturity your organisation currently finds itself. You can do this test on your own, but in my opinion it is better to do it with a number of people from the same department or business unit. If you work in a small company, I suggest you involve everyone from product development, marketing, sales and communication, as well as the senior management team. For each domain and dimension, just tick the box that you think best describes the current situation in your organisation. For each line (dimension) note down in which level (1 to 6) you are positioned. Be as honest as you can and be aware that overestimation is more common than underestimation when dealing with the professionalisation of innovation management. Just because you have read a book or listened to a keynote or attended a workshop, this does not mean that innovation is effectively embedded in the practices and processes of your organisation!

If you find yourself in level 3 for the first dimension, that means that you have a score of the 3 for that dimension. If you are in level 4 for the second dimension, you have a score of 4 – and so on. Once you have a score for each dimension, add up the total and divide this by twelve to give you an average innovation score. For example, 2.3 out of 6. At this stage, this presupposes that the same weight should be attached to each dimension and domain. Bear in mind that

Figure 37 – *The six levels and twelve dimensions of innovation.*

this might not necessarily be the case, but can vary from company to company and from sector to sector, and is also dependent on the organisational culture. Plotting your results on the spider's web below will give you a clearer picture of your overall situation and the relative strength and weakness of each dimension. The closer you are to the core, the less mature you are. The nearer you are to the rim, the more mature you are. In this way, you can see at a glance which dimensions you need to improve and which dimensions you need to further fine-tune. This will allow you to set priorities.

On page 170 you can find an example of this test that we completed with a number of people involved in innovation at Procter & Gamble. (For understandable reasons, I have slightly adjusted some of the scores). We worked in five groups with a total of 120 managers from 21 P&G innovation teams operating worldwide.

Do not be disappointed if your organisation fails to get such good scores when you first complete the test. As I have already mentioned, Procter & Gamble are innovation superstars. This is a field where they are not only extremely well organised but also highly streamlined. The P&G culture is steeped in the innovation ethos, which becomes clear when you see how the results for each of the five groups is broadly the same for the 'culture' and 'metrics' dimensions. The situation becomes more interesting when you look at some of the more divergent results for dimensions like 'people' or 'idea management'. Perhaps it is no surprise that people have different opinions or that some groups are indeed further behind in some dimensions than others. But once you have plotted things in this manner you can at least see where the discrepancies exist and start trying to find some explanation for them.

If you add up all the individual dimension scores for this exercise, you will see that Procter & Gamble has an average innovation score of around 4 out of 6. Believe me, this is a high score. Even so, there are still points for improvement, such as 'people', 'tools & tech' and 'strategic innovation plan'. As far as the latter dimension is concerned, there was a reason for the low score. The five groups were all part of a newly formed worldwide division and the test was carried out as part of a workshop they were attending in response to a recent P&G decision to realign for the future and develop a new common strategic innovation vision to make this possible. In other words, this dimension was still a 'work in progress'.

Figure 38 – This is an example of an exercise we did with a group of innovation people at Procter & Gamble. (I have slightly modified the result for understandable reasons.) A total of 120 managers were involved, divided into 21 teams from around the world.

			LEVEL 1	LEVEL 2	LEVEL 3
			DEFICIENT	INDIVIDUALS	TEAMS
1	CULTURE	Culture	Risk-averse. Not open to new ideas. Status quo focus	Ideas pop-up by individuals but any further development is not possible. Innovation is not defined, inconsistent and present in sparks	Innovation need is recognized, valued and defined. More risk-tolerant, new ideas are documented and become traceable
2		Outside-in ecosystem	not present, only collaborations with customers and suppliers in development	accidental opportunity spotting, one-off partnerings, individual initiatives, very protective legal & IP, knowledge not shared	Repeated external partnerships based on affection & experience, focus on few dominant partnerships, no structural plan, skills through experience
3		Skills, People	People are seen as productivity units, not as sources of innovation & ideas	ideas by employees are welcomed, mainly to serve in product/process optimization initiatives	human capital awareness in relation to innovation - idea champions move ideas forward
4	KNOWLEDGE & COMPETENCIES	Digital savvyness	Digital is a necessary commodity, unaware of the innovation capabilities behind digital technology, only short-term focus on digitalisation.	longer term digital initiaves to create digital business are limited and isolated. Limited insight and projects are a response to market analysis. No structural data gathering for innovation purposes.	leadership allows limited scope digital experiments to enhance innovation. First structural data gathering to connect with customers and make products better. The ICT organisation is supportive towards business. Agile ICT development and project management in place.
5		Training & future	not present	introduction to basic innovation concepts as creative problem solving, design thinking, ideation is available for management (eg yearly innovation day)	training on idea generation, innovation processes like design thinking. Senior leadership and execs are trained in innovation, foresight and early warning
6	ORGANISATION SUPPORT	Strategy	maintain status quo, protect market share, strategy is limited to forecasting	innovation ideas are not aligned with strategic coporate strategy. Innovation is short term (next quarter) focussed and initiated by market needs or pressure	ideas get aligned with project or department strategic challenges. The intent is locally communicated.
7		Leadership	short term focus and looking at past performance	leaders understand the difference between focus on today and innovation that looks at the future	Senior leadership relies on middle mgmt to do the innovation job to achieve quick wins (short term)
8		Facilities	not present	limited enterprise support for innovation. Volunteers play the most important part. No real infrastructure nor governance	need for innovation infrastructure recognized but not formalized. A dedicated room is available for internal innovation; exceptional external parties attend.
9	INNOVATION PROCES	Processes & Practices	not present	great ideas are rewarded. Ad hoc processes for innovation are used by indivuals	idea mgmt and innovation processes are established. Teams document and share best practices. There is no standardisation.
10		Tools & Techniques / data to wisdom	not present	ideation software is used for problem solving /data in the organisation is only used for process control and only available via standardized reporting	innovation ideas are harvested in all areas / Data generated through monitoring business processes is used for understanding the as is situations in differerent areas and leads to deeper insights on business challenges.
11		Idea generation, capturing, mgmt	ideas not captured	ideas captured by front line mgmt, no alignment with corp strategy, only quick wins	ideas captures, logged, documented. Internal, and external (customers, 3rd parties), digital feedback data, Idea champions take ideas forward and check alignment with department or strategy
12		Metrics on innovation	no innovation-related metrics	elementary metrics as there are #ideas submitted / % managers with innovation trainging / % performance rewards linked to innovation activities	%revenue invested in innovation / idea campaigns, external hackatons / ratio succesful ideas to submitted ideas / #new product launches / data from products provide real-time usage insights

LEVEL 4	LEVEL 5	LEVEL 6
STRUCTURES	**CLIMATE**	**ECOSYSTEM**
Culture encourages risk-taking. All employees are encouraged to participate. Formal roles start to exist. Innovation becomes part of the strategy and culture. Innovation output becomes consistent and sustainable.	Culture embraces innovation. Innovation becomes a company wide collaboration effort with sustained results in market share and positioning	An innovation culture is fostered. Culture encourages risk-taking collaborative innovation efforts. Employees have dedicated time to work on outside-in, long term focused future projects
informal standardization on partnerships, champions share experience & knowledge, strategy applied in finding the right (non-comfort) partners, mentorship widely available	OI & ecosystem training to all employees (not only R&D), partnership in all parts of the value chain, strategy & foresight applied in finding, selecting and evaluating partners(hips), start-up mentality in new partnerships	written OI strategy, dedicated ecosystem team, centralized reporting with open innovation facilities, knowledge sharing and trust-based IP & legal attitude, focus on win-win. Divers stakeholders in a strong ecosystem
employees are encouraged to take calculated risks to solve problems and testdrive new concepts. Limited time is available, there is support from a (small) dedicated innovation team	employees are supported to collaborate with others on new ideas during business hours, besides optimization there is strong focus on new business models and outside-in collaboration seeds	human capital is an innovation key element. Everyone gets dedicated time to generate and prototype new ideas that are validated and rewarded. Everyone gets professional innovation training and support to maximize results
topdown culture change with strategic goals in mind. Enterprise wide adoption of digital technologies to produce data and nurture first (limited) AI initiatives to make products better. (Maintain parity with competitors.) The ICT organisation is integrated in business. ICT is the full responsibility of the business departments.	digital leadership by continuous evolution of vision to product/service experience. Customers are constantly connected and drive new innovations. A digital ecosystem is build and culturally adapted. Strategy to manage the rapid and continuous change in technology is in place.	management at all levels have a digital disruption mindset leveraging data, exponential technologies and digital interaction models, foresight techniques to create a continuous evolving strategic vision. This results in new products, business models and partnerships. Ecosystem grows rapidly thanks to high scalability and agility of ICT in the business organisation and because the organisation is taking crucial roles in platform models
continuous training and evaluation of all employees and management in innovation practices, concepts and methodologies. Foresight is a structural process, an early-warning team supports decision making. Idea champion training	continuous training for all. Outside-in facilitators and experts are involved to avoid any status quo or missing creativity. Foresight is a part of innovation. Foresight team & dedicated innovation training team	customers, vendors and ecosystem partners are involved in outside-in training, brainstorming sessions. Continuous training & evaluation. An internal team is dedicated to detect, empower high potentials. Venturing principles are part of each training
Executives discuss strategic need, goals and intent. Innovation portfolio is systematically aligned with coporate strategy. Execution procedures are in place and outcomes are monitored	Enterprise-level committed strategic planning includes trend analysis, scenario planning and foresight, business model innovation and open innovation sourcing	the organization is well-known as innovator and has a vibrant open ecosystem. Corporate strategy includes future farming, continuous foresight efforts, early warning, innovation portfolio mgmt, innovation-related metrics for senior leadership
leaders create and market targeted innovation campaigns. Senior leadership communicates innovation strategy & processes with long-term vision	Chief innovation officer or similar leadership is appointed to structure all innovation efforts and align with corporate strategy.	leadership is actively engaged in innovation portfolio mgmt and a culture that embraces uncertainty, foresight and bold innovation steps. Top execs meet frequently with outside-in ecosystem execs
dedicated innovation & idea team & center, software, training facilities. Funding = reliable support and infrastructure. Exchange programs with partners.	off-site collaborations, inspiration missions, open innovation congresses are organized. Dedicated innovation facilities. Open for smaller partners, intense collaborations.	innovation center of excellence is established and is accessible for external partners
goals related to innovation systems are established. Methods / tools are formalized and company wide available. Best practices shared. Focussed on business results	Success and failures (!) are documented and communicated and even celebrated. Efficient processes with high participation, rapid decision making, reliable funding	innovation is a business process with well-defined processes, roles, policies, guidelines, funding, metrics with focus on business objectives, success rate and future proof developments
hybrid, targeted innovation campaigns to solve specific problems / This is supported by periodic analyses of integrated data views as data is managed for coordination between different areas.	company-wide idea generation tools are installed & hackatons take place. Digital connectivity with the customer is standardized / Data strategy follows business strategy and is focussed on improvement of business processes thanks to techniques of prediction and forecasting.	"Hackatons are a mantra in the enterprise, supported by well-trained people / Digital technology is used to measure real-time usage of products/services which immediately leads to contextual execution. Data driven decision making is entirely in place and data discovery processes lead to meaningful innovations. "
all ideas are captured, digital data is analyzed and used for wisdom creation, idea implementation systems installed, aligned with strategy before implementation	centralized idea mgmt, quality control, digital data is fed to neural networks, trained data = new insights = available to build new products/services, feedback systems are standardized. Digital twins for testing are experimented.	ideation is included in an overall innovation management, maximum usage data is captured, early warning system in place to detect new-to-the-world concepts/ideas, software to track, monitor status through the process. Digital twins, digital dashboards
%worktime devoted to innovation, idea generation, open innovation / % employees with innovation-related goals / %exec time spent on H1/H2/H3 / %products are online monitored (generate insights)	%H1/H2/H3 innovations in portfolio / time from submission to launch / %teamdiversity / NPV launched products / %open innovation rate per project (how many external partners involved) / % external expertise involved in new ideas	%revenue derived from new products/services year over year increase / %change in company value, market share from new innovation / digital leadership perception topscore / frequency of business model re-evaluation / foresight stress-testing of porfolio, pipeline & partnerships / %outside capital attractiviness (willingness to invest)

Identifying and analysing different scores in this way can lead to new insights, certainly when the differences are considerable. What are the reasons? Is there a problem we are not aware of? These are matters that are at least worth discussing and often provide important new perspectives. Is the level really too low? Or is the distribution of knowledge between different members of the same team unequal? Or are there differences of opinion within the team about the vision and/or the culture? To clarify the situation, the team scores are charted in a different graphic (see below), with additional information about the most extreme scores, the average scores and the standard deviation in the scores. This latter figure gives a good indication of the extent to which the teams were generally 'in agreement' about the scores. The yellow bars indicate the minimum and maximum scores. Sometimes, this might be caused by a particular individual who likes to work with extreme scores. These can be filtered out by plotting the median score or (in this case) the average score, indicated by the blue dots. The red bars show the standard deviation in the score within each dimension, which reflects the degree of consensus among the group.

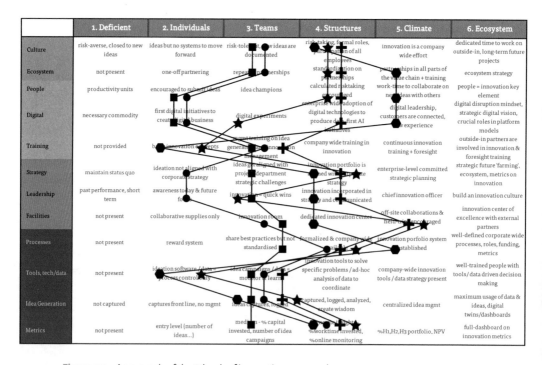

Figure 39 – An example of the 6-levels of innovation scorecard.

In the first graphic you can see that 'culture' has a fairly high score, and this is also the case in the second graphic. You can also see that the standard deviation is small and tends towards higher scores. For 'training' and 'strategic plan', it is noticeable that – notwithstanding the sometimes extreme scores – the scores in general were fairly uniform. 'Tools & techniques' clearly has the worst scores and this is something that was discussed at length in the remaining days of the workshop.

The scores for 'idea capturing' and 'idea management' were also the subject of further discussion. In both cases there is a broadly comparable average score, but in both cases there is also clear disparity between the scores of the different groups. Why was this? After a free and frank exchange of views, it became clear that the groups had widely divergent approaches to outside-in idea capturing; in other words, to open innovation. One team had already built up an ecosystem of partnerships, whereas other teams had hardly started. In the first team, this was largely attributable to a number of team members who had transferred in from other divisions where open innovation was already standard practice.

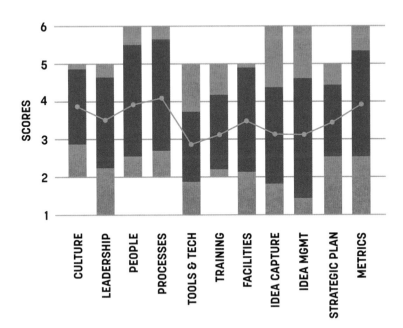

Figuur 40 – How united is the team on the level of innovation?

In some of the other teams this knowledge had not yet been acquired, so that it became evident that knowledge and experience transfer between the teams would mark an important step forward for the new division. In P&G, this was possible using a software platform that was already extant and could be used by the all the teams in question, so that everyone would soon be operating on the same wavelength. Problem solved – and a good example of the benefits that this kind of test can produce!

On the basis of this insight and bearing in mind the ever-growing attention to outside-in idea capturing, collaboration and ecosystems of partners, an additional dimension – 'outside-in ecosystem' – was added to the original eleven-dimension scan used for the P&G test, resulting in the standard twelve-dimension scan that I now use today.

In a nutshell

With this third key, I have outlined the eight obstacles that can block or slow down your innovation momentum and have identified the six levels and twelve dimensions of innovation that can help to anchor an innovation culture in your organisation.

KEY 4
A WINNING INNOVATION TEAM

One of the most frequently asked questions at the start of an innovation trajectory is this: "Who should I include in my team?" My answer is always this: "The more diverse your team, the more you will achieve." In this respect, 'multidisciplinary' is the magic word. You need to find the right balance between strategy, execution and communication.

But perhaps this sounds too simple. So let me share some other pieces of advice, based on my decades of working with large companies, small companies and even start-ups, supplemented by the experience of setting up, running and occasionally even closing down a number of companies of my own. There are two elements in particular that you need to bear in mind when putting together your innovation team:

1. What does a potential team member do best? For which step in the innovation process is he/she the ideal person? I often found useful insights by viewing these questions from the perspective of the person's **dominant learning profile**.
2. How much complexity can the potential team member deal with? Will he/she struggle if things are too complex? Will he/she lose interest if the challenge is not complex enough? I often found useful insights by viewing these questions from the perspective of the person's **personal complexity level**.

By viewing the problem of team composition from these two perspectives, we have been able to help many companies to put together the right innovation teams, a factor which made all the difference between a failed and a successful innovation trajectory.

Kolb's learning circle: learning profiles

David Kolb is an American learning psychologist and pedagogic adviser who has investigated the different aspects of experience-based learning. In his opinion, we learn how to learn by working through a systematic process in four phases:
1. Discovering, exploring and observing new things: dreaming.
2. Reflecting on these things, so that we have a clear understanding of what we have seen: thinking.
3. Translating these thoughts into concrete steps and concepts: deciding.
4. Experimenting with and implementing the knowledge you have acquired: doing.

According to Kolb, people who pass through these four phases of learning will undergo sustainable behavioural change. Fundamentally, this cycle is based on a combination of four very different and sometimes contradictory ways of looking at the world. And no matter how many times we repeat this learning

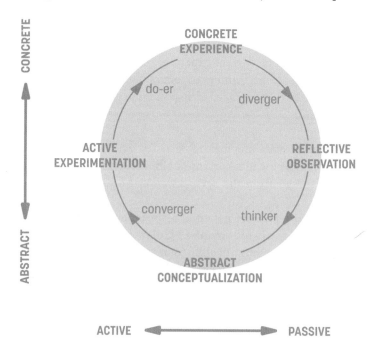

Figure 41 – *Experimental Learning Cycle.* SOURCE: KOLB, D. ET AL. (1984). EXPERIENTIAL LEARNING: EXPERIENCE AS THE SOURCE OF LEARNING AND DEVELOPMENT. ENGLEWOOD CLIFFS, NJ: PRENTICE-HALL

process, every one of us will always feel more attracted to one or other of these learning forms: the one in which we excel.

Thinking about new things, getting a feel for them and exploring them: these are the kind of divergent activities that are typical for a dreamer or **inventor.** Reflecting and conceptualising abstractly on the content of hypotheses and theories is typically something for a **thinker**, a theoretician who can calmly create order out of chaos. Translating ideas and concepts into concrete steps are the convergent activities of a **decision-maker**, someone who makes decisions and likes putting them into practice step by step, so that a clear direction is followed. The actions of the decider are complemented by those of the **doer**, who is keen to move forward through a process of active experimentation and is prepared to take the initiative, even if this involves the risk of possible failure. Please note that I have not used the word 'visionary' in any of these descriptions, because it is possible to be visionary in each of these four dominant profiles by excelling in creativity, courage and charisma.

This model can be applied beneficially to the composition of innovation teams. An innovation process is also a deep learning process that you do not undertake alone, but with a team of other people. It is a good idea to know how each of these people deals with information and in which of the four profiles they excel. Each of the quadrants in the diagram of Kolb's model contains important qualities that are necessary in order to innovate successfully. Each quadrant therefore stands for a dominant characteristic that the different team members possess: inventor, thinker, decision-maker, do-er. Within each of the four quadrants, it is also possible to make a further distinction between three sub-profiles, resulting in twelve different profiles in total. Anyone who takes part in an innovation team must excel at (or at least be dominant in) one of these learning phases. Take a look at your own innovation team and try to match one of the profiles to its members. You will be amazed just how insightful this can be!

INVENTORS:
- **Explorer**: is curious, impatient, keen to learn and driven to discover new things; in other words: "to boldly go where no one has ever been before".
- **Idea developer**: embraces uncertainty, sees the big picture and always finds new possibilities and alternatives.
- **Storyteller**: turns every idea into an earth-shattering idea, thanks to his/her enthusing, passionate and effective communication.

THINKERS:

- **Translator**: investigates options, removes obstacles and gives the first impulses to the following steps to be taken.
- **Catalyst**: is uncertain and wants to listen to the advice of external parties without providing answers himself/herself; in other words, builds the bridges that lead to an ecosystem.
- **Questioner**: always asking questions and always wanting more certainty.

DECISION-MAKERS:

- **Analyst**: initiates the first steps of a more concrete approach.
- **Planner**: organises everything in 'if-then-else' plans.
- **Activator**: the one who says 'go' or 'no-go'; more the latter than the former.

DO-ERS:

- **Supervisor**: monitors and directs all aspects of the operations, with an emphasis on efficiency, eliminating bottlenecks and time management.
- **Pioneer**: has an excellent knowledge of tools, a flexible approach to concepts and develops fast prototypes.
- **Accountant**: excels at the collection, measuring and interpretation of facts and figures.

Getting the right people for your innovation team

To get the best possible composition for your innovation team, you need to have a balanced mix of the right profiles. It is difficult to find intrapreneurs who have both the necessary business and technical skills. For this reason, some organisations contract out or buy in all or part of their innovation process. Or else they put together a group of high-potentials to create a new start-up or spin-off. If, however, you want to keep your innovation process in-house, you need an innovation team with different learning and performance profiles. They process information differently and make themselves useful in different ways, depending on the type of innovation project. Is it an incremental innovation project or is it something completely new and disruptive, which will take the team outside the comfort zone in which the organisation usually operates? Is it an incubation project or an open-innovation project with numerous external partners?

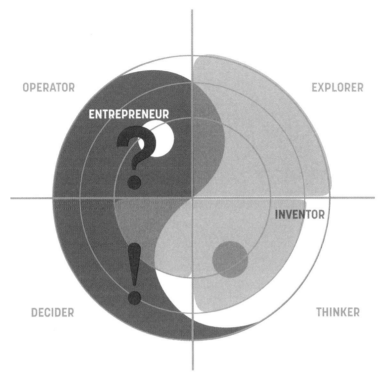

Figure 42 – *A winning innovation team possesses 4 types of skills that are complementary and necessary to succeed.*

By getting to know your team members and learning how they function, you will discover that they have one or sometimes more of the above-described dominant learning profiles at which they excel. It is important to identify these profiles and give them a score. Is the profile weak, moderate or strong? Give each team member a score of 1 to 5 on their individual spider, based on your personal dealings with them and/or your experience of them in other processes. You can do this either for the four quadrants or for a more detailed 12-element profile. It is important to involve your HR people in this assessment. In particular, it is useful to compare your profile evaluation with the MBTI or other personality scores that the HR department possesses for the people concerned. If you add up all the different scores, you will be able to see who are the best people with the best skills for the type of innovation project that you have in mind and also get a good idea about where any profile gaps might occur.

In the example above, it is clear that the doer and decision-making factors are wholly absent. As a result, this project will get bogged down in searching, thinking, reflecting and uncertainty, because nothing will be decided and nothing will be implemented. You need to add a strong entrepreneurial type to this team, someone who is not afraid to take risks and make mistakes, someone who 'walks the talk'. In this way, you can ensure that the project either accelerates or is killed quickly if it looks like going nowhere. The lack of decision-makers is one of the most important reasons why radical innovation projects sometimes end up as zombie projects. There is nobody who dares to pull the plug, because everyone's dominant learning profile is still being stimulated.

If you want to give your investment in an innovation team the maximum chance of success, it is crucial to carry out this evaluation process at the onboarding stage. Do you have all the essential profiles you need for this specific

'If you do something and it turns out pretty good, then you should go do something else wonderful, not dwell on it for too long. Just figure out what's next.'

STEVE JOBS

Figure 43 – *This message is on display in the Apple Campus.*

innovation project? Even in smaller teams, it is important not to expect skills
from your team members that their learning profiles indicate they do not possess. Expecting people to do things they cannot do not only leads to frustration
and fatigue, but above all causes them to lose the complete absorption in their
task that is essential if any complex process –like innovation – is to succeed.
Train your innovation team in these matters. Make them aware of the different
types of learning, so that they know who to approach for help when they get
bogged down. You cannot change people, but you can make them aware of the
different learning profiles that are dominant or present in your team. Where
possible, you can also strengthen your team with the profiles you know are
missing. Do you have too many over-dominant types in your team? Give them
a coaching or mentoring role, so that the effect of their dominance on the innovation process is moderated. If this does not work, pull them out of the team
altogether.

You can also use these same insights to create a balanced innovation commit-
tee, which will serve as a sounding board that guards your organisation against
conservatism and complacency.

The team makes the difference – even in start-ups

As you can see, the right-hand side of the learning circle is primarily concerned
with the characteristics possessed by inventors, whereas the left-hand side is
concerned with the characteristics of entrepreneurs. In a start-up, the founders usually meet each other either by chance or during training. In start-ups
that develop into successful organisations, you often see this chance combination of yin and yang. Think of Microsoft: Paul Allen the inventor, Bill Gates
the entrepreneur who converted MS-DOS into lucrative partnerships and pure
cash. Or Apple: Woz was the brilliant engineer, but without entrepreneur
Steve Jobs Apple would never have become the biggest company in the world.
However, the opposite is also true: without Steve Wozniak, Jobs would never
have had a working computer to sell. He saw the opportunity and ran with it.
And it was the same story at Xerox Labs, when he stumbled by chance on the
user interface and the mouse during a visit to the innovation park. And Google? Larry Page and Sergey Brin now have a reputation of being both inventors
and entrepreneurs, but their more mature management skills only came later:
for the first ten years, the shareholders placed them under the 'parental super-
vision' of Eric Schmidt.

Perhaps it was different at Tesla? Not really. Few people know that 'employee no.7', J.B. Straubel, was really the person behind the company's revolutionary electric car. But JB would never have driven out of Silicon Valley in his electric Porsche 944 – developed at the age of just 14! – without the brilliant business brain of Elon Musk, who in addition to being a serial entrepreneur is also an inventor in his own right, as well as possessing charisma and passion by the barrel-load. As if that were not enough, he also has the gift in everything he does of being able to attract any learning profiles that he lacks: Tesla, PayPal, SpaceX, Starlink, Neuralink and Boring Company all require different skills. And if wants something that is not possible internally or if he doesn't have the time, he is not afraid to allow his ideas be developed externally. For example, via the SpaceX Hyperloop Competition Prize he mobilised the best engineering teams in the world to compete against each other to further develop and refine his space exploration project at top speed. And you can be certain that as soon as his product is good enough in any of his ventures he will take it to market and turn it into a global success, in a new company that employs the best inventors, recruited via the learning profile method outlined above. The main projects still in the Musk pipeline include the TeslaBot robot and the Tesla Smartphone π (pi), which will be linked directly to the Starlink satellite and perhaps even with our brains, via Neuralink technology. The prospects are truly fascinating.

Tesla is obviously a unique case, but you can find this same balance in the successful incubators and accelerators of other major companies. If the yin-yang combination of dominant learning profiles is not present, the project is destined to fail, no matter how good the basic idea might be. Of course, intrapreneurship is much more difficult and more complex in a corporate or public organisation than in a free-spirited start-up. This is one of the lessons we have learnt from our Kodak and Philips CCF examples. In companies of this kind, you often need a larger team in which each member can roll out his/her excellence – dominant profile – in each phase of the K3 trajectory. The insights in this section will help you to get this balancing act right. And never forget the golden rule: "a fool with a tool remains a fool". Don't make the mistake of relying too heavily and too blindly on tools. Innovation is essentially something human.

The Time Span of Discretion and the complexity of innovation

Having identified the way in which your team members absorb knowledge and learn during the innovation process, the next crucial step is to identify the extent to which they can deal with complexity. Every innovation project has a different level of complexity. This is not only (or even primarily) dependent on the technical complexity, but on the nature of the future horizon that needs to be surveyed and the decisions that need to be taken. In the past, I have always been unable to find a telling way to described this challenge – but not any more. I have found the insights and the terminology I need in the research of Dr Elliott Jaques. Jaques (pronounced 'Jacks') was a Canadian psychoanalyst and social scientist who died as long ago as 2003. His passion was the study of organisational cultures and the ways in which people collaborate to get their work done. At the start of the 1950s, he was asked by the British Glacier Metal Company (GMC) to develop an employee participation plan. The company asked him to find out whether it was important that the low-skilled workers were paid per hour or per day, while their managers were paid per month or even per year. This simple question set Jaques thinking and led him in the direction of the work that would occupy him for the rest of his career: requisite organisation.* This involved him investigating the importance of time in the context of the job content that a person is required to perform. He had previously carried out a study for the US Army Research Institute into mental complexity, which revealed that people process complex information in four different ways: declaratively, cumulatively, serially and in parallel.

His new study for GMC revealed (not illogically) that the higher the position in the management hierarchy, the more complex the tasks to be performed. Complex tasks require information to be processed in a different way and every individual has a limit to the degree of information complexity he/she can deal with. This limit increases as we get older, up to and even beyond pensionable age. (Makes you think, doesn't it?) Put all of this together and it means that within an organisation the different hierarchical levels need to be matched as closely as possible with the complexity levels of the activities that need to be performed. With this in mind, Jaques investigated the link between the complexity of a job and the longest time horizon of a task for which we can be held

---

* https://www.requisite.org

Table 4 – *TSD = Maximum time horizon of the tasks for which we are acountable that we can successfully manage = complexity of the job to be done.*

STRATUM	ORGANIZATION LEVEL	TSD	TYPE OF WORK - RESPONSIBILITIES	WHAT CAN BE ACHIEVED?
6	Board, global CEO	10+ years	Future talent/skills strategy – long-term innovation strategy - disruptive transformation – lead in uncertainty	Future Vision – Scenario planning with disruptive options – long term strategic collaborations – disruptive innovation synergies – H3
5	Directors, BU President, Large corp staff VP	5-10y	Strategy – globalization – bus dev – open innovation – r&d – strategic hrm – optimize total business system – transform an entire business to future vision (5y+ outlook)	H2, future options hypothesis testing – competitor analysis – value chain analysis – co-creation / open innovation successes
4	General Management	2 – 5y	Product & BU strategy – integrate and manage departments - manage uncertainty on mid-long term	H1 operational collaboration – joint marketing efforts – joint manufacturing / hardware collaboration – platform collaboration
3	Senior Management	1 – 2 y	PNL driven – optimization - detect mid long term trends & challenges/ opportunities	Practical targets for (open innovation) projects
2	First Line Management	3m – 1y	operations - project driven – gather the right information to diagnose + anticipate problems	Project support
1	Shop or Office Floor	1d– 3m	Operational tasks, follows procedures, seek help when obstacles are encountered, no anticipation of problems is expected, reporting is	Operational stability & performance

accountable with success. Imagine that the longest task for which a person can be held accountable with the expectation of satisfactory completion has a duration of six months. This is the maximum time span for which the person can manage the task successfully. This is expressed as the Time Span of Discretion (TSD). In this case, TSD = 6 months. All the different roles with the same TSD are roughly equal in complexity, irrespective of the department, company or sector to which they belong. Roles with a shorter time horizon are less complex; roles with a longer time horizon are more complex.

Jaques gave the TSD a graded scale to indicate levels of complexity, expressed in units that he called 'stratum'. This scale runs from stratum 1 to stratum 6. The scale covers a duration of just a few days (stratum 1) to more than 10 years Not everyone is capable of working at every stratum level. Some people can deal with complex tasks better than others, although until recently we did not have the language to express this properly. Some people can implement procedures reliably, but they do not have the ability to anticipate problems. They cannot solve these problems by themselves and need assistance to sort them out. With the help of the above table and the Jaques terminology, we can describe this person as someone with potential competence at the stratum 1 level. But how does this all link in with innovation? Incremental innovation demands smart attention, while market-expanding and radical innovation is even more complex. In other words, it is clear that you cannot ask just anyone to carry out any kind of innovation task. What kind of innovation task is it? What level of complexity does it involve? What is the time horizon? The thought horizon? The decision-making horizon? These are the kinds of questions you need to ask before compiling your innovation team.

Someone who is responsible for a routine daily project with (primarily) daily accountability works in stratum 1. The first line manager who has quarterly responsibilities works in stratum 2. The divisional leader who works with an annual PNL plan is in stratum 3. The VP (vice-president) is in stratum 4 and the GM (general manager) in stratum 5. Elon Musk, who launched the adventurous and high-risk SpaceX project without a moment's hesitation or doubt, has been operating in stratum 6 for years – although for him they might need to invent a stratum 9! Be aware that every increasing step up the stratum ladder involves a massive increase in complexity and remember that most managers have a tendency to overestimate their own stratum level. In addition to identifying a person's dominant learning profile, it is also vital to accurately identify this complexity level if you want your innovation team to function effectively.

Talent management can also make beneficial use of this TSD principle. If you allow someone to permanently carry out a task that is above their maximum TSD, the result will be burn-out – which is obviously something you want to avoid. To fulfil their responsibilities (or at least try), the person in question would be forced to perform over the limits of their capabilities day after day. The opposite extreme also applies. If you give someone work over a long period that is significantly below their level of complexity, this will eventually lead to bore-out. Tedium prevails and your talented employee will soon be looking for a new job elsewhere! If you are not careful, this can also happen in your innovation team: you have to make sure that you give the right tasks to the right people at the right level, which is something that will largely be determined by the time horizon of your project. Only then will this project have a chance of success.

Conclusion: a fit in terms of complexity (what people can deal with) combined with a balance of learning profiles (how people process information) are the two most crucial elements in putting together your innovation dream team, both for internal and open innovation projects. Understood? Okay, so let's get started!

Innovators dream of the future; operators think about the present.

In our company we also use this same principle to match the correct profiles in round-table discussions about the future of certain topics. We have more than 20 years of experience in this process, yet even so we still sometimes have to ask ourselves why some of these discussions fail and others are so worthwhile. Once again, the conclusion is that the failures are primarily the result of the absence of the required matches in horizon thinking. The discussion will not work if you have a person with a TSD of one year sitting at the same table with a person with a TSD of ten years. Throughout my entire career, I have met very few people who have been able without hesitation to take on and accept the responsibility for a project with a time horizon in excess of ten years. Or people who can converse confidently and fluently about future ideas for the year 2040, without feeling limited by the complexity of the discussion. Many people think that they have the ability to do this, but in practice few of them are right. This is not a criticism. As with all of us, the wish is often father to the thought.

If you have a mismatch of horizons in a discussion, you will actually end up with a non-discussion. Consider the YouTube debate between Elon Musk and Jack Ma about artificial intelligence and the future. From about the fourth minute onwards, the whole thing actually becomes quite painful to watch. When asked whether AI represented a threat for the human race, Elon Musk answered: "We will just be too slow for AI. Human speech for a computer with exaflops of capability will sound like very slow tonal reasoning, like a whale sounds." And what did Jack Ma answer? "AI stands for Alibaba Intelligence. Computers are never going to be more clever than humans. Not now, not in the future. Of course, it is difficult to predict the future. 99.9% of predictions about the future that mankind has made were wrong." To which Elon responded: "...including this one?"

In my conversation with Professor Emile Aarts of Philips, already mentioned earlier in the book, I asked how Philips Research managed to recruit and retain the right people on his watch. He referred me to the 'Ten Commandments' of Gilles Holst, who was the founder of the Philips NatLab (Research). Although the search for talent at Philips involved a degree of serendipity (as it does everywhere), Holst's Ten Commandments are still an excellent guide for setting up a well functioning industrial laboratory. Check to see if they apply to your innovation lab. I have listed the commandments below, in a slightly updated form.

Holst's Ten Commandments for finding the right R&D innovation people:
1. Recruit smart researchers, young if needs be but with at least some experience in academic/innovation research.
2. Do not pay too much attention to the details of the work that they have done so far.
3. Give your people as much freedom as you can and accept their idiosyncrasies.
4. Allow your people to publish and take part in international scientific activities.
5. Avoid rigid organisational structures. Allow authority to be based on expertise.
6. Do not compartmentalise an innovation lab into different disciplines, but create multi-disciplinary teams.
7. Give as much freedom as you can to the choice of work, but make the lab's leaders aware of their responsibility to the company.
8. Do not budget for an innovation lab per project but by portfolio and do not allow the production department to have budgetary control over research programmes.

9. Encourage and facilitate the transfer of competent older researchers from the lab to the product development and production units.
10. The choice of research projects must not only be determined by market opportunities, but also by current evolutions in (academic) technological research.

In a nutshell

Key 4 shows you how to put together your innovation dream team by making use of two crucial insights: the learning styles of Kolb, whose four-quadrant model I have extended to create twelve dimensions or characteristics that need to be balanced in your team; and the concept of the Time Span of Discretion, which maps out the complexity of the different roles and tasks in your organisation.

KEY 5
THE THREE HORIZONS LEADING TO YOUR FUTURE

You can never man your organisation completely with "crazy ones, rebels and troublemakers", but you can at least develop your processes in the right way to make sure that the 'crazy' people that you do have can do their thing in their own unique way, so that they will want to carry on working for your company. To make this possible, you need to think and plan in terms of three different future horizons. In this section, I will explain why having a belief in a distant future is so crucial and also how these crazy ones can be fitted into the organisations of tomorrow, not only in start-ups, but also in established companies and government authorities. I will also outline where you need other innovators, who are slightly less crazy.

Organisations look for risks in the wrong places

It makes perfect sense to focus on the future, because that is where we are going to spend the rest of our lives. In reality, however, many people spend most of their time living in the present and the past. In this respect, Matt Shinkman of the American CEB research bureau (now owned by Gartner) published an interesting survey of 10,000 companies in the *Harvard Business Review*. His survey started with two simple questions to senior managers:

> *"What does your working week look like?"*
> *"What do you spend time on in your job?"*

Let me challenge you to answer these questions for yourselves!

What Shinkman discovered is that a large part of management time is spent on financial reporting (39%) and dealing with operational matters (42%). This was followed by legal and compliance activities (13%). The remaining time was used on what might be called strategic activities (6%). I often show the results of this research in my presentations and for many people in my audiences it looks all too familiar. For you as well?

These results are a clear indication of where most human capital is spent in our organisations. The researchers were interested in finding out whether these activities had any connection with developments that lead to growth or shrinkage, with shrinkage being defined as loss of value – and therefore as a risk that needs to be well managed. To find the answer, Shinkman monitored his 10,000 respondent companies over a period of ten years. If the company

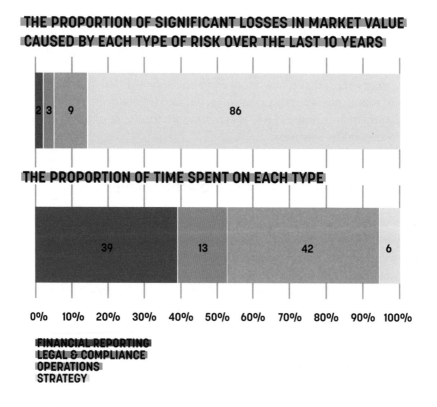

THE PROPORTION OF SIGNIFICANT LOSSES IN MARKET VALUE CAUSED BY EACH TYPE OF RISK OVER THE LAST 10 YEARS

2 | 3 | 9 | 86

THE PROPORTION OF TIME SPENT ON EACH TYPE

39 | 13 | 42 | 6

0% 10% 20% 30% 40% 50% 60% 70% 80% 90% 100%

FINANCIAL REPORTING
LEGAL & COMPLIANCE
OPERATIONS
STRATEGY

Figure 44 – As managers we focus strongly on doing things right, but doing the right things makes the difference in the long run. SOURCE: HBR, HOW TO LIVE WITH RISKS, 2015.

had lost market value during that period, had mistakes been made? Of course, this is something that is easier to assess post-factum or even post-mortem, and it gives a good idea of where hidden risks for a company's future might lie. Were the activities on which managers spend most of their time to blame? No, not at all! In only 2% of cases was loss of value a consequence of financial reporting. Legal and compliance, even with the addition of intellectual property rights, only accounted for 3%, with operational shortcomings in comparison with the competition following on 9%.

In other words, in just 14% of cases loss of value was caused by THINGS THAT WERE NOT DONE RIGHT. In the remaining 86% of cases, the loss resulted from NOT DOING THE RIGHT THIINGS AT ALL.

Companies make too many bad strategic choices or even fail completely to devote attention to strategic choices. Or to put it in slightly different terms: managers spend 94% of their time on trying to improve the things they hope are the right things and just 6% on strategic consideration of the organisation's future, whereas this is the area where 86% of the risks are concentrated. This should be a huge wake-up call for the vast majority of companies: they are looking at the wrong horizon, ignoring the direction from which the most dangerous threats are likely to come.

This distorted method of working is something that people have been taught for decades. For the 20 years or more that we are in the educational system, we are trained to do things right. What these things are, is something that is decided for us by others. This is as true today as it has ever been. Many modern curricula and training courses devote huge attention to the past and the present, and hardly any to the future and the best way to prepare for it. We hope that if we carry on doing things the right way, everything will turn out well: we will get a job, get promoted, make a career... In essence, we are provided with a series of tools and models that allows us to co-ordinate today's activities on the basis of yesterday's information. You can see this in many people's jobs: we are always busy, busy, busy, as Shinkman's time-use study clearly showed. This often gives us a good feeling: "It has been a hectic week"; "We always stick to the rules"; "We never deviate from the agreed procedures"; etc., etc. In other words: we feel we are being productive. By contrast, developing a strategy for tomorrow is more often than not a personal initiative rather than an organisational one, so that it happens in an unstructured and uncoordinated way. And the problem is not just a shortage of time; we also lack the right models for the task. We think about the future with the methods we use to manage the present and to map out the past. Typical tools like SWOTs and budget plans are always based on what has already happened. Of course, no manager is ever going to be able to spend four days a week on strategy. Nor would it be a good idea if he/she could. However, the CEB research demonstrates beyond doubt that more attention needs to be devoted to strategy and future development than is currently the case.

A massive 86% of organisations are still not asking the right questions, even though these are simple and logical questions that have a huge bearing on the future. Yet even when we ask the right questions, without the right methods to deal with the challenges and without the right organisational culture it will be difficult to succeed. Uncertainties can never be dealt with in black-and-white terms. Classic management tools are wholly inadequate to answer the questions that need to be answered in the rapidly changing times in which we live. We need to create a new generation of tools that are better suited to thinking about the future and evolve a culture that accepts open questions as the new norm. In short, an organisation that embraces change, instead of rejecting it. That is the subject of this chapter.

Past, present and future

To see if my assumptions were correct, I decided to test them out in practice. During my lectures on scenario planning at the University of Ghent I asked the students to draw three circles, the size of which should reflect the amount of time that they spent during their studies on the past, the present and the future. If you like, you can do it yourself for your present job,

Sketch A in different variations was the most common response: past, present and future divorced from one another, with attention to the past being greater than for the present, with the future hardly featuring at all. I asked the same question to the managers of companies, both public and private, where no foresight strategy was in place. In this instance, sketch B was the most frequent. Managers of this kind were constantly telling me that they spent nearly all their time dealing with the problems of the present, based on experience gained from the past. If they wanted to know where the organisation would stand in 12 or 24 months' time, they used procedures that had existed for decades to extrapolate the evolution of recent years into the future. Are we on schedule? Are we living up to expectations? Looking further ahead than two or three years was simply something that did not happen. For me, this was clear evidence that Shinkman's research was correct and that the majority of companies fail to select the right things, fail to innovate and fail to look ahead to the challenges that await them.

Would it help to change people's approach if they were made more aware of the importance of strategy and looking to the future? Can the exclusive focus on doing things right be supplemented with some curiosity about whether the right things are actually being done? I asked my same questions to the managers of organisations where I knew they already had some experience of strategy scenarios and future thinking. This led to the production of sketches C and D. In sketch C, the present is still the main focus of attention, in which insights drawn from the past still play a role. Past and present are no longer separated

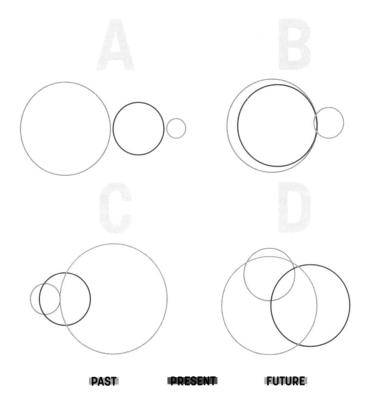

PAST   PRESENT   FUTURE

Figure 45 – How do you view the past, present and future?

from each other and no longer dominate to the same extent as in sketches A and B: the future circle has become much bigger and overlaps with the present. Here it is clear that people query whether they are doing the right things and take important decisions in the present with a view to developing an even more promising future. One of the managers I questioned came up with sketch D. I asked her what it meant. She said that for every important decision taken today, the company worked with an impact analysis drawn up in the light of a dynamic future plan that had been developed with the backing of the entire leadership. Experience and insights from the past are still heard and usually come from the top downwards, which she did not think was negative per se. However, she had had to learn to deal with recurrent scepticism about new pilots, because "something like that was tried in the past and it never worked". I was interested to hear this, since the organisation in question is a reasonably flourishing family business in which some members of the founding family are still in control, but who clearly seem to find it difficult to let go of their successful past and allow the next generation to look at the future and perhaps do things in a completely different way.

> *So how would you draw your circles? And how do you*
> *think your fellow managers would draw theirs?*

Be on your guard if you see that your circles for the past and the present are significantly bigger than your circle for the future. Is the future present at all? Are the circles nested? Or are they separate from each other? Why is that? Does your organisation have cross-business knowledge transfer? Do you analyse your successes and failures from the past to make a direct link to your plans for tomorrow? Do you involve your managers who have had foresight training? This can have a huge impact on how the circles are drawn and will certainly raise a number of interesting topics for discussion. As a management team, you must know how you look at the past, the present and the future.

Divide the future into different horizons

It should by now be clear to you that the three horizons of innovation and management time – past, present and future – can help you to divide up tasks, skills and resources. Large companies are not start-ups – although a few years ago it was a hype to have a few 'hoodies' running around in your company, in the hope that this would stimulate an entrepreneurial culture – but they can no longer behave like the slow, heavy and rigid institutions of the past, basing their activities on a slowly evolving range of products and services, which they then take to market with the same equally rigid business model. To develop an innovation ecosystem, today's large companies need to see themselves as a dynamic portfolio of products and services. They need to throw open their doors and windows to the world, imitating the approach of Cargill that I described earlier. For decades, the big companies have been organising themselves to position their products and services ever more firmly and more extensively in the market. Nowadays, developing a balanced innovation portfolio is a crucial task, if you want to continue to grow. Fast-paced changes in the business environment mean that portfolio models are now evolving with equal speed. So let's take a look at this evolution.

From the old Ansoff matrix as the basis for future product innovation...

The oldest (but still useful) strategic model was developed by Igor Ansoff, an American economist and mathematician with a Russian background and the founding father of strategic management. At the end of the 1950s, he published the Ansoff matrix, which soon become fundamental information for every marketeer in the world. The model argues that in good and stable environments there are four growth strategies that can be implemented. The logic behind this theory is simple: when consumers earn more, they also spend more, so that more products need to be produced. According to Ansoff, this growth can take place in one of two dimensions: the development of new goods and services or the exploration of new markets. This results in a matrix of four possible strategies that are still applied today in growth markets.

1 – Market penetration: This involves increasing the sale of existing products in existing markets through price-setting, design and packaging innovation, freemium models (first try a product and then pay for upgrades or else pay on completion of a test period), upselling, robotisation, feature innovation (extra options), (creative) advertising, partnerships, influencers, reviews and ratings. Greater market penetration leads to economies of scale and, eventually, to a dominant position. Competitors then respond with lower prices to limit your growth or win back market share. This can sometimes provoke a fierce fight for market position and generate savage price wars, as is often the case in the supermarket sector. In recent times, smartphones have also become a battle-

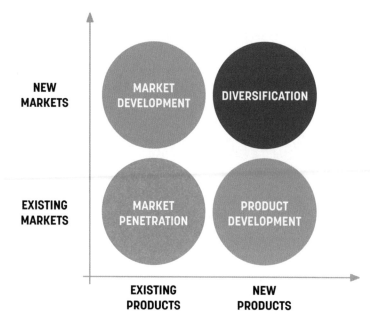

Figure 46 – *The old trusted Ansoff matrix no longer suffices.*

ground for this kind of strategy. All smartphones are basically the same, but seek to attract new customers through the best camera, the biggest screen, the flashiest cover, etc. This is the least risky of Ansoff's four strategies, but it is not the most profitable in the long term.

A simple example of how this strategy works is the use of influencers to convince people that they are using the right products and that others should use them as well. For instance, Brad Pitt is now the new De'Longhi Perfetto coffee drinker. He does everything in the promotion video himself, from riding his motor bike to buying, making and drinking coffee. Perhaps this is a nod to the legendary clip with Danny DeVito and George Clooney, who created the instant coffee moment with Nespresso – What Else? I am curious to see how many (female) fans will now be willing to swop George for Brad!

2 – Product development: This involves developing new products and services, and then selling them in existing markets. Cross-selling is often used for this purpose, sometimes in creative new partnerships. Strava measures and records your sporting performance, but for a monthly fee can also act as your ideal sports coach. Steve Jobs' 'one more thing' routine became legendary, as the brain behind Apple revealed yet another new feature or product to take the market by storm.

A more recent and perhaps less well-known example is the Foodmaker Smart Fridge, a health fast-food caterer that started in Belgium as a challenger to the much larger EXKi and Le Pain Quotidien. As a result of the Covid-19 pandemic, the company restaurants that formed Foodmaker's biggest market suddenly closed their doors, so that Foodmaker needed to switch to supermarkets and home deliveries in order to survive. Now that many people are working more and more online, the future of these restaurants is increasingly in doubt. Foodmaker's response was to create an innovative unmanned shop, a kind of smart fridge that aims to be the replacement for the 'unhealthy' snack machines (crisps, chocolate, etc.) that are still found in many workplaces. A related app with a smart personal health coach even suggests which salad might be best for you today. What's more, its stand-alone nature means that the smart fridge can also be used at other locations, such as battery charging points, schools, function rooms, co-working spaces, etc. It is an excellent example of how you can use smart technology to expand your market and follow your public.

3 – Market development: This involves the sale of existing products in new markets that have not yet been served, which is a useful option when growth opportunities in existing markets have become limited. Of course, moving into a new market also involves a greater degree of risk, which is why in recent years this option is often accompanied by partnerships that allow 'instant' experience of the new market to be obtained. This approach is particularly useful for companies wishing to move into unexplored foreign markets. In recent times, selling online has also become a way for many companies to develop a new market. In a reverse process, online traders have also started to develop physical stores as a way to pull new consumers 'over the line'. This typical segmentation of the market may sound outdated, but is still often used in this context.

If you have a good and simple product that responds to the frustrations of consumers, the internet and the app stores of Apple and Google have made market development much easier than it once was. A good example is the Canadian Shopify. In 2006, two friends, Tobias Lütke and Scott Lake, wanted to start a web shop to sell snowboards. They were unhappy with the existing e-commerce software for the purpose and so decided to make their own platform, which skyrocketed almost overnight. By 2010, Shopify was the fastest growing company in the Ottawa region of Canada and today their platform model forms the basis for 1.7 million online stores in more than 175 countries worldwide.

4 – Diversification: This involves the sale of new products in new markets that have not yet been served. This is by far the most high-risk of Ansoff's four strategies and for this reason is less frequently applied by large corporate companies. In fact, diversification involves a double risk. One the one hand, you launch an entirely new product, which gives your competitors time to develop a better or cheaper version. On the other hand, you are venturing into a new market, where you are less familiar with the needs of customers than some of your rivals. This 'new market' risk was evident in the case of Google's smart glasses. Nobody attempted to copy the product, but the target group for the glasses was not clearly defined, so that customers more or less had to find out for themselves what the glasses could offer. I first tested them in 2014, courtesy of a newspaper publisher in Belgium. If you wore the glasses while reading the paper, you saw extra information. But it was all too elaborate, too time-consuming, too early...

A more successful example of this strategy is the collaboration between Miele, with its new Dialog oven, and the M Chef start-up, which does home deliveries in Germany. The Dialog is a totally new technological concept for ovens. Through a system of sensors, the oven communicates continually with every different ingredient that is being cooked in it. Its revolutionary use of electro-magnetic multi-frequency waves and radiant heat makes it possible for the Dialog to cook, thaw and reheat fish, meat, vegetables and bread all at the same time. M Chef focuses on providing high-quality gastronomy that you can make quickly and easily in your own home, providing you have a Dialog. When you order your gastronomic meal via the app, it is made by a top chef and delivered quickly to your door on beautifully dressed porcelain plates. You put everything in the oven, scan in the menu code and the Dialog does the rest, preparing everything in the right way at the right time and at the right temperature. It is an interesting concept and one that seeks to explore the market for top-class food for people who do not have the time, skill or inclination to make it for themselves. I am curious to see how it will develop in the rest of the world. If you would like to know more or see for yourself, the Dialog will be part of the Miele Kitchen of the Future that will be launched as part of our innovation platform in Brussels at the start of 2023.

It is worth noting that some products work their way through the entire Ansoff matrix. Apple's iTunes came onto the market as a solution to allow Mac computers to easily burn CDs and archive your MP3s. This was a market penetration strategy designed to avoid the loss of customers, who might otherwise seek a solution from Microsoft. It was followed by a second product innovation strategy in the form of the iPod, which in turn was responsible for new market development, since people worldwide became interested in being 'liberated' from CDs. Finally, there was diversification into a totally new product with the iPhone, which was also able to conquer a much broader market. At first, you needed to install Mac or Windows, but this was later superseded by iCloud web services. As a result, you no longer needed a Mac or a PC to activate your iPhone. The cycle was complete.

... via a three-stage product road map for the future

The Ansoff matrix is a clear and reliable instrument for the allocation of an organisation's resources to a number of growth initiatives in production lines. But it is less applicable in breakthrough and radical innovation contexts. This was noted by the researchers Bansi Nagji and Geoff Tuff, who in 2014 defined a new matrix that has not two but three stages per dimension. In addition to 'existing' and 'new', they added an 'adjacent' stage. The playing fields of 'market' and 'product' remained the same. As a result, the new matrix gave a deeper overview of three different types of products that you can launch in a market, each requiring a different strategy: core, adjacent and transformational products.

The **core products** are equivalent to the market penetration products in the Ansoff matrix.

Adjacent products are by no means ground-breaking innovations, but still manage to reach new target groups with new products. For example, the Swiffer developed by Procter & Gamble was quickly able to reach a much broader target group with a simple product that went further than classic detergents and mops. Adjacent products of this kind also fit within the Ansoff matrix.

In contrast, **transformational products** go beyond the standard Ansoff range. These are the products that generate lots of buzz. Suddenly, everyone is talking about them. They are radical and new-to-the-world. Think, for example, of

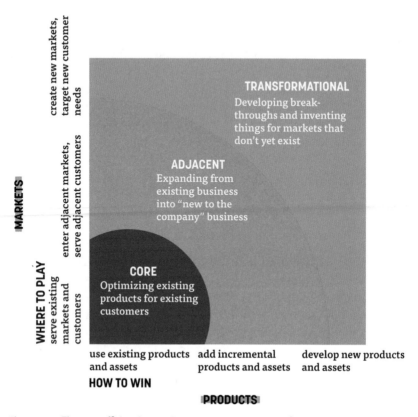

MARKETS

WHERE TO PLAY

create new markets, target new customer needs

enter adjacent markets, serve adjacent customers

serve existing markets and customers

TRANSFORMATIONAL
Developing break-throughs and inventing things for markets that don't yet exist

ADJACENT
Expanding from existing business into "new to the company" business

CORE
Optimizing existing products for existing customers

use existing products and assets

add incremental products and assets

develop new products and assets

HOW TO WIN

PRODUCTS

Figure 47 – *The most efficient innovation management consists of investing in 3 levels of ambi-tion.* SOURCE: BANSI NAGJI AND GEOFF TUFF, HBR

Napster, Netscape, Starbucks, Netflix and Uber. Or more recently, the Apple Watch, Hyperloop, Neuralink, Starlink and future Elon Musk projects like TeslaBot or Tesla Phone π. These are products that have the potential to rede-fine, create or destroy entire sectors.

In which segment would you position the above examples from the Ansoff ma-trix? And where would you position your own innovation initiatives?

Is there an ideal balance for allocating my resources?

You will probably have noticed that the more you move to the outer edge of the Nagji and Tuff graphic, the higher the level of risk inherent in innovation becomes. This makes transformational innovation a far-from-evident choice for companies that are risk-averse, but it is music to the ears of the start-ups, who like nothing better than a 'go for broke' approach.

Let us focus for a moment on the 'corporates', the larger organisations that have been in business for quite some time. The research conducted by Nagji and Tuff in various sectors analysed the extent to which the percentage allocation of resources to core, adjacent or transformational initiatives correlated with a significantly better performance and a higher stock market value. They discovered that there was indeed a correlation and concluded that companies that allocated their innovation resources on the basis of a split between 70% core initiatives, 20% adjacent initiatives and 10% transformational initiatives performed better than their competitors and realised a growth in profits and/or stock market value of between 10% and 20%. Interesting, don't you think?

Of course, differences were seen between sectors. FMCGs focus primarily on core products and less on transformational projects. In contrast, tech companies invest less heavily in the core and immediately seek diversification via breakthrough products that will allow them to differentiate and grow. This what happened when Steve Jobs returned to Apple for the second time at the end of the 1990s, sparking off a metamorphosis that turned the company from flop to top with a series of transformational and adjacent products like iMac, iTunes and later the iPhone and the iPad.

Established companies will nearly always have a preference for innovating in the core and adjacent zones. Transformational projects, which require a high level of genuine intrapreneurship, are much more difficult for them to implement successfully. They often make attempts via incubators, accelerators and outsourcing to venture studios, but usually with disappointing results that achieve little other than to waste time and resources. This is where the ROI obstacle to innovation – which I mentioned earlier in the book – has its origins.

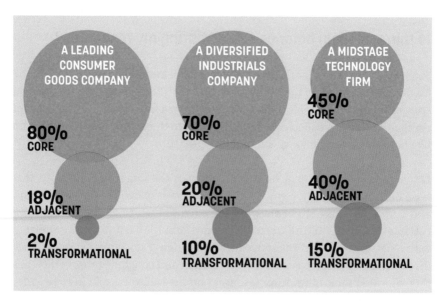

Figure 48 – On average, companies were found to invest 70% of the innovation resources in the core, 20% in adjacent and 10% in transformational. This may differ depending on the ambitions, risk profile and sector. SOURCE: BANSI NAGJI AND GEOFF TUFF, HBR

Start-ups looking to attract venture capital in the tech and internet sector focus much more on the high-risk 'wow' products that are found in the top right of the graphic. This kind of product brings them to the attention of the media and venture-minded investors, who provide them with sufficient cash burn to guarantee that they will get their breakthrough or adjacent products to market.

Of course, getting them to market is no guarantee of success: high risks go hand in hand with a high rate of failure.

The rule of thumb for venture capital is that three to four out of every ten start-ups fail and three to four never fully take off. In other words, three-quarters of them never yield an added value for the investors. The remaining one to two are successful, but of these less than 1% are able to generate significant value creation, although this value can sometimes be astronomically high; so high, in fact, that I sometimes wonder where valuations of this kind will take us in the future.

The term 'unicorn' was first devised by Aileen Lee, founder of Cowboy Ventures, a US seed-stage venture capital company. She used it to designate companies worth more than 1 billion dollars. By extension, a decacorn is worth more than 10 billion dollars and a hectocorn more than 100 billion dollars. Worldwide, there are some 800 unicorns, like Facebook and Google used to be. There are roughly 40 decacorns, including SpaceX, the American space exploration company of Elon Musk. At the time of writing, there is only one hectocorn; namely, ByteDance, the Chinese company behind the hugely popular TikTok platform. ByteDance had plans to go public in the summer of 2021, after President Biden had revoked the ban on TikTok in America. As a result, the company's grey market valuation shot up to 425 billion dollars, a figure never previously seen. In the meantime, however, we now know that the Chinese government has blocked the initial public offering of Jack Ma's fin-tech Ant Group and the Didi taxi-app, which has tilted the whole tech sector out of balance, since it is now clear that President Xi wishes to rein in the growing wealth and power of the new tech giants. For this reason, ByteDance decided that it would be a good idea to postpone its IPO indefinitely and seek instead a closer working relationship with the regime in Beijing, so that it can continue to grow in a manner acceptable to the authorities. In this way, for example, the maximum gaming time for Chinese youth has been restricted to 90 minutes a day. These developments make it uncertain what value ByteDance will finally reach, if or when it eventually launches its IPO.

Be that as it may, we are still talking about huge figures, but these are the kinds of return that venture capital-backed starter companies can sometime yield. That being said, some of the established names are also capable of super-rapid growth. There are now officially six stock-listed companies with a value in excess of 1,000 billion dollars: the MATAMA group (temporarily minus Facebook/Meta) and Saudi Aramco.

On paper, it seems as though the key to innovation success for these and other less well-known companies is just a question of moving around your available resources to create the right innovation portfolio. Unfortunately, it is not quite as simple as that. Because in reality there are many factors that determine how and when you can – or cannot – shift your resources to change your innovation strategy.

... to innovation in a three-horizon future portfolio

In this respect, the three-horizons concept of David White, Stephen Coley and Mehrdad Baghai sheds interesting light on what is possible and what not. This three-horizons idea was first developed in their book *The Alchemy of Growth*, published in 2000. It is still one of the best tools for assessing and deploying your innovation strategy and determining the resources that will be necessary to achieve it. It provides a terminology that can be used in the boardroom to explain why a different approach to innovation and resources is dependent on the kind of road map that the company wishes to follow. In my experience, the model works well for commercial companies, public organisations and even start-ups (although in public organisations innovation success is not measured in terms of profit or turnover, but in terms of the overall success of the chosen policy and the resulting legislation and/or services it creates). Its application is the best guarantee of a continuous pipeline of new products, which are ready as a succession of S-curves to form the next successful core.

According to this methodology, your innovation efforts can be sub-divided into three horizons, the expected future value of which increases as you pro-

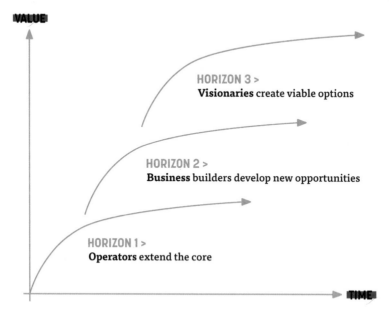

VALUE

HORIZON 3 >
Visionaries create viable options

HORIZON 2 >
Business builders develop new opportunities

HORIZON 1 >
Operators extend the core

TIME

Figure 49 - *The 3 levels of ambition, the value and the type of skills you need.*
SOURCE: DAVID WHITE, STEPHEN COLEY AND MEHRDAD BAGHAI, THE ALCHEMY OF GROWTH

gress through the horizons. The model is also useful in brainstorming sessions for immediately categorising the different horizons in which the different ideas fall.

In my opinion, it is equally useful for putting together your innovation team, who need to share the appropriate innovation horizon if you wish them to collaborate successfully on a challenging project. We saw earlier that for every concrete task you need to take account of the complexity level (TSD) and dominant learning profile of your team members. The different horizons will each require the use of different skills.

HORIZON 1: Quick wins or improvement projects

Typically, these are the products with which your organisation is traditionally associated. You are good at making them and already have them on the market. They are the core of your success and provide the majority of your revenue. Even so, innovation continues to be necessary to maintain your position. You need to work at greater cost efficiency, digitalisation, product and service expansion, etc. It is also the domain where you need to look at productivity gains, cost-cutting and restructuring. Developing your existing portfolio into a collaborative model with others – an ecosystem – is certainly an interesting option.

Platform models like Facebook, Uber, Airbnb, Wikipedia, Apple Pay and Itsme are good examples of ecosystems that remain successful through incremental innovation that adds new features to existing products and services. The best way to plan your approach to horizon 1 is to draw up a tactical plan with your operational management team, linked to incentives based on profit and loss. The necessary talents are often already present within your organisation and with a little extra training can perform excellently in this horizon. The results can be measured using your quarterly figures, ROI (look at future profits) and net present value (look at future income). This will give you some idea of the investments you can make. If we compare horizon 1 with the product-market matrix, it is situated in the core zone or at the start of the adjacent products zone.

HORIZON 2: The development of new business or services

The second horizon is an extension of your existing business model and organisation, and is situated somewhere between standard operations and undertaking something new. It is often referred to as 'emerging business' or 'new business development'. The best plan of approach is to set up a sufficient number of new ventures divorced from horizon 1, for which you need to attract the right skills, give the necessary freedom of action, provide sufficient budget and install the right metrics. For this horizon, you need proper entrepreneurship; in other words, you must be bold and accept a (controlled) degree of risk tolerance. It is important to develop different fast-moving initiatives (or consider a merger or acquisition), which will transform the future of your organisation. The way in which you do business will change, because you will be launching new products, and these changes will be felt both in terms of new business models and new technology.

The necessary capabilities will probably be less easy to find in-house than was the case for horizon 1. Some of the technologies you need will be unfamiliar to you. In some areas knowledge will also be lacking and you may have to deal with new markets and new customers that you do not know. For all these reasons, it is important to work sufficiently outside-in with new partners who can help you to reach your objectives. You can attract the talent you need by giving them the resources and the room to manoeuvre that they need to score. And when they do score, you must give them the recognition they deserve. This can sometimes lead to the setting up of an entire new product division, which in some cases (as experience has shown) may equal or even overtake your core business within five or so years (although it is difficult to predict an exact time frame).

The measures for success in horizon 2 are no longer ROI or NPV, but ROV: Real Options Valuation. This involves you attempting to keep your options open for as long as possible. Each venture can be assessed on the basis of milestones, which will allow you to accelerate, slow down, put on hold or cancel, as seems appropriate. This demands a much more dynamic planning than horizon 1 and you will work in an environment of constant uncertainty. The best approach is probably to use a combination of forecasting (extrapolating known certainties to the future) and foresight (assessing future uncertainties and how they affect the present) to plan for a three-to-five year period. In terms of comparison with the product-market matrix, we are now situated in the heart of the adjacent zone, but seldom in the transformational zone.

Horizons 1 and 2 are focused primarily on the operational working of the organisation in which innovation needs to take place. This is not the domain of Steve Jobs' 'crazy ones'. Nor would they be happy here. No, this is the domain of the specialists and the business scouts. These are also the horizons where the corporates feel most comfortable, because they can go a long way with rules and procedures. The processes in H1 and H2 can be institutionalised to create an innovation machine. Companies in FMCG, vehicle manufacturers, banks and retailers have all built perfectly functioning innovation machines of this kind, run by senior managers who earned their spurs in operations. In contrast, horizon 3 plays by very different rules and demands very different skills.

HORIZON 3: Transformation and revolution

In addition to a well functioning operational base engaged in incremental innovation (H1) and the further exploration of new markets and collaborations (H2), it is also crucial to invest in longer-term innovation, if you wish to remain relevant in the future. Every organisation – whether it is a start-up, a corporate company or a government institution – must have a long-term ambition, an innovation doctrine, a set of beliefs that place the innovation effort in the right context. You need to understand why you innovate, so that later on you can continue to play the game. "Execution pays your salary; innovation pays your pension," as innovation professor Steve Blank once said. A one-liner that hits the nail very firmly on the head.

H3 is the horizon where you sow new seeds for the organisation's future business harvest. In terms of the product-market matrix, you are now right in the middle of the transformational zone. You explore new options intensively via new technologies, new business models, new partnerships and new markets. You are dealing with the products and services that your company will have in five years' time. This exploration can take different forms: research projects, alliances, minority interests, investment in start-ups, scale-ups, pilots, etc.

Horizons 1 and 2 are often closely associated with P&L organisations (business units) in the corporate sector and this is where they are most frequently implemented. Horizon 3 is a very different place. Because this is indeed where the 'crazy ones' – the misfits and the mavericks – live and work. If you tried to implement horizon 3 in a P&L structure, it simply would not work. The result would be internal conflict and failed innovation. This is where the obstacles to viable innovation efforts are mainly to be found and this is often determined by what is allowed and what is not allowed within the organisation – which is why since the turn of the century H3 has largely become the preserve of start-ups financed by risk-taking venture capitalists.

What is allowed and what is not allowed?

Start-ups have very few or no rules to hold them back. In fact, nothing excites them more than looking at a saturated market and finding ways to break all that market's conventions. Think, for example, of Uber, Airbnb and (earlier) Napster. By contrast, in corporate organisations you can only do what the rules

> "HERE'S TO THE CRAZY ONES,
> **THE MISFITS.**
> THE REBELS, THE TROUBLEMAKERS,
> THE ROUND PEGS IN THE SQUARE HOLES.
> THE ONES WHO SEE THINGS DIFFERENTLY.
> **THEY'RE NOT FOND OF RULES.**
> YOU CAN QUOTE THEM, DISAGREE WITH THEM,
> **GLORIFY OR VILIFY THEM,**
> BUT THE ONLY THING YOU CAN'T DO IS IGNORE THEM
> **BECAUSE THEY CHANGE THINGS.**
> THEY PUSH THE HUMAN RACE FORWARD.
> AND WHILE SOME MAY SEE THEM AS THE CRAZY ONES,
> **WE SEE GENIUS.**
> BECAUSE THE ONES WHO ARE CRAZY ENOUGH
> TO THINK THAT THEY CAN CHANGE THE WORLD,
> **ARE THE ONES WHO DO."**
>
> **STEVE JOBS**

made by the company allow you to do. This works for H1 and H2, but creates conflicts in H3. Because of their structure, it is more difficult for larger companies to break the rules, even if they are only internal ones. Just think back to the stories of Kodak or the Philips CCF earlier in the book. Governmental organisations have even greater problems in this respect: they not only have to follow the rules, but also have a certain mandate that they have to respect, written down in formal agreements and policy notes. In this way, creativity and innovation are stifled or at best limited by short-term objectives and the kind of 'quick wins' that elected officials love so much. This may gain them popularity in the short term, but it does very little to generate added value in the long term.

H3 and the need for ambidextrous organisation

The conflict between H1 and H2 on the one hand and H3 on the other hand can only be effectively resolved by what Emile Aarts of Philips refers to as ambidextrous innovation. You need an ambidextrous organisational structure: a two-handed organisation, where one hand can (and is allowed to) do something completely different from the other hand, even though both hands are attached to the same body and directed by the same guiding brain. The conflict situation that is created by H3 – the breaking of rules – arises because H3 needs plenty of freedom to do what it needs to do. You must give the crazy people, the radical visionaries, the chance to experiment, the chance to fail, the chance to think and act differently. If you don't, your H3 project will never succeed. This will only be possible if the organisation allows these teams more privileges than the rest.

When I said at the beginning of this chapter that it is impossible to staff your organisation completely with innovators, so that it is necessary to create the right procedures to allow the crazy people to do their work, it was the Horizon 3 procedures that I had in mind. If you let everyone in the organisation experiment to their heart's content, you are a start-up. But start-ups are small and have no rules and regulations. In a large company, this kind of unrestrained freedom would immediately cause huge and potentially dangerous problems, because your operational execution would suffer. H1 and H2 need rules and procedures; H3 does not (or not much). Does this mean that you cannot implement H3 in larger organisations? Is it the exclusive preserve of start-ups? No, but radical innovation in large companies will only work if you have an ambidextrous approach. In the past, people used to argue for the total separation of the disruptive innovation unit (H3) from the rest of the organisation. This is not a bad idea per se, but it has two major drawbacks. It means that the unit is less able (or not able) to make use of some of the assets of the mother company (production options, sales channels, etc.) and the distance of separation often leads to the weakening and even collapse of the unit as a whole. Start-ups and spin-offs are often set up in locations remote from the home base, where all sense of connection with the mother company is lost, persuading many of the brilliant talents that it is perhaps a better idea to set up their own business with the venture capital that is there for the taking from the venture capitalists in Silicon Valley. Similarly, in Europe we have also seen in recent years that it has become much easier to get start-up funding.

Even H3 needs structure, but above all an innovation vision

For this reason, the corporates now prefer to keep their innovation projects in-house, but this requires them to adopt a different approach. It is not easy, but it is not impossible, either. It means, however, that you must train the entire organisation to think constantly in terms of long-term solutions. You need to preach the innovation faith. You need to develop an innovation doctrine, creating a culture of innovation that is less about the stimulating of creativity and more about understanding the three innovation horizons and the different ways they work. Everyone – I repeat, everyone – must realise that the organisation needs both short-term scores to survive in the present and more high-risk success in the long term to remain relevant in the future. The senior management plays a hugely important role in this respect. Based on their belief in the innovation doctrine, it is they who must ensure that H3 can be implemented as effectively as possible. They must avoid friction wherever they can and resolve it wherever it occurs. They must add the necessary annexes to the organisation's innovation manifesto that defines the free playing area for the H3 team and make clear that the rules for this area are different from the rules of the P&L divisions. For example, an H3 innovation boffin must be given a certain innovation project budget without the need to justify how he/she spends it. Whether it is the fast-track development of a prototype, the purchase of a new AI tool or attendance at an international conference, neither HR nor the finance department will be able to veto the plan. The only guide that the 'crazy ones' must have is the metrics that chart every step of their progress. In short, as an organisation you have to accept the need for two sets of rules and processes. Without this ambidextrous approach and the freedom and confidence it creates, your disruptive (H3) innovation unit will never be a success. Without preaching and actively implementing a long-term vision, your 'two-handed' organisation will be nothing more than a castle in the air. Conclusion: start developing your innovation doctrine today!

But how do you begin? My experience with companies who succeed in this task suggests that drawing up foresight scenarios is the best way, not only for the development of the doctrine, but also for the vision, the H3 definition and the creation of an ambidextrous culture supported by everyone in the organisation. The most important thing of all is to define and implement the three-horizons portfolio.

You need to accept that there will be a fairly long time horizon before you are successful. Most of the practical examples from the past show that between five and ten years is the norm. Think of Tesla, SpaceX, Ryanair and Booking. com, but also wider concepts like car-sharing, blockchain and alternative energy concepts. They all took time to get off the ground. To be able to approach this level in the right manner, you need visionary thinkers: people who have the guts to think in radically different ways, who are not afraid to formulate moonshots and have the ability to motivate teams to achieve them.

A classic example (as in so many other things) was Steve Jobs, who was known and sometimes feared in Apple for his 'reality distortion field'. I read the biography of his life by Issacson with much interest. At one point, it describes a perfect horizon 3 moment. During the development of the Macintosh computer in 1984, Jobs asked Larry Kenyon, one of the Apple engineers, to cut the Mac boot time by 10 seconds. Kenyon told him that this was not possible. Jobs asked him a second question; "If it would save someone's life, could you find a way to do it?" Kenyon slowly nodded. Jobs then went across to a whiteboard and explained what this would mean: "Well, let's say you can shave 10 seconds off the boot time. Multiply that by five million users and that's 50 million seconds, every single day. Over a year, that's probably dozens of lifetimes. So if you make it boot ten seconds faster, you've saved a dozen lives. That's really worth it, don't you think?" A few weeks later, Kenyon came back with a rewritten code that cut the boot time by 28 seconds... This is typical of the way visionaries often think differently from the rest of us. They refuse to believe that something cannot be done, even if everyone else tells them the opposite.

Another good example is Johan Thijs, the CEO of KBC, a Belgian bank. For years, he has been on the list of the world's top ten CEOs and he is unquestionably visionary in his approach. During a speech at a CEO summit meeting in 2017, he indicated his intention that by 2025 companies should be able to get loans in less than 10 seconds by using a simple app, in contrast to the existing three-day long process of interviews and form-filling. I can still see how many of the other CEOs smiled and shook their heads in disbelief. Last year, I asked Johan how the project was progressing. He told me that the bank had invested heavily in blockchain and artificial intelligence systems to make his objective achievable. For most loans the lead time was down to 30 minutes, but from then on this would be improved quite quickly. This proves the point yet again: you have to have the courage to pick the right radical moonshot – and then just go for it!

The following table is a summary of the most important conclusions relating to the three horizons.

Table 5 – *The core elements of the 3-horizon innovation portfolio methodology*

	HORIZON 1	HORIZON 2	HORIZON 3
Business	Core	Growth	Future
Strategy	Optimize	Entrepreneurship	Visionary, radical
Innovation	Incremental	Adjacent	Radical
Innovation comes from	**Ecosystems**, partnerships. Make things better, not different.	**Products** that change the way you do business. Serves customers in new ways	Emerging **technologies** that disrupt or create radical new approaches
Type of plan	Tactical plan	New business development plan	Foresight & options milestone plan
Required leadership	Operational managers	Networkers and business building	Visionairs, think different
Skills needed	Engineers, operational excellence, PNL incentivized	Business builders with freedom, autonomy + intrapreneurs	People that think different, mavericks
How to attract & maintain talent	PNL incentivized	Provide freedom to build new things	Freedom to experiment, marketing of radical innovation ideas
Metrics	ROI, Net Present Value (NPV)	Real Options Value	ROV + Cost of not innovating
Time to cash-flow	1 year	5 year	10 year

The three horizons concept is an innovation portfolio methodology. You must work on all three horizons, if you wish to maximise your organisation's chances of being successful tomorrow. Ignoring certain horizons or failing to devote sufficient attention and resources to them is very risky, especially in our rapidly changing times.

It is important to understand that working with horizons is far more than a simple translation of your existing short, medium and long-term (SLM) planning. This is an error I often see. SLM planning makes it possible to set priorities and to postpone or advance certain projects, depending on operational requirements and external circumstances. But it lacks the structured and visionary approach to innovation that is inherent in the three horizons model.

CASE: THE THREE HORIZONS IN THE CAR INDUSTRY

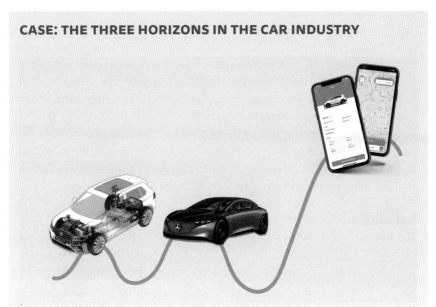

Figure 50 – An example of how the 3 horizons translate in the automotive industry.

The car industry is in the process of a fast-moving transformation, with several different initiatives making their impact felt all at the same time. The days of the internal combustion engine are coming to a close and will be replaced by electric alternatives. This not only casts a pall of uncertainty over the future of the car manufacturers, but also threatens the car dealers and garage owners. Let's put ourselves in the position of these three groups and look at the situation from the perspective of the three horizons.

Horizon 1

Horizon 1 deals with innovation in the existing products and market. Most car brands have already launched hybrid models that combine a normal diesel/petrol engine and an electric engine powered by a small battery. In this way, fossil fuel consumption can be reduced, providing you use the electric engine as much as possible. The biggest impulse for innovation was the tax benefit for the buyer. In horizon 1 – the horizon of sustaining innovation – the main aim is to see how next year's car can use even less fossil fuel and drive for longer on the electric battery. To make this possible, you need 'operators'; in this case, design engineers who can optimise the software installed in cars, integrate lighter materials into their production, develop more performant batteries, and design and roll out more and faster battery charging stations. However, this will not transform today's generation of cars into something that is revolutionarily different, nor will it immediately attract a different target group of customers. In other words, the impact on existing business models, sales, channels, distribution, maintenance, etc. is limited. Essentially, it is all 'more of the same' and it primarily generates short-term added value for the manufacturer and the chain. The consumer notices the changes even less, except perhaps in marketing terms. Companies are able to accurately assess investment in hybrid engines against future revenue from the sale of these cars, which is likely to increase because of the tax incentives offered to the buyers. As a result, there will be an immediate impact on turnover, although everyone in the sector knows that the lifespan of these innovations will be relatively short.

Horizon 2

This horizon takes things a stage further. Cars will become fully battery-powered. This will create numerous innovation challenges: a new chassis, extra-light materials, special software for energy management, hyper-powerful batteries, charging systems that allow maximum charging in a minimum time, etc. Many of these challenges will not be in the comfort zone of the existing manufacturers, so that collaboration with partners will become increasingly necessary to create fit-for-purpose products. In other words, collaboration with business builders and intrapreneurs.

The advent of the all-electric car will also herald in many other changes. The cars will need no maintenance, so what will this mean for garage owners, for whom maintenance is currently a large part of their income? Car dealers, who in the past built up a relationship with their buyers from the moment of purchase, so that they could be confident that these buyers would also give them their maintenance custom, will become almost superfluous. People will buy their electric cars online, just like they buy a new iPhone. And having made their purchase, they just need to follow the instructions in the related app, which will also provide assistance whenever necessary. This is all going to cost the manufacturers and the dealers a significant amount of their margin.

But the disruption of the sector will go even further than that. Petrol stations will no longer be required, to be replaced by large-scale battery charging stations. You can see that the battery companies are already trying to develop fuelling options that work quickly and efficiently for all types of cars – as was the case with diesel and petrol engines – but this is proving to be difficult and will not get any easier.

It is clear that there will be many new ventures on the launch pad in horizon 2: cars with batteries, charging stations, new dealer networks, new business models based on online sales, new insurance perspectives, and much, much more.

It is interesting to see how many manufacturers, who have waited too long before committing to electric cars, are now investing heavily in the hope of closing the innovation gap with their rivals. But this will not be easy, because they are a long way behind. Their rivals are already in a position to start with horizon 2 projects, whereas the slow-coaches are still stuck in horizon 1, which means that they must first take action to work more efficiently. This has been noticeable in recent events, which saw the established brands slash their number of dealerships. In 2021, GM sold one in five of its dealerships. Daimler sold its dealerships in the UK, Spain and Belgium to a private investor. Daimler top man Ola Källenius referred to these dealerships as "a relic from the last century". In contrast, new solutions like IONITY, the charging network started by the largest car companies, are helping to facilitate the shift from horizon 1 to horizon 2 through the fast adoption of fast-loading technology. Hopefully, the manufacturers will have sufficient pipeline in horizon 2 to offer adjacent services for CASE (connected, autonomous, shared, electric) cars in the near future. By 2025, there will be more than 100 million smart cars on our roads. They will be able to communicate with other vehicles and react to conditions in the environment. The smarter these cars become, the closer they get to becoming data hubs.

The manufacturers who want to give themselves a chance of survival in the future will need to start dozens of ventures in horizon 2 in which data forms the core, with the aim of forming new and future-minded partnerships that go beyond the straightforward sale of cars. This does not just mean smart navigation and autonomous driving, but also associated in-car options like online shopping, entertainment and games; or a virtual guide that explains where you are and what you are passing; or 'agents' who will make reservations of many different kinds for you (hotels, restaurants, health centres, etc.), taking account of your start time, destination and arrival time. There will also be new and customised forms of insurance, depending on whether you drive alone or with others, whether you share your car or not, whether you combine car use with public transport, etc.

In this way, the large brands will be able to offer important customer experiences of a kind that scarcely exist today. It will come as no surprise to learn that Tesla already has dozens of pilot projects up and running to explore these various new fields, testing what works and what does not work and what has sufficient margin to make it viable. For example, it may be possible on cold winter days to hire seat heating with just a single click or buy an upgrade that significantly increases the acceleration of your car. At the opposite end of the spectrum, many of the traditional car manufacturers still seem to be in the stone age when it comes to digitalisation. They think that the only purpose served by a car app is to monitor and control the vehicle at distance: where is the car now, can I turn the heating on before I get there, do I have enough battery range to get me home, etc.? In horizon 2, things have already moved far beyond this simplistic approach. Even so, the car industry still has an awful lot of work to do before it can meet the future with confidence. Learning the lessons of the Kodak story will do much to help them on their way: combat inertia and full steam ahead!

Horizon 3

In this horizon, the entire car industry will be turned upside down. In fact, the future of the entire sector will be called into question. Companies will no longer sell cars per se but will sell mobility as a service, with the car, e-bike or e-drone included, not to mention energy, insurance, films, podcasts and (autonomous) chauffeur services. Cars will become mobile hotel rooms, mobile meeting places, mobile shops, mobile cinemas and so much more. In this new world, who will want to own a car when it spends 92% of its time standing still? We still want this today, just to be sure that our mobility is always available to us. But this advantage will disappear when it becomes possible with the click of a button to have the hire car of your choice delivered to your door in less than five minutes.

At the present time, the car is not only a status symbol, but also – and above all – a heavy investment. In fact, after your home it is probably the largest investment you make. In horizon 3, however, mobility-as-a-service will become the new norm: self-driving, electric, autonomous and shared. Not that you will notice much of that sharing. It will still seem as though you are driving (or being driven in) your own car, which can be personalised to suit your requirements, which are then memorised for future reference. No matter where you are, you will always be able to call up a car that matches your specifications. At the same time, the car manufacturers will also bundle together all their services: their own insurance, their own AI for accident-free autonomous driving, their own maintenance-free engines, their own energy and recharging systems, etc. These developments will turn the automobile world on its head. Not in your lifetime? The above scenario is expected to become a reality around 2030. If you know what you are looking for, you can already see the first signals today.

On 24 August 2021, Elon Musk announced that Tesla in Germany is planning to move into the energy market, creating shockwaves throughout the car and electricity industries. Customers who buy a Tesla car, Tesla solar panels and a Tesla battery can benefit from an extremely advantageous green energy contract. The threat to Tesla's rivals in both sectors is to be found in the smart software, Autobidder, which ensures that the consumers who produce energy are also allowed to make maximum use of it.

This means that less solar energy will be pumped back into the public net and more into the batteries and the domestic circuit of Tesla car owners. When energy is cheap, because too much is being produced nationally, the surplus will simply be stored in the car and in the house battery. If (or rather when) Tesla connects together all its batteries and all its cars, it will have an energy storage and provision capacity that is unrivalled anywhere in the world. It will form an AI-controlled energy network with countless gigawatt hours at its disposal, which can be sold for profit. Even though these developments are only in their infancy, the energy sector is monitoring the situation with a mixture of suspicion and trepidation.

CASE: THE FACEBOOK ROAD MAP

Figure 51 – Mark Zuckerberg presents the Facebook road map.

At the F8 Conference in 2016, Mark Zuckerberg, the CEO of Facebook, revealed his organisation's road map for the next ten years. To do this, he made use of an updated version of the three horizons methodology. In this respect, I am convinced that he was a pioneer, who not only set out a clear vision and strategy for Facebook, but also indicated to investors where the future of the company will lie. The stock markets and shareholders (public ownership) often force companies to think in the short-term, because they expect their investment to yield quick profits. This is why Facebook's focus on 'horizon 0' problems, like privacy issues and misleading information, sometimes seems to occupy too much of their attention. These are topics that take up a great deal of the organisation's energy and which, without a well-considered strategy for the future, could simply get bogged down in a messy status quo, possibly even threatening the end of the company. It was precisely for this reason, if for no other, that the unveiling of a ten-year strategy was such a clever move. Zuckerberg applied perfectly the steps that I have outlined above, the steps that you too ought to apply in your company – if you are smart.

Horizon 1
In this horizon, Facebook focuses on the ecosystem that they built up with their platform and which they wish to develop further in the future. It is

their core business, the thing that makes them who they are, the thing for which they are recognised: connecting people. The majority of their operational personnel are engaged in this task, which ensures that Facebook's users will stay with the platform and keep it turning as a cash machine. This involves investment in adverts, tools for adverts, getting local businesses on the platform, opening second-hand markets and much more. The ecosystem that they need to make this possible are the developers, traders and their partners, who, for example, you can reach via a single sign-on with Facebook. It is clear that this approach has worked. The number of Facebook users has increased from 1.5 billion to 3 billion in just five years. During the same period, turnover rose from 20 billion dollars to more than 100 billion dollars – a fivefold increase.

Horizon 2

In 2016, Facebook's focus was fixed on new products. Their key question was this: how are we going to grow these products alongside the core platform and encourage people to use them more? Direct communication or unified messaging has always been crucial for Facebook. In addition to their own FB Messenger system, in 2012 the company bought Instagram for 1 billion dollars, followed in 2014 by WhatsApp for 19 billion dollars. Instagram was a new way of communicating for Facebook: more photos, less words. WhatsApp offered a simpler alternative to the old SMS and was popular because it made the forming of groups possible. Grouping is also a core function of Facebook, bringing people together (temporarily or not) to exchange photos and information. However, searching for and finding the right messages and photos is becoming increasingly difficult, given the growing number of platforms on which we communicate. At the same time, the shift to video was pushed by challengers like TikTok and Snapchat. For this reason, from 2016 onwards a series of massive pilot projects was developed with a time line of five years, which resulted in a range of horizon 1 products that generated huge amounts of cash.

At the end of 2020, five years after Zuckerberg first revealed his horizon 2 strategy, the company announced that it wanted to integrate all its direct messaging platforms with the main Facebook platform: in other words, WhatsApp, Messenger and Instagram would soon become a single tool. All the users of the different systems would be able to communicate directly with each other and search through the different tools. Applying this strategy would make it easier for Facebook to reach the right target groups in terms of age, gender, place of residence, profession, hobbies, purchasing history, etc. This involved more than making use of the company's own existing cohort of programmers: video engineers were recruited to take the fight to TikTok, and Reels (a rival for YouTube) and Facebook Messenger Rooms (a rival for Zoom) were both launched in the middle of 2020. Full-screen video was also integrated more deeply into Facebook's operations, above all in Instagram, which evolved from a photo-sharing service into a genuine video content platform. By adding direct messaging to the platform, it effectively became a form of interactive television, a development that people have long been waiting for. Zuckerberg used this channel repeatedly during the Covid-19 crisis, organising live broadcasts with Dr Anthony Fauci, a well-known American immunologist, who answered questions submitted by the public. The stream was watched by 40 million viewers, which far outclassed the 3 million viewers attracted by mainstream television's popular *Late Show* with Stephen Colbert. Throughout the Covid-19 crisis, Facebook was the most efficient channel to reach people, inform them and, regrettably, also misinform them. This prompted the company to bring in independent fact-checkers to assess and remove false information about Covid-19, which is something they previously did during the Trump-Biden election campaign, in the hope of avoiding a repeat of the Cambridge Analytica scandal.

This, of course, gave rise to a horizon 0 discussion about whether or not Facebook has the right to act as judge of the information that is spread through its channels. The fact that this is not a simple 'yes-no' discussion was something that was also seen in the summer of 2021, when Apple announced that it intended to use AI technology to cleanse its iCloud photographic library of all possible images of child pornography. After furious protests from privacy campaigners, including the Washington-based Center for Democracy and Technology, Apple has decided to shelve its plan indefinitely.

This shows that horizon 2 ideas, no matter how well intended and justifiable, can fail as a result of unforeseen external factors. So to what extent has Facebook's own horizon 2 strategy been a success? The company certainly has grounds to be more than satisfied. It is true that the anti-trust authorities continue watch its operations very closely, but significant progress in the right direction has been made. In 2016, revenue from Instagram accounted for 13% of Facebook's total turnover. By 2021, this had risen to over 40%. The company has a solid base as it prepares for its move into horizon 3.

As became clear in 2021, one of the flagships in the years ahead will be WhatsApp Business. Advertisements on Facebook and Instagram can give potential customers direct access with a single click to make purchases via WhatsApp and also bring those customers into direct contact with the selling companies. Via WhatsApp Business Catalogues, it is already possible to build virtual stores, which with another single click can generate personalised adverts via Facebook or Instagram. These projects are now all ready to be absorbed into horizon 1. At the quarterly meeting held at the start of 2020, Zuckerberg said: "I want to be clear – we have a long way to go to build out a full featured commerce platform across our services, and this is a multi-year journey, but I am very committed to getting there."

Horizon 3
In horizon 3, Facebook will focus neither on the platform nor on new products, but on emerging technology. This is undoubtedly the right way to deal with this horizon. It is not necessarily a smart move to translate potential new ideas into concrete concepts and business models too quickly. It better to first wait and see which way the wind is blowing; to research and assess the new tech trends thoroughly. Which ideas will win? Which ones will lose? What impact will this have on your business, both in horizon 2 and in horizon 1? With this in mind, Facebook has now opened its doors to explorers. Visionaries can experiment with the latest technological wizardry and take far-reaching risks in the hope that the reward will be worth the effort at some point within the next ten years. In 2016, a focus was set on three specific technologies: connectivity, artificial intelligence and virtual reality. It was clear that this would require Facebook to attract people with different kinds of skills and they have succeeded in doing so.

In 2014, Facebook purchased Ascenta, a start-up founded by a group of aviation engineers. It had already previously started its own Aquila project to develop solar-powered aircraft that will take internet connection to parts of the world where the internet is currently scarcely available. The acquisition of Ascenta was designed to get this idea literally and metaphorically off the ground. An important element in Facebook's future survival is its ability to provide its users with greater connectivity worldwide. In Western countries, the number of users is starting to fall slightly. Future growth must therefore come from new regions, where the internet is currently less accessible. The project was already in an advanced test phase, when it was put on hold in 2018. Since 2019, there have been rumours that Facebook is now collaborating with Airbus to develop a follow-up to the Airbus Zephyr drone, although this is far from clear.

Another 2014 acquisition was Oculus, purchased for 2 billion dollars. Since then, Facebook has invested further and heavily in VR. The company is determined to become the leading platform for easy access to virtual worlds. To make this possible, the improved Oculus Quest was launched, the best-selling VR glasses in the world. In 2021, VR only accounted for 3% of Facebook's income, but Zuckerberg is convinced that within the foreseeable future it will come to represent the bulk of the company's revenue. He might well be right. It is anticipated that the market for VR will increase twentyfold during the next ten years and Facebook intends to be a core player. As part of the plan, the company made a further twelve acquisitions during the Covid-19 period, primarily in gaming and VR (although it also paid 1 billion dollars for Kustomer, a customer relations management start-up). Zuckerberg recently said that the way we currently communicate with each other via digital 'clay tablets' is not ideal for virtual interaction. This needs to be improved, to make possible the creation of a life-like virtual world for everything we do. The first steps are being made. For example, the Covid-19 pandemic stimulated a boom in online meetings, a trend to which Facebook responded with Facebook Horizon Workrooms, a virtual meeting system via personalised avatars that was launched in the summer

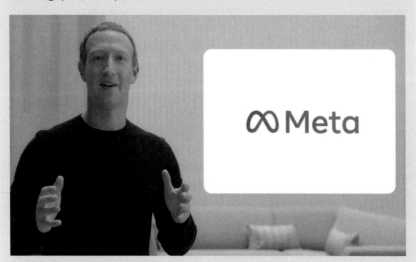

Figure 52 – With the launch of Meta, Zuckerberg takes a risky Horizon 3 step with his entire company Facebook.

of 2021. It is a first step towards a system that will allow VR to measure human movements and reproduce them in the meeting room.

Facebook recently decided to change its name to Meta to underline that the company is much more than just the Facebook platform alone. On 28 October 2021, Zuckerberg launched the Metaverse. This is the world in which Meta hopes to generate hundreds of billions of dollars in online turnover by allowing everyone to shop, travel, learn, work and relax in a virtual environment, where you can also buy and sell virtual real estate, to which you can then add your own bank, museum, theatre, government authority, shop or school. A phygital world in which the real one is upgraded with augmented reality via Meta-AR glasses, the first tentative test examples of which have been marketed in collaboration with Ray-Ban. But the plans go even further than that and aim to achieve total virtual reality, whereby the virtual avatar will be difficult to distinguish from a real person and can mimic facial expressions in real time. As a result, you will be able to spend a virtual night on the town with your favourite film star or take a trip around the world with your family, even though you will never leave your own front room. Zuckerberg is convinced that by 2030 at least a billion people will be using the Metaverse in every aspect of their daily life, a prediction he is prepared to back up by investing 10 billion dollars a year in this successor to the internet. In his eyes, he must be – and will be – the winner-takes-all.

The Metaverse requires gigantic computing power, an AI tour de force and massive experimental work with the AR glasses and other tools of tomorrow. But you can already see how horizon 3, first outlined back in 2016, is slowly starting to take shape. Some matters will be accelerated; others terminated or put on hold. One thing is certain: the pipeline is full and even if there are plenty of failures there are also guaranteed to be plenty of successes that will become the new cash cows for Facebook – sorry, Meta!

If you want to get an idea of what the Meta world could be like, I recommend you to read the book *Ready Player One* by Ernest Cline. It will give you plenty of food for thought about the world of the future, which in the book is called OASIS. The film version by Steven Spielberg was slightly less chilling, but you can watch the trailer here.

In a nutshell

Research has shown that the time horizon of organisations is all too often fixed on the past and the present and not enough (if at all) on the future. This results in companies looking for risks in the wrong place. The Ansoff matrix is a useful instrument for strategic planning in relatively stable markets. More recently, this matrix has been extended to become a three-wave product road map for the future, which results in a three-horizon approach to develop a balanced innovation portfolio. I analysed and explained this model with reference to the examples of the automobile sector and Meta, a company which has shown that it is already thinking and planning in terms of the three horizons.

"The future depends on what we do in the present."

MAHATMA GANDHI

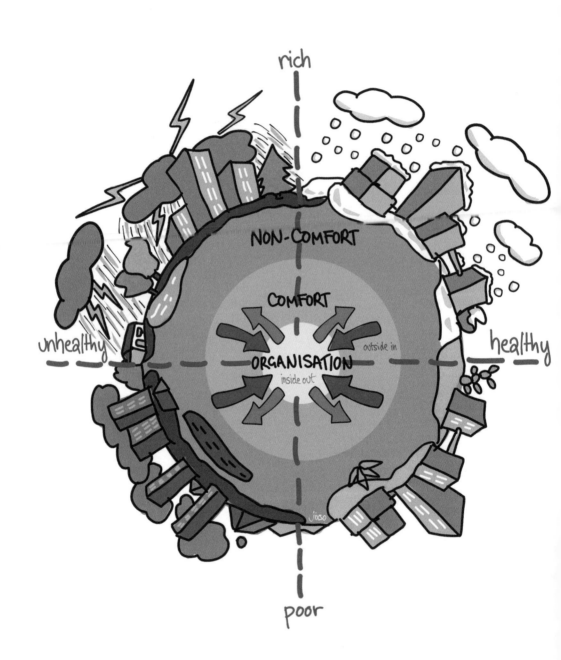

KEY 6
SCENARIOS AS THE CORE OF YOUR INNOVATION STRATEGY

Horizons 1, 2 and 3 are all situated in the future. This means that they all have a significant degree of uncertainty. When you have to make important decisions, wouldn't it be nice if you had some idea of what this future might look like?

One thing is already certain: the future has not yet taken place. It does not yet exist. It is still approaching, which means that you can philosophise, fantasise and make suppositions about it. The future is, however, inescapable. It might be expected. It might be feared. It might offer us hope. There are few standard definitions of the future. In thermodynamics, it is said that the future is the direction of time during which entropy – the process of gradual decline from order to chaos – increases.

Change defined

Uncertainty is connected with changes that occur and the manner in which these changes will develop in the future. There are two types of changes: gradual changes and sudden changes.

Megatrends

Megatrends or gradual discontinuities are evolutions that usually happen as a result of human behaviour over a long period of decades or even centuries. Megatrends nearly always have a global impact. It takes at least five to ten years before their first effects start to be seen. Think, for example, of urbanisation, climate change, technological progress, the ageing of the population,

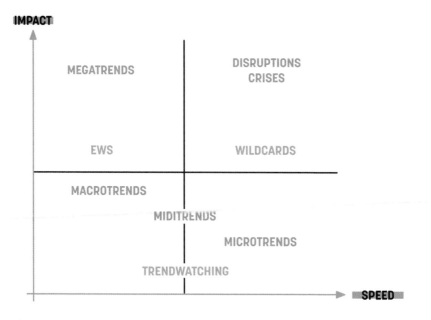

Figure 53 – *Types of change based on speed and impact.*

etc. Megatrends also occur in the societal domain. They can change a society or even the entire world.

Megatrends can be sub-divided into two categories. On the one hand, there are the inevitable trends; the trends we know are coming, whether we like it or not, such as climate change. Every future that we can imagine will be affected to a greater or lesser degree by climate change. It cannot be avoided. At best, we can mitigate its effects by taking effective corrective measures today.

On the other hand, there are also uncertain megatrends. Think in this case, for example, of the possible health risks associated with the use of wireless communication or genetically modified foodstuffs. At the present time, there is no single study that establishes a clear connection between the non-ionising radiation emitted by cell phones and the development of brain tumours. Nevertheless, many governmental authorities, including the World Health Organisation, are cautious when asked to confirm that there is absolutely no danger. They recommend low emission norms, especially for children, and suggest that no mobile devices should be used too close to the brain. You can almost feel the uncertainty that this kind of situation creates. However, such situations will only have an impact in a limited number of scenarios, even if there is a suspicion that this impact might become more significant than is currently the case.

For example, one of the great uncertainties about the future is the way in which AI will develop. Will it form a threat to mankind if we develop machine-based intelligence that will eventually be smarter than the brain capacity of the entire human race? Or will it simply be used to strengthen our own human creativity? You cannot say that one or the other is inevitable, but nor can you say that one or the other will not happen. When there is maximum uncertainty, we speak of a 50-50 situation.

Trend watching: macro, midi and microtrends

Megatrends often give rise to other trends that generate further influences. We classify these trends according to their speed of change: namely, macrotrends, miditrends and microtrends.

Macrotrends occur over a longer period of time; typically, five to ten years. They have a greater impact than microtrends and persist for longer. Some recent examples include AI, big data, space tourism and self-driving cars. Macrotrends can sometimes develop under their own impetus to become full-blown megatrends. We can see this already with artificial intelligence, which is developing at phenomenal speed and with such far-reaching effects that it is approaching the scale of a megatrend. In turn, AI will stimulate the emergence of other megatrends, such as humanoid companions like Alexa or Siri, but far more sophisticated. Macrotrends generally have less impact at the societal level, but more direct impact on individual consumers.

Microtrends arrive quickly and disappear just as fast. Having greater awareness for sustainability and what we eat is a megatrend; the emergence of meals boxes like Hello Fresh is a microtrend, which seeks to respond to the megatrend. Microtrends are highly recognisable and suddenly you see them everywhere, but within a few years they have vanished. Or else they have been replaced by a different concept, like the Segway has been replaced by the e-scooter, which in turn will no doubt be replaced by another mobility idea within the next five years. Microtrends are mostly present at market level and can be strongly influenced by many kinds of techniques, such as marketing, social media, influencers, etc. Microtrends are often referred to as hypes.

Miditrends are trends that are halfway between a macrotrend and a micro-trend, and generally last for a period of one to five years.

Abrupt discontinuities and crises

Sometimes, disruptive changes appear out of nowhere, creating abrupt discontinuities. Overnight, the past no longer seems relevant and all our existing systems are shaken to their core. This forces us to change the way we think, resulting in a true paradigm shift. Abrupt discontinuities of this kind often occur in the form of an unexpected crisis. If we look back at the events of the past two decades, we can see that we have experienced a number of these destabilising crisis situations.

- 1989: Mad cow disease. The meat industry is hit hard. Public confidence drops to zero, especially when it is shown that this condition, which the industry has done little to combat, can be transmitted to humans in the form of Creutzfeldt-Jakob disease. This was the start of the search for vegetarian and vegan protein alternatives.
- 1991: The Gulf War heralds in the further destabilisation of the Middle East.
- 1999: The dioxin crisis in Belgium leads to the creation of the Federal Agency for Food Safety, which seeks to make Belgium the safest country in the world for consumers.
- 2001: The 9/11 attacks spark off the war on terror, leading to even greater destabilisation in the Middle East, with an impact that is still being felt today by our companies, in the way we travel, in geopolitical tension and in the sad and never-ending flow of refugees.
- 2003: The start of the worldwide energy crisis, in which we still find ourselves today. This has resulted in a huge volatility in prices and supply, with negative consequences for the environment and the level of geopolitical tension. It signals the start of the race for alternative sources of energy.
- 2004: The tsunami in the Indian Ocean kills 230,000 people and causes untold human suffering, making the world more aware of the dangers and power of nature.
- 2008: The financial crisis re-draws the financial markets for good. The first cryptocurrencies are developed in an attempt to escape centralised monetary regulations.
- 2012: The continuing financial crisis brings Greece into difficulties. The rest

of Europe needs to intervene to prevent the country from going bankrupt.

- 2014: Ebola, a highly infectious and deadly virus, breaks out in Africa, killing tens of thousands and making the rest of the world concerned about its possible pandemic effects, a possibility to which Bill Gates alluded in his famous TED talk.
- 2015: Europe is faced with a huge stream of migrants fleeing from war-torn regions in Africa and the Middle East. Draconian measures are imposed to restrict this flow and thousands die in hopeless attempts to cross the Mediterranean. It is the start of a more intense phase of the refugee crisis.
- 2016: Terror comes to the streets of European cities with violent extremist attacks in Paris, Nice and Brussels, echoing the attacks in London and Madrid a decade earlier. Soldiers patrolling our streets become a normal sight.
- 2017: Brexit: the UK decides to leave the EU, sending economic shockwaves throughout the world. It takes years of difficult negotiations to reach a leaving agreement, but many internal problems for the UK are likely to remain.

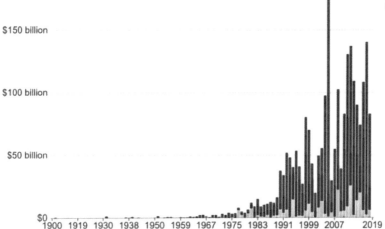

Economic damage by natural disaster type, 1900 to 2019
Global economic damage from natural disasters, differentiated by disaster category and measured in US$ per year.

Source: EMDAT (2020): OFDA/CRED International Disaster Database, Université catholique de Louvain – Brussels – Belgium
OurWorldInData.org/natural-disasters • CC BY

Figure 54 – *The financial impact of natural disasters increases enormously. It points to the serious consequences of climate change.* SOURCE: EMDAT (2020), INTERNATIONAL DISASTER DATABASE.

- 2018: In North Korea, Kim Jong-un's nuclear tests pose potential danger to the world, although no one knows just how seriously this military threat should be taken.
- 2019: Natural disasters precipitated by climate change ravage the planet: hurricanes, floods, heatwaves, tornados, earthquakes, tsunamis… The WHO published a report which says that by 2030 natural disasters are expected to kill 250,000 people a year, although most experts regard this as a serious underestimation. The cost of repairing the damage increases annually and is now around the 100-billion-dollar mark.
- 2020: Covid-19, a global pandemic, brings the world to a standstill for a year and a half. Populations are hit by successive waves of infection, which cripple the economy and change the way people interact with each other, perhaps permanently.
- 2021: In Afghanistan, 20 years of de facto occupation by the United States comes to an end, forming a prelude to the take-over of the country by the Taliban. The situation destabilises rapidly and America and the other Western powers seek to evacuate their people, but often fail as panic and chaos increase.
- 2021: In the aftermath of Covid-19, the cost of materials increases dramatically as scarcity grows, thanks to the stockpiling of resources by some countries to power their economic recovery. Silicon chips are in particularly short supply, so that the high-tech and car industries are forced to reduce production. Energy prices also reach a new peak as a consequence of the recovery and growing geopolitical tensions between China, Russia and the Western world.
- 2022: The omicron variant of the Covid-19 virus sweeps the world. Is this the beginning of the end for the Covid-19 pandemic or will new and even more infectious variants develop with the potential to overwhelm our health care systems and perhaps even threaten the foundations of our society?
- 2022: The Russian invasion of Ukraine. World War III?

Black swans?

The above events are sometimes referred to as 'black swans', after the title of the well-known book by Nassim Taleb. However, this description is not entirely correct. A black swan is always an abrupt discontinuity, but not every serious crisis is a black swan. By definition, you do not see the black swan coming. You cannot predict it. At best, you can only expect it, although you do not know where or when. In this sense, the Covid-19 pandemic was not a black swan

(even though that is what I said in the opening sentences of this book!). The
pandemic was perfectly predictable and was therefore a 'white swan', as Bill
Gates, Laurie Garrett and others have shown. They warned us – and rightly so
– that a pandemic needs to be tackled in its embryonic stage. This would have
been possible with minimal resources, but instead we are now spending trillions worldwide as a result of the delayed reactions of the governments and
institutions that are supposed to protect us.

Decision theory

When faced with uncertainty, how do you take decisions about the future?
The future can actually be divided up into two main categories of phenomena:
things that you know and things that you do not know. In other words, the
knowns and the unknowns. You can then further sub-divide these categories
into a second layer of knowing and not knowing. This results in the following
four possibilities.

- Known knowns: These are the things you have learnt or of which you are
  aware through experience. In other words, your knowledge, the things you
  know. You know, for example, that you cannot build a new factory unless
  you have planning permission. You know that you will find it hard to expand because the skilled personnel you need are in short supply. You know
  the interest rates that the banks will charge you for a 10-year loan.
- Known unknowns: These are the things you know you do not know. They
  are unknown factors whose possible emergence you need to take into account. You do not know how the market adoption of your new product will
  turn out. You do not know how the shortage of microchips will develop. You
  do not know how the price of gas will fluctuate.
- Unknown knowns: These are the things you thought you knew, but later it
  turns out that you did not. You thought that a competitor would emerge to
  bring a much better product on to the market than yours. You thought that
  you could ignore the development of digital photography.
- Unknown unknowns: These are the things you do not realise you do not
  know. These matters are simply not on your radar. You cannot see them approaching and you have no idea of the impact they can and will have on
  your activities. The above list of crises offers several very good examples of
  events that we never imagined, but which nonetheless had a massive impact on every organisation and every society.

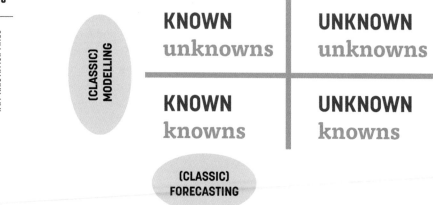

Figure 55 – *The future divided into four uncertainty quadrants.*

This terminology was made fashionable at the time of the Gulf War by the American Secretary of State for Defence, Donald Rumsfeld. During a press conference held on 12 February 2002, following the invasion of Iraq, he was asked whether the advancing Allies had so far found any evidence for Iraq's possession of weapons of mass destruction. Rumsfeld answered: "Reports that say that something hasn't happened are always interesting to me, because as we know, there are known knowns; there are things we know we know. We also know there are known unknowns; that is to say we know there are some things we do not know. But there are also unknown unknowns – the ones we don't know we don't know. And if one looks throughout the history of our country and other free countries, it is the latter category that tends to be the difficult one." It transpired that the Americans were completely mistaken: they invaded Iraq because they thought Saddam Hussein had such weapons of mass destruction at his disposal, but in reality he did not. In other words, their assumption was an unknown known. Perhaps not surprisingly, this was the title chosen by Errol Morris in 2013 for his documentary about Rumsfeld's career.

In your company, you should take these four quadrants of the future into account for every decision you make, and above all in your strategic planning. However, if we look at the tools organisations currently use to make their five-year or long-term plans, very few of them pay significant attention to the future.

As part of this same process, it should also be noted that the future can be divided into other different categories: the desired future, the probable future, the possible future, etc. Every company has a desired future, a dream: which of us has never dreamt, for example, of annual growth of 15%?

Extrapolation or forecasting is typically a model that takes account of known knowns: by and large, the current dotted lines on the graph are simply extended further. Sometimes, a small deviation might be plotted as a result of a limited uncertainty, but for the most part the forecast depicts a probable future. In this way, the evolution can be better (+10%) or worse (-10%) than expected, but the uncertainty and its consequences can be kept within reasonable bounds. This is how most company budget plans are made, which is surprising, because this kind of extrapolation can be very dangerous. Consider, for instance, the horse manure syndrome...

The danger of extrapolation

During the 19th century, the horse and cart was one of the most popular methods of transport. As a result, the streets of many Western cities were covered with horse manure, which needed to be cleared away and dumped. As the end of the century approached, some of these dumps in London were over 10 metres in height. In 1894, the respected *Times* newspaper sounded the alarm about what it called the 'Great Horse Manure Crisis' and predicted that if horses continued to soil the streets at the same rate the city would be covered in a three-metre-deep layer of manure in less than 50 years' time! So great was the panic in England and in other countries that in 1898 a 10-day international conference was convened to tackle a global challenge that seemed to be growing out of control. The delegates soon reached the conclusion that the problem had simply become too big and therefore could not be solved. After just three days, they all went home. 'Fortunately', the advent of the motor car meant that the problem of horse manure was eventually replaced by the problem of exhaust fumes, and the Great Crisis of 1894 was quickly and quietly forgotten.

We can probably all think of examples in our own experience when simple extrapolation was used to predict a probable future in alarming, misleading or downright ridiculous terms.

"In fifteen years' time more electricity will be used for electric cars than for electric lighting," declared Thomas Edison in 1910. Today, 112 years later, his prediction has almost come true. At least he was more accurate than *Popular*

Mechanics, which in 1949 confidently assured people that the computers of the future would weigh no more than one and a half tons. In 1979, the RAND Corporation, a future institute that perhaps should have known better, predicted that by 1984 all the cinemas would be closed, because everyone would be sitting at home watching videos on Betamax. More recently, of course, we have heard the same said about Netflix. But let us return to the past. The technological domain has always been a favourite for wildly inaccurate predictions. In 1984, the respected *Science* magazine said that the cloning of mammals was impossible. In 1943, Thomas Watson, the president of IBM, said that there was a world market for a maximum of five computers. In 1981, Bill Gates estimated that 640K of memory would be enough for everyone. In 1977, Ken Olson, the CEO of Digital, argued that there was no good reason why everyone would want their own computer in their home. In 1999, Ray Kurzweil was convinced that average life expectancy would rise to one hundred years by 2019. Even the usually more reliable Elon Musk boasted at the start of 2021 that by the end of the year Tesla would have a fully self-driving car with level 5 autonomy.

All these claims show just how risky it can be to develop a strategy for the future based exclusively on an extrapolation of the situation in the past. I can well remember a conversation with a global VP of the food giant Cargill, who confided to me in 2015 that their entire three-year budget plan had been consigned to the dustbin because they had seriously misjudged the likely cost of oil. This was a very important factor in their calculation of prices for the purchase and sale of raw materials and finished products. The oil price had been fairly stable for five or so years at around 100 dollars per barrel, and they had allowed a margin in the budget of +/- 20%, which was regarded as being sufficient to cover volatility. However, in mid-2014 the price per barrel fell from 110 dollars to 45 dollars in just a few weeks. The slide continued until a rock-bottom price of 25 dollars was reached in the course of 2016. Cargill was forced to realise that the forecasting models it used were no longer adequate in today's VUCA world. Moreover, it was a lesson that cost the company billions, because the price of food follows the price of oil: empirical research carried out between 1990 and 2020 has concluded that this kind of oil price shock has a clear short-term effect on food prices and a long-term effect on meat prices.*

---

* The Linkages between Crude Oil and Food Prices, Institute of Economics and Finance, Warsaw University of Life Sciences, Monika Roman, Dec. 2020

The Cargill story is just one of many I could have chosen to illustrate the danger of over-reliance on extrapolation. When you are dealing with high levels of uncertainty, it is much better to switch to predictions based on possible futures or scenarios, which are much better suited to prepare your organisation for what lies ahead.

How scenarios originated

The term 'scenario' was first coined by Herman Kahn, who is now regarded as the father of scenario analysis. This American futurist worked during the 1950s for the RAND Corporation, a non-profit think tank that was set up by the Douglas Aircraft Company in 1948 to carry out research and analysis for the United States armed forces. At that time, the Cold War between Russia and the US threatened on more than one occasion to provoke a nuclear conflict and it was Kahn's job as an expert on military strategy to dare to think the unthinkable: if a nuclear war ever broke out, what would be the best way to survive it? He called his approach to this challenge 'future now' thinking and it involved drawing up a number of possibilities for what might happen and their likely outcome. In 1960, he even wrote a chilling book on the same subject, entitled *On Thermonuclear War*, in which he outlined various synopses that would each result in the death of millions, which he referred to as 'megadeath'. However, he did refute John von Neumann's 'mutually assured destruction' principle, which argued that both superpowers should have such massive nuclear arsenals that neither could dare to attack the other and expect to survive.

His book was read on both sides of the Iron Curtain and led people to the insight that the MAD principle was precisely that: mad. Kahn described his 'future now' thinking as scenarios, a term he first used when explaining his methods to the press: "They are not predictions! They are only scenarios, intended to be used as thinking tools, nothing more!" In 1963, he founded the Hudson Institute, a political research organisation, which helped the US government to develop scenarios that would better direct national policy. It was the forerunner of the institutes for the future or foresight institutes we still see in many countries today. Kahn understood that it was (and still is) important for policies at all levels to be based on long-term scenarios, which make possible structured reflection on the future and stimulate discussion about likely outcomes, which can then be subjected to stress tests. It is broadly these same principles that in recent years my TomorrowLab.com organisation has attempted through a process of intense collaboration to introduce into various official bodies in the fields of mobility, health, air traffic control, public transport, sport and movement: a major step in the right direction.

Via Amazon I recently found one of the few remaining original books by Herman Kahn, dating from 1967 and entitled *The Year 2000*. A rarity indeed! The book is a work of reference in which Kahn for the first time made extensive use of scenarios to look from a strategic perspective at the possibilities for the world as it reached the end of the century, which was then still 33 years in future. He involved many other experts in his project and many of his conclusions – such as the various applications for lasers, new methods of birth control, the ability to make long-term weather forecasts, new types of planes, etc. – were close to the mark. Perhaps most telling of all was his suggestion that by the year 2000 there would be more PCs in the world than cars and bridges.

Scenario planning made its entry into the business world with the setting up of a scenario team at Shell under Pierre Wack. By the late 1960s, financial planning was well established in most companies and accountancy departments worldwide made a habit of collecting and analysing data. This formed the basis for 'management by objectives', whereby various targets were set, but with an allowable range of deviation for uncertainties. The operational divisions strove to achieve these targets, but on the assumption that the environment in which they worked would remain relatively stable. To refine this process, in 1967 Shell launched what it thought was the ultimate system that would make all other planning systems superfluous. The new system was known as the Unified Planning Machinery. Its manual was huge and explained in great detail all the necessary accounting procedures, how they must be carried out and how they must be reported to Shell HQ by every division in the world. On the basis of extrapolated figures from the past, a strategy for the following three years would then be drawn up.

Less than a year after the launching of this 'ultimate system', the world proved that it had become too volatile to allow the development of any manageable strategy for budgeting. The Roaring Sixties were in full swing: student riots in Europe and the US, war in Vietnam, the landing on the moon, the first Club of Rome report suggesting that the world was heading for environmental disaster if things did not change soon... Shell responded well to these challenges and replaced the UPM with a team of specialists under the leadership of Pierre Wack, who were tasked with plotting Shell's path forward by using new scenario techniques. The idea was that the new unit would look at the world in general to see what was happening and what was likely to happen, before translating this into terms and recommendations that were relevant for the company. However, Wack and his team were very soon confronted by one of the main obstacles to strategic long-term thinking, an obstacle that still exists today. The problem was not how to develop the scenarios. The problem was how they would be received by the company leaders and operational managers for whom they were intended.

How scenarios are used

When organisations look towards the future, there are a number of questions they want to have answered.

First of all, we want to know where we stand today and where we want to get to in the future. (These are subjects I dealt with in earlier chapters and do not need to be repeated here.) Next, we want to know what is happening around us and what impact this will have on the environment in which we function. Bearing these factors in mind, we then need to know how to reach our objectives: do we need to take action and, if so, what action, and how should we do it?

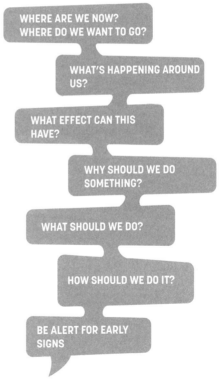

Figure 56 – *When you look to the future you have to ask the right questions.*

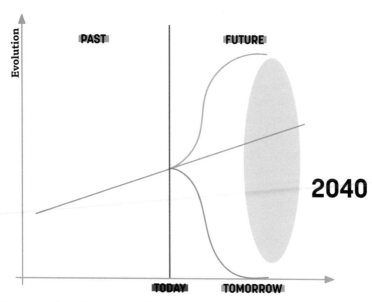

Figure 57 – *Scenarios move away from extrapolation and provide a lens for the future.*

In the above diagram, extrapolation is shown as a dotted line: the probable future. But in a year's time you could just as easily find yourself on the green line or the red line. But how can you know? What you really need is a kind of lens through which to view the future, which will allow you to calculate and take account of the range of uncertainty in which you might find yourself. In the above example with Cargill, the company suddenly found itself on the red line, as did every other company that was heavily reliant on oil. As a result of the outbreak of Covid-19, some retailers unexpectedly climbed their way up the green line, while almost everyone else slid down the red one, thanks to the strict regulations that were in force.

The above graphics illustrate two examples of the cone of plausibility, which can be used to help you assess your range of uncertainty. The central circle in figure 58 is the projected future, which is a straightforward extrapolation of the past and the things you know. If a few trends are added into the mix, the level of uncertainty increases, with a limited deviation from the extrapolation of, say, +/- 10%. In this way, you arrive at the probable future, the future you think is most likely to happen.

CONE OF PLAUSIBILITY

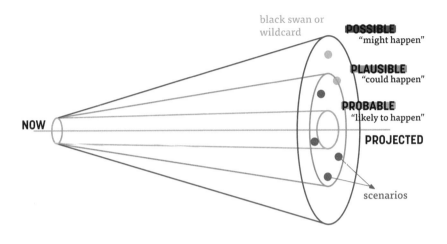

Figure 58 – *The further into the future the more uncertainty, the cone of plausibility.*

The more unknown elements you continue to add, the more the level of uncertainty continues to rise, taking you from a probable into a series of plausible futures: they could happen, but you cannot be sure. It is with these plausible futures that scenarios are used to try to find the best way(s) forward. If you keep on factoring in more uncertainties in the form of black swans and abrupt discontinuities (wild cards), you will move into the zone of possible futures. In theory, you can still take things yet another stage further, by letting your fantasy run wild to speculate on a number of quasi-impossible futures (for example, the world is hit by a meteorite or World War Three breaks out) although this is hardly relevant for the future strategy of your organisation.

Scenario planning goes much further than the quantifiable models that were frequently seen during the Covid-19 period and were also often referred to as scenarios, whereas in reality they were designed to indicate projected and probable futures. This same confusion is also common in the press and in many boardrooms. Part of the problem is caused by the similarity of and the subtle differences between the terminology used: probable, plausible and possible. They might seem close together, but are actually worlds apart in terms of their ascending order of uncertainty.

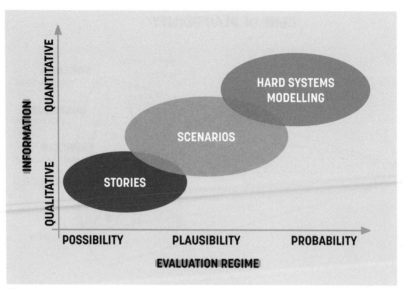

Figure 59 – *Scenarios are in between stories and models.*

In addition to uncertainty as a factor, the type of information at your disposal will also determine which is the best tool for you to use to describe your future.* There are two types of information: qualitative information (words, conversations, interviews) and quantitative information (things you can measure). If you have quantitative probable information, it is more likely that you will use hard systems modelling for your calculations. Stories, passed on by word of mouth, are at the opposite end of the spectrum. They are built up on the basis of qualitative information about a possible future, which does not necessarily need to be credible. You never know: it might one day happen. Think of films like *The Matrix* or Ridley Scott's *Blade Runner*, which are no longer as science-fiction as they once seemed.

Scenarios are found somewhere in the middle. Above all, they want to identify plausible futures, worlds that on the basis of the uncertainties involved might reasonably be assumed to exist. With these kinds of worlds, it is possible to develop a more robust, stress-resistant strategic planning, in which account is taken of relatively extreme changes caused by uncertain events over which we have little or no control.

---

* Source: Oxford – Scenario Programme – Prof. Dr Rafael Ramirez

Scenario planning is a methodology whereby scenarios are developed to explore the future for the purpose of making strategic decisions more efficiently and more effectively. Scenario planning is not an end in itself, but a means to gain insight into future developments and better understand their complexities. Scenarios typically focus on the areas of greatest uncertainty in the environment where your organisation operates, the matters over which you have no control.

It is an outside-in instrument. This makes it a highly important tool for our times. The majority of strategic exercises in today's companies are inside-out; they extrapolate the known knowns. An outside-in approach takes unknowns as its starting point and then, as it were, turns them into knowns, which can work out differently in each scenario. In this way, you end up with a series of plausible future worlds, in which you can make your strategic plan. This will put an end to the habit of staring blindly at your preferred probable future. It will force you to explore worlds where you would prefer not to come or where you thought you would never find yourself.

In other words, scenarios are not predictions. Nor do they contain preferences. They are logical, coherent and challenging descriptions of alternative futures that could happen.

Strategic conversation: how differences of opinion and discussion become positive instead of negative

Everyone in management will be familiar with the reflex to ignore or minimise certain things during strategic discussions designed to set policy for the years ahead. You often hear comments like: "That will never happen" or "We thought that ten years ago as well".

It is remarkable that so many decisions are still taken on the basis of gut feeling, with very little or no in-depth research. In the past, this seemed to work, but the amazing acceleration in technological change, the volatility of external factors and the sheer complexity of today's world means that this is no longer possible – if you want to be successful. Scenarios, if properly constructed, give decision-makers a framework for thoroughly discussing, analysing and understanding all possible futures, allowing them to determine the best way to react strategically, should any of these futures actually occur.

By developing skills in scenario planning and future thinking, it is possible for organisations to reduce future risks and maximise future potential. Risk reduction can result from the earlier detection of problems and threats or because you have made preparations to meet the unknown. Similarly, the methodology can also be used to facilitate change. At the same time, scenarios broaden your view of future horizons, making your company more agile and helping you to overcome your current limitations. This all contributes toward the maximisation of your future potential. Thanks to your thorough scenario analysis, you develop a kind of 'memory from the future' with the following characteristics:

- It makes the future manageable.
- Strategic decisions are better grounded.
- Patterns are recognised in events, leading to a better realisation and understanding of the effects.
- Future risks and opportunities can be better anticipated.
- It provides leadership within the organisation.
- It aligns stakeholders, often with different interests, around possible futures and strategic options.

Scenarios are best used whenever there is a high degree of uncertainty; or in situations or organisations that are complex and/or operate in a dynamic environment; or if a situation or sector is subject to major changes with a high level of impact; or if an organisation has experienced too many costly surprises in the past; or to free companies from tunnel-vision thinking; or simply to view all your alternatives in a row. But let's be honest: is that not necessary in every situation today?

'It is not the strongest of the species that survives, nor the most intelligent ... but the one most responsive to change in the environment.' CHARLES DARWIN, NATURALIST

Types of scenarios

Basically, there are three different types of scenarios. They are each used to answer a different question about the future: what is going to happen, what could happen and what can we do to realise a particular objective? They are known as extrapolating or forecasting scenarios, target scenarios and exploratory scenarios.

Forecasting or extrapolating is something that every company does. This is the symbolic dotted line, drawn straight from the past into the future. This type of planning can be divided into two categories: projections and prognoses. Examples of projections are the anticipated level of world population in a hundred years' time or the expected evolution of life expectancy in the coming decade. An example of a prognosis is predicting on the basis of historical data the expected future demand for water in a large city or country. Forecasting looks primarily at known knowns, which can be varied to a limited extent.

Target scenarios look at a particular objective that you want to realise. We have become familiar with this approach during the recent Covid-19 pandemic. Whenever a new wave of infection arrived, every country drew up a target scenario to ensure that intensive care units were not overwhelmed. This was known as 'flattening the curve' and to achieve this there were basically three options: doing nothing, controlled social distancing and total lockdown. Depending on the measures you took, you hoped that the number of cases would follow the projected curve or even fall below it. These models first came into prominence during the first Covid-19 wave, when some countries thought the best option was to do nothing, with the aim of developing herd

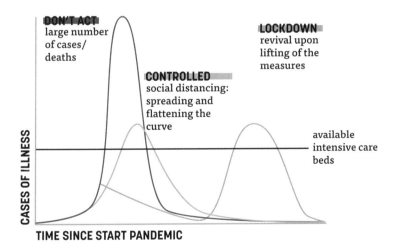

GOAL SCENARIOS IN THE FIGHT
AGAINST COVID-19

DON'T ACT
large number
of cases/
deaths

LOCKDOWN
revival upon
lifting of the
measures

CONTROLLED
social distancing:
spreading and
flattening the
curve

available
intensive care
beds

CASES OF ILLNESS

TIME SINCE START PANDEMIC

Figure 60 – *Three target scenarios for fighting the coronavirus. Source: TU Delft, RIVM, 2020*

immunity among their populations. This soon resulted in overfull hospitals and heart-rending scenes of patients lying in corridors for the lack of beds to put them in. Stringent lockdowns had to be introduced in order to get the curves back down to an acceptable level. Target scenarios are primarily used in the 'knowns' domain and try to give answers to known unknowns, such as the likely number of infection cases resulting from the Covid-19 virus.

Exploratory scenarios are much broader in view and are primarily used in the 'unknowns' domain. They apply an outside-in approach, taking uncertain factors in the wider environment around the organisation as their starting point. It is this kind of scenario that I will examine in more detail below. Exploratory scenarios are not only useful for making better strategic decisions and facilitating innovation, but also for aligning teams and building a culture that has the courage to embrace uncertainty instead of trying to avoid it.

Exploration is nothing new. In past centuries, it was how the world was discovered and opened up. Consider, for example, the explorers who first went in search of the 'Wild West' in the United States. A team of thirty pioneers under Lewis and Clark set off into the unknown lands across the Mississippi, aiming

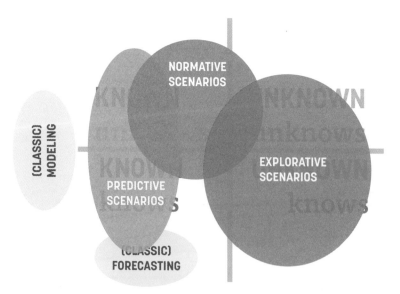

Figure 61 – *Exploring the future with forecasting, models and scenarios. - scenarios look at the four uncertainty factors of the future.*

to see how far they could get. A group of scouts went ahead of the main party, to see what lay in front of them and to find the safest way forward. Each of the scouts had to write down what he had seen, so that the leader could then decide how best to proceed. There was no discussion, because every scout had only seen his own version of the path that could/should be followed. It is the same in future thinking: no one has a monopoly on the truth and there is never certainty. It is all a matter of the leader interpreting what the scouts have seen and deciding which interpretation should be accepted as the true one. The purpose of scenario planning – whether in the Wild West or the modern business world – is to take the best decision and to find the way forward that is likely to lead to the most desirable result.

Thinking in terms of ecosystems

An important element in the development of scenarios is the use of an outside-in focus. This focus needs to be applied in three different environmental domains: the organisation, the comfort zone and the non-comfort zone.

Figure 62 – The three levels of outside-in interaction.

- **The organisational level** encompasses your familiar fields of activity, on the basis of which you determine your strategy. This includes your brand, product, service, systems, resources, infrastructure, etc.
- **The comfort zone or transactional environment** is the ecosystem of actors with whom you most frequently interact. You know this environment like the back of your hand and it includes your employees, customers, suppliers, investors, rule givers, lobbyists, competitors, channels, etc. This comfort zone is the place where you carry out your transactions. As a result, this transactional environment is influenced by your organisation, especially if your organisation is a major player. Facebook, for example, is a major and influential player in the social media world. Apple, Spotify, Uber, Ryanair and Netflix all have that same status in their respective comfort zones. Sometimes, they have even expanded their comfort zone to move into new sectors, sectors that never saw them coming. The transactional environment has gained in importance in recent years and has even been graced with a sexy new name: the ecosystem. The boundary between the transactional environment and your organisation is the place where your strategy unfolds.
- **The non-comfort zone or contextual environment** is the domain where you find the 'driving forces' that have an impact on your comfort zone and over which you have no control. These forces are something that just happens to you, whether you like it or not. There is not much that you can do about it, but the result can be to transform the environment in which you are used to working in a matter of just a few years. Forces of this kind include legislation, international trade, geopolitics, ecology, world health, energy prices, technological development and social values, to name but a few. We can probably all cite examples of how changes in the environment have caused abrupt discontinuities that have turned entire sectors upside down. The crises that I listed earlier all had this effect, but you could say the same thing about major legislative changes – think, for instance, of the drastic effect that the EU's REACH directive had on the chemical industry in Europe – and ecological measures, such as the increasing restrictions on combustion engines as a means to cut CO_2 emissions, which is causing multiple headaches for the automobile industry.

Most organisations still have an inside-out focus: their comfort zone is their world. This is a fault that Shell has avoided making since the end of the 1960s, which was when it first created a futures or foresight team under Pierre Wack, another of the founding fathers of scenario planning. Arie de Geus, one of the team's leading members, describes it as follows: "The first scenarios were ready in 1972. It is worth noting that only one of the eight scenarios we presented related to the question of oil supply. In this scenario, we explored a possible world in which the price of oil would rise to 8 dollars per barrel by 1976, in just four years' time. Back then, this was a highly unlikely scenario. For decades, the strategy of a whole generation of oil managers had been determined by the price of oil from Kuwait, which in 1972 cost 1.85 dollars per barrel, in comparison with 2.25 dollars in 1951. In 1972, there were not many Shell managers who were able to envisage a world in which oil might one day cost 8 dollars a barrel. For them, this was 'unthinkable' and so they found it difficult to think about the measures that might be necessary to deal with this situation, should it ever arise. A year later, Shell and everyone else was taken by surprise when the oil crisis erupted, causing the price per barrel to rocket up to 12 dollars during the next two to three years. By that time, Shell had concluded that it was probably wise in future to listen to Pierre Wack and his team."

In this way, Shell became the first company in the world to make permanent use of scenario thinking in its strategic planning.

In a nutshell

The future always means change and since ancient times people have been trying to find ways to predict that change. But what kind of change do we mean? There are megatrends, which evolve gradually and are quasi-unavoidable, but there are also macro-, mini- and microtrends. In addition, there are abrupt discontinuities and crises that can seldom be foreseen, with black swans as the most extreme examples. Experience has shown that extrapolation is a dangerous method for predicting the future. I believe above all in the value of future scenarios. In this chapter we looked at the types of scenarios, how they originated, how they are used and how they can help to transform differences of opinion in strategic conversations from something negative into something positive. An important principle when creating scenarios is the use of an outside-in focus, in which the world can be divided up into three circles or domains: the organisation itself, its comfort zone and its non-comfort zone. These sub-divisions can be useful when thinking in terms of ecosystems.

In-depth: How do you build a scenario?

How do you build scenarios? By following a sequence of six steps. I will take you through each of these steps and give you further insights by conducting a simplified but nonetheless real-life study for the expansion of a hospital in the future.

Step 1: What is the core question that you wish to research?

The research question encapsulates the subject or reason for making an exploratory scenario. What is it you want to explore? The future of cars? Your future competitive position in the market? It might seem easy to decide this, but practical experience suggests that companies should spend some time to consider this carefully. If you don't formulate the right question, you won't get the right answer. Often, companies choose a theme they would like to explore, but without a specific question. Having a clear question is essential, because this defines above all the things that you will not be exploring. For example, 'the future of Europe' is a very wide-ranging theme. But what exactly is it that you want to know about Europe's future: likely political developments, demographics, the economy, social and cultural relations, its international position in the world? All of these things together?

Ask yourself the following questions:
- What exactly do you want to investigate?
- Why do you want to investigate this?
- What is the business idea that you wish to investigate in this context?
- What is the policy idea that you wish to investigate in this context?

If your core question is too broad, you will end up with general scenarios that cannot be used for the purpose(s) you had in mind. All you will get for your troubles is a report full of outdated clichés and 'classic' ideologies. So think carefully about the core question you want to answer.

Here are some examples of 'bad' core questions, because they are too broad:
- How will organisations learn in the future?
- How will the world deal with the growing health care problem?
- What will retail look like in the years ahead?

The broad questions in the above list are all inside-out, which is one of the most common mistakes. The internal problems of the organisation or sector are included in the wider question. In other words, these are not exploratory scenarios but at best forecasting or target scenarios. This is also often the case when the scenarios have been developed by so-called 'experience' scenario consultants. Recent examples I have seen include 'How can I make sure I have enough battery charging points?' and 'How can I replace the loss of advertising revenue by the commercialisation of big data?' These are both valid questions, but they are not good core questions for a scenario analysis, although they might later become strategic questions in each of that organisation's plausible scenario worlds or occur as options that arise spontaneously in those worlds, which can serve to answer the relevant questions sufficiently.

At the opposite end of the scale, it is also possible to set your question too narrowly, so that it once again misses your real objective(s).

Here are some examples of 'bad' core questions, because they are too narrow:
• How do I make electric cars?
• How do I find the right people for my company?
• How do I integrate telemedicine into my hospital?

You must ensure that your questions are always set outside-in, taking unknown unknowns as your starting point. If people in 19th century London had focused on known unknowns and had asked how horse manure could be collected and processed efficiently or how sufficient water could be found for the operation of steam locomotives, this might have prevented the development of the internal combustion engine and the electric train, since neither of these inventions were on the radar at that time.

Finally, here are some questions that have been well set by particular organisations:
• Amazon: What will Amazon mean for shopping in the future?
• Mobility Flanders: What is our mobility vision for 2040?
• London: What does the 'smart city' concept mean for London 2035?
• Stanford University: What does my university of the future look like?
• Karolinska Hospital: What hospital should I design today with the future in mind?

For me, the last of these questions has a personal resonance, since I was once asked to explore the future for hospitals and care centres. It is a few years ago now and that means that I can explain the case in detail in the following pages without giving away any confidential information. It will also serve to underline that a well-developed scenario stands the test of time. They can often be used for a decade or more, with the necessary reframing of certain areas in response to early warning signals. But more about that later.

Scenario thinking can also be a change instrument for your organisation. If you make it part of your culture, it is a very effective way to combat complacency – or 'future laziness', as I like to call it. You need to remember, of course, that a scenario exercise is resource-intensive, both in terms of budget and in terms of the time commitment it requires from your top managers. Even so, it is worth it. If you carry it out properly and in the necessary depth and allow enough time for the adoption of the necessary cultural change, it will represent a valuable step forward for every organisation, city, policy-making unit or knowledge institution that makes the effort.

But let's now return to my hospital case. Imagine that we are sitting in the boardroom of a hospital that has decided to develop a new greenfield site. The cost of a development of this kind can quickly run into hundreds of millions and even if you take your decision today it will be at least another eight to ten years before your new facilities are operational. So, what should this hospital of the future look like? This is what we will now explore via plausible worlds – scenarios – in which this hospital might function.

One of the basic questions that needs to be asked is why the patients of the future will come to the hospital. What care needs will this involve? Answering this question will have implications for both the optimal layout and the services of the hospital, which may be very different from what we know now. Should the hospitals of the future be built in the same way as the hospitals of today? Once again, these are valid questions, but as we have already seen a general question about 'the health care of the future' is too broad. We need to have a narrower core question, so that our exploration can be more concrete. Something like:

"What will the health hub of the future look like?"

The next step is to question the people in the organisation who will be involved in the foresight exercise, in order to find out what they know and do not know. In terms of the future, what is known terrain for them and what is unknown terrain? Above all, it is important to name known unknowns. The unknown unknowns will come to the surface during a later stage of the exercise.

You need to ask what keeps these people awake at night when they think about the long-term prospects for their hospital or about the health hub of the future. It is with these known unknowns that you will need to start. The following step is to appoint a team of experts from outside the core organisation, who you can interview about the uncertainties raised by the organisation's own people. These experts should be chosen as far as possible because their knowledge will allow them to say something relevant about one or more of these uncertainties, which they will approach from the different perspective of their own individual expertise. If we are talking about the evolution of medical care in the future, matters as diverse as regulations, technology, artificial intelligence and affordability will all need to be discussed. So, at the very least you need to find experts in all these outside fields.

Step 2: Outside-in interviews with experts

The most important thing you want to find out is not what the experts are certain of, but what they are not certain of. You need to discover where the boundary between certainty and uncertainty lies, and just how great the uncertainty on the other side of this boundary really is. In this way, you will get some idea of the scope of the uncertainty you are dealing with. It is a good idea to try to surprise your experts with questions that might not normally be asked. You want to confront the expert with the boundary between his/her own certainty and uncertainty about the future. If you can succeed in doing this, these interviews will provide far more valuable insights about the future than you might otherwise obtain through 'standard' questioning. Every question has a deep meaning that will only emerge later in the process, so it may be useful to pause and look at this in slightly more detail.

Allow at least 45 minutes for each interview and ensure that you are well prepared, so that you can follow all aspects of the conversation and can pick up on any points that need elaborating. As the scenario researcher, you should not attempt to 'lead' the conversation. You should do no more than ask the questions you have prepared in advance. Of course, you must ask for clarification if something is not clear to you. You should do this with open questions like: "What do you mean?" or "Can you clarify that?" or "Can you give an example?" Avoid closed questions like: "Do you not think that...?" or "Do you agree with X when he says...?" This type of intervention never leads to worthwhile information, because they involve an opinion or a judgement, and therefore have no bearing on the known unknown.

Discovering the most important uncertainties

You first need to go in search of the most important uncertainties. You do this by using, as it were, the techniques of a clairvoyant. You tell the expert that you have come from the future. Pick a year that is sufficiently far ahead, so that it is beyond the comfort zone of the topic you are discussing, but not so far ahead that you are moving into the realms of science fiction. As far as the future of health care is concerned, it is enough to look forward 15 or 20 years into the future. This meant that for my research in 2012 I chose the year 2030. If I was starting today, I would choose 2040, because 2030 is now too close. Having told the expert which year you come from, tell him (or her) that he can ask you three questions about the subject under review, so that he can see how it has evolved during the intervening years and can establish where it is positioned in relation to its present-day environment. These must be questions for which the expert would be willing to pay a fortune to know the right answers. But emphasise that he can only ask three questions – and no more. This will force him to think very carefully about the questions he asks you in your persona as a visitor from the future. To start the ball rolling, you first ask an opening question:

QUESTION 1:

Imagine that you can ask three questions to someone who lives in the future and can therefore answer your questions about the years ahead. What three questions would you ask him/her (in relation to your business, job, etc.)?

Note down the answers briefly. You will need to return to these themes during your second and third questions (see below). Ask the following subsidiary question:

Are you certain that for you these are the most important challenges in the years ahead? Have you forgotten anything or is there anything you would like to add?

The expert has just given you what he/she regards as the three greatest uncertainties during the period you are interested in. You now need to try to find out just how uncertain these uncertainties are. Where are the limits of the uncertainties? What is their ultimate scope? With this in mind, ask the following question:

Let's reverse the roles. Let's imagine now that you are the one who lives in the future. Assuming the future develops positively and turns out the way you would like, what answers would you give to your own questions?

Note down his/her answers and ask the following new question:

QUESTION 3:

Let's now imagine that the future does not turn out positively, but develops in the worst possible way from your point of view. What answers would you give to your own questions in that case?

Of course, you will notice in every conversation that the expert has a certain bias, but it is not your task as a foresight researcher to make comments about people's preferences or convictions, or to filter them out of the interview. If you do this, you will introduce your own bias! At the end, make a summary of all the certainties and uncertainties that came to the surface.

Each interview will give you important information. In total, it is a good idea to talk with a minimum of ten experts, using the same process each time. Naturally, you will get different answers from each one. After all your interviews, you will have a considerable amount of highly relevant data.

For the scenario for the hospital, I interviewed ten national and international experts about their vision and about the greatest uncertainties they had about the future. These included leading men and women in health care, DNA specialists, politicians (including a prime minister), and respected authorities from the worlds of health insurance, med-tech and pharmaceuticals. I also talked to top researchers in Google, Microsoft and Amazon, as well as university professors in the fields of sociology and ethics.

Here is a simplified summary of the experts' answers and the uncertainties that mentioned.

Having looked to the future, you now need to ask follow-up questions that look back to the past and draw on the experience of the expert. You will immediately be confronted with *hic-et-nunc* answers that are situated in horizon 1: what is the current position and what have we learnt from the past? Even so, it is important to include this backcasting in your scenario evaluation.

Table 6 – *Core uncertainties.*

RESPON-DENTS \ ANSWERS.	UNCERTAINTY 1	UNCERTAINTY 2	UNCERTAINTY 3
Resp. 1	Breakthrough in prevention?	Old age diseases cured?	Evolution in home hospitalisation and home care?
Resp. 2	Will sickness and disease still exist?	Ethical problems with DNA predictions: can we solve them?	Overpopulation: can we stop it?
Resp. 3	Will we achieve P4 (prevention, prediction, personalised, participative)?	Breakthrough in regenerative medicine?	Stopping aging succeeds?
Clones?	Will we stop ageing?	Technologische revolutie vindt doorgang of niet?	Ageing continues or not? (again die faster?)
Resp. 4	Affordable health care?	A technological revolution or not?	Further ageing of the population or not?
Resp. 5	Technology replaces transplants?	Personnel shortages?	Personalised medicines?
Resp. 6	Affordability of current health care model?	Technology for everyone or just the happy few?	Home care? Drastic cut in duration of hospital admissions?
Resp. 7	More responsible patient mentality?	Breakthrough in personalised medicines?	Financing of health care: will it remain available for all?
Resp. 8	Can the economy support the health care system?	Breakthrough in preventative medicine?	Genetics? Personalised treatment?
Resp. 9	Mentality and healthier living?	Affordability?	Effects of overpopulation?
Resp. 10	Technology?	Prevention and the will to invest? Mentality towards health?	Affordability? Care for all or just the happy few?

What are the crucial moments or developments that occurred in your field in recent years; the ones that you will never forget, whether for good reasons or bad? What lessons can these moments or developments teach us for the future?

Below you will find a summary (after clustering) of the answers of the ten expert respondents and from twenty or so other people with whom we also conducted scenario interviews in the same way. The list contains some important turning points in medical and health care history, many of which played an important role in helping to shape the care landscape of the future. This is an important step in foresight research: looking briefly backwards to help you move forwards.

Step 3: Determine the key drivers - looking backwards

You can order the suggested turning points in a PESTLE analysis, which will sub-divide them into the following categories: Political, Economic, Social, Technological, Legal and Environmental. You will note (as in this case) that you can often group together major pivotal events within a certain period of time. On this basis, you can predict when there is a strong likelihood that changes will lead to a drastic shift in the landscape of the future. In this case, you can see that this happens roughly every twenty years. This means that we can prepare ourselves for the next major shift in the health care landscape, driven by PESTLE changes, to occur around 2040. This means that if we were to re-do this scenario exercise today, we would set 2040 as the time frame. 2030 would be too close; 2050 too far off.

Step 4: Determine the core uncertainties - looking forward

When we look forward at the future, we base our conclusions on the most important factors of uncertainty that were mentioned during the interviews with people who have vision and insight into the care system of today and tomorrow. It will be seen that many of these factors are related to each other. This allows any redundancy to be eliminated and leaves us with a number of important clusters of uncertainties. The shape of the transactional and contextual environments for health care is outlined below. We will focus primarily on the contextual aspects.

Table 7 – *PESTLE-analysis.*

	< 1960	1980-1990	2000-2010	Future
Politics	Socialism/ care becomes more accessible	Subsidiarity principle, residential care centres instead of chronic in the hospital	Budget de-railment	Strong savings after pandemic? Breakthrough home hospitalization? E-health services and apps? care platform models?
Econo-mics	Golden Age	Wealth migration	Budget cuts	World recession due to pandemic, war in Europe, materials crisis? Instability in financial markets
Social	Babyboom	Immigration Numerus Clausus	Ageing / HR challenges	Overpopulation / depopulation? Ageing or new baby boom? Unhealthier life or just more consciously healthy?
Techno-logy	Narcose, röntgen, X-ray	Radiotherapy, microsurgery	DNA, bio-tech, ro-botisation, non-invasive procedures	DNA corrections, m-RNA, prevention? Internet-of-medical-things, healthcare data operability, VR/AI/AR
Legal	Subsidizing care	Reimbursement patient	IP expiration, generics, FDA, medical records	Privacy? Prescribing behaviour? Data act EU? Strict environmental rules
Environ-ment	Smoking, pollution	Unhealthy living environment: dead watercourses, acid rain, air pollution, waste	Diseases of affluence, awareness of prevention through bet-ter nutrition and the envi-ronment	Global warming? water scarcity? Environmental pollution? Biodiversity is declining?

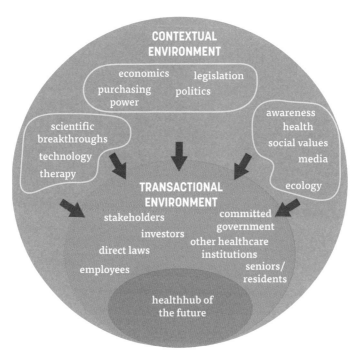

Figure 63 – *The uncertainties cluster in the contextual zone.*

All the uncertainties that we have detected, both in the 'known' zone and the 'unknown' zone, are now positioned in a graphic, in which we attempt to assess the impact of these uncertainties on our research question. To do this as accurately as possible, we give transcripts of the interviews to participants in a special workshop with a foresight team. The participants should all be people from the organisation under review (in our case study, the hospital). The only condition is that they should have a sufficient horizon (time span of discretion) to reflect on the future.

You discuss the uncertainties and determine together the extent to which these uncertainties will have an impact on the organisation. It may well happen that the participants have very different views. It is a fascinating process to then look more deeply at these divergent opinions about impact versus uncertainty. This makes it possible to understand precisely where the uncertainty resides and to identify the underlying reasons (systems thinking) that can explain why these uncertainties could have an impact.

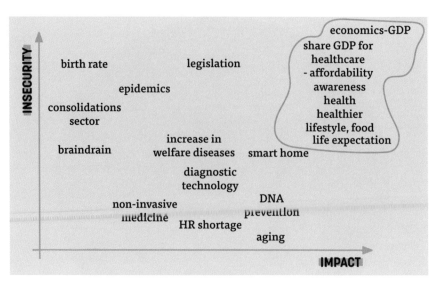

Figure 64 – *Scale outside-in uncertainties on the degree of uncertainty and impact for your organisation.*

You eventually end up with a graphic on which impact versus uncertainty is plotted. This is not an exact science, but it will give a good general indication of future changes in the environment. Typically, the trends that we can already see today will be positioned at the bottom of the graphic. This means that their impact may be great or small, but their level of uncertainty is limited. In the first instance, we take less account of these trends, because they will appear in each of the different scenarios we make to a greater or lesser degree.

We next look at the top right-hand corner of the graphic. Which of the factors have the biggest impact on our core question, our organisation and are also the most uncertain to predict in terms of their likely direction of travel? In our hospital-health hub case, you can see that there are two clusters of uncertainty: the economic cluster of uncertainty and the patient cluster with life expectancy, well-being, health awareness, etc. How will people deal with their own health in the future? Will they be more aware and have a more responsible attitude? If so, to what extent?

It all sounds very simple and logical, but it often arouses lively debate in the core team that takes part in the scenario exercise. Sometimes the decision is taken to ask for further outside-in information from the experts, in order to gain a more nuanced picture. The more information you collect, the more sharply defined your end picture of the future becomes. But you need to be careful. Sometimes you can attempt to explore a subject too deeply, so that you spend too much time and too much budget on too many interviews that yield no additional information that is relevant. Finding the right balance is key. I have seldom seen a scenario where more than fifteen experts have been interviewed, except in cases where the purpose of the exercise was different; for example, to create a consensus based in part on these expert opinions, which is more a culture-shaping and alignment project than a true foresight project.

Step 5: Building up the future worlds

The time has now come to further examine the two clusters. We position them on different axes and let the uncertainties vary between different extremes. Ensure that the axes are independent of each other. The extremes of these axes represent the range of uncertainty and they are more or less defined by what the experts had to say. It is important to think in terms of extremes. If you think incrementally, your scenario worlds will be too close to each other and therefore insufficiently challenging to be used effectively.

There are different methods for building scenarios: the inductive and the deductive or the incremental and the normative. The most important difference is that the deductive method – which was the method used in our case study – is more methodical in its approach and spends time in setting the right axes accurately. In other words, you structure your data before you build your scenarios. The inductive method works more associatively. You take one uncertainty as your starting point and this moves you on to the next one. In this way, you end up with different paths and different scenarios.

In my experience, the deductive method is more insightful for strategic planning, policy, innovation and entrepreneurship. The inductive method is more interesting for short exercises like brainstorming.

In the health hub exercise for the hospital, we discovered two important driving forces, which we then simplified:
• The affordability of health care.
• The behaviour of people in relation to healthy living.

Be aware that it took several discussions and work sessions before settling on these two driving forces. This is not uncommon. Sometimes different teams reach different conclusions, which need to be resolved by a steering group that will take the final decision about the axes and coordinates to be used. In some exercises, we decided to use three axes, which complicates things significantly. If you are ever contemplating this, ask yourself whether or not there is redundancy (dependency) in the three elements, so that you might be able to reduce them to just two. Perhaps you are dealing with a certain trend that you can investigate subsequently in each of the scenarios.

We place our two driving forces – the two greatest uncertainties with the greatest impact – on our double axes in order to create four worlds in which our future hospital may have to function.

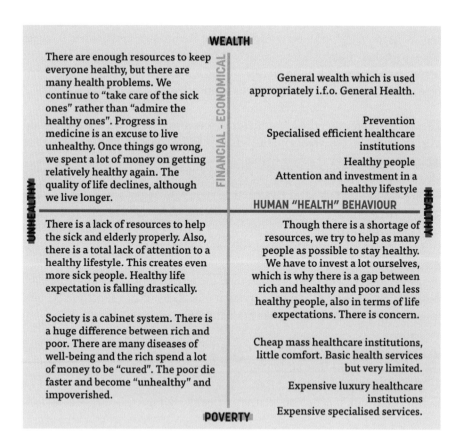

Figure 65 – The axes of the scenarios formed by the main driving forces.

In the next stage, we allow our two parameters to move towards the challenging extremes we have set. In this way, we create stories that make it possible to explain the different worlds. To do this, you can split your team up into smaller groups and let each of them think about one of the four future worlds that you have called into being. Once they have prepared a text to describe their world, these are shared with the other groups and, once agreed, placed on the relevant quadrant. This is often known as 'the art of storytelling'. By doing this, you work yourself more deeply and more insightfully into these challenging but plausible worlds. They are worlds that could actually happen. By applying the 'implication wheel' technique, you focus above all on cause-and-effect implications: if this happens, what will be the results? Letting your imagination run free is important: creativity is a crucial element in scenario thinking.

In the hospital-health hub case, the two axes chosen were the 'financial-economic' axis and the 'healthy human behaviour' axis.

Vertical axis: financial-economic

The extremes of this axis are 'rich' and 'poor'.

By 'rich' we mean that there are sufficient resources to allow everyone access to guaranteed and high-quality health care. This includes sufficient resources for the use of the latest technology and expensive therapies.

By 'poor' we mean that the medical-social safety net as we know it today has disappeared completely. The care system is bankrupt. There is no (or only very limited) access to quality care and there is no freedom of choice. The gulf between rich and poor is more pronounced than ever, but even the rich find it harder to obtain good care at all times and in all places.

Horizontal axis: healthy human behaviour

The extremes of this axis are 'healthy' and 'unhealthy'.

By 'healthy' we mean that people are concerned about their health, but also about the environment, the food they eat, leisure, exercise and education. In other words, they pay great attention to everything that can lead to better health.

By 'unhealthy' we mean the opposite of all these things: no attention to diet, relaxation, exercise, ecological matters, etc. People simply do what they like with no thought for their health, assuming that if something goes wrong 'science' and 'medicine' are there to save them.

It is a good idea to try to visualise the four future worlds you have created. You can do this using collages, video clips or other image material. Use anything that can help people to work their way deeper into the different worlds. This will be beneficial when you come to draw up your scenarios.

Figure 66 – Visualise the different future worlds.

Choosing an appropriate name for each of the scenarios is also an important step in helping to bring these worlds to life. In many of the organisations where we create strategic scenarios, these names are valuable points of recognition for everyone involved and make it possible for management to make a statement or frame an event by reference to a particular scenario.

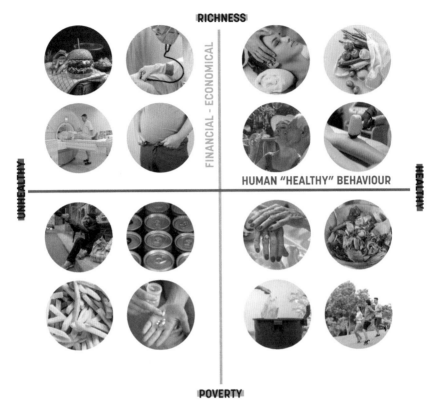

Figure 67 – *Give the different worlds an evocative name.*

You can also capture the various outcomes of your core question by using a single image for each future world. Once again, this can be a film, or a collage, or a cover from *Time* magazine: anything that helps to get your message across and allows you to show what the worlds of the future might look like. In our case study, this means hospitals in the year 2040. This does not need to be super-precise. After all, we are dealing with an exercise. Even so, the images you choose will probably say more to people than a thousand words, because an image can evoke certain emotions, insights and ideas associated with that particular world.

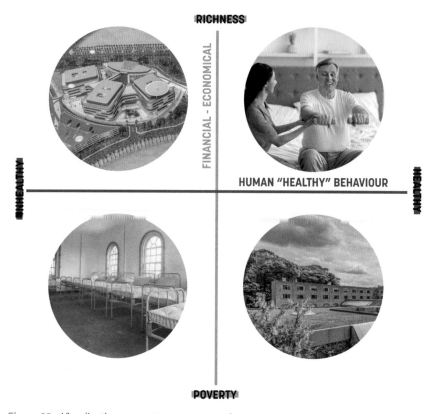

Figure 68 – *Visualise the answers to your core question.*

Step 6: Writing and telling stories for your future worlds

It is important that people can understand and use your scenarios, even if they were not directly involved in the scenario exercise. This means that you need to think carefully about your plausible worlds and the message you wish each of them to put across. Telling the right story is the core of this sixth and final step. There are different ways you can do this. One option is to use mood boards or customer (or in this case patient) journey maps. Alternatively, you can use a fictive diary or make a mini-newspaper for a day in 2040.

It is a good idea to use between three and five different personas to tell your story, so that the story-listener will get a sufficiently wide-ranging experience of the future you want to project. These scenarios are your crystal ball to illustrate your possible futures, in which you must identify with much more depth the right needs, problems and possible solutions. Well-developed scenarios are so rich in stories that you can even infer the willingness-to-pay from the future worlds you depict. Or that, at least, is how it should be, if your scenario team is sufficiently diverse and creative; if your scenarios have been developed outside-in; and if your hypotheses (options) have also been tested with external input.

For larger organisations, we often make video clips to visualise the future worlds; short films that allow their viewers to get a real feel for these worlds in just a few short minutes.

As an example of this storytelling aspect, below you can find the story for one of the future worlds in our hospital-health hub case. The text is written as though the future it predicts has already arrived. You can discover the other worlds via the QR-code.

Paradise

In this world, there is a strong awareness of the importance of healthy living. Economic and – above all – technological progress has ensured that medical treatment and preventative care have both experienced a significant positive evolution. DNA scans make it possible to assess a person's health risks at birth. As a result, people take better care of their bodies through daily exercise and appropriate diet. Good food, fresh air and stress-free relaxation are important priorities for the inhabitants of this world. The efforts made by both society and individuals to continually improve in all these directions are considerable.

In this society, sufficient resources are available for everyone. Thanks to decades of education and modernisation, the health care system has become more performant and more efficient. Doctors are prescribing fewer medicines and fewer people are getting sick as a result of extensive preventative measures. Getting enough exercise and eating a balanced diet have cut the number of 'prosperity' diseases. Greater attention to the environment and living conditions has reduced disease, allergies and cardiovascular disorders, which used to be the No.1 killer. People are getting older more healthily. This has not dramatically increased life expectancy but it has increased quality of life in old age. These are now largely years without medical problems. The mobility of seniors (90+) is still good and they like to meet, which they do regularly. Better health and longer life expectancy means that the active population is greater than it has ever been. The pensionable age is now 70 years. This higher employment rate means that there is a reduced pressure of work, since there are more people to do it and robots are also increasingly being used. This leads to knock-on reductions in stress and unhealthy habits, combined with more time for relaxation and greater attention for quality of life. The four-day week is now the rule, as are home working and flexible working hours. The overall result is that society is much more stress-free than in the past, so that the incidence of many of the traditional prosperity diseases and psychological problems has fallen significantly.

The focus of medical care has shifted from treating the sick to keeping people healthy and active for as long as possible. Improved awareness about the need for taking care of your health has played an important role in this. Of course, people do still become ill and they are given the care they need. That being said, fatal diseases and malignant conditions have been drastically reduced as a result of rapid evolutions in technology. Transplantations can now occur with cloned tissue or by implanting mechanical nanotechnology systems into patients, both of which can quickly restore quality of life. Most operations now take place in specialised and comfortable health centres, following which patients can nearly always revalidate at home or in a specialist care hotel. A high-performance team of experts is now available to intervene anywhere in the world at the first signs of the possible emergence of a new pandemic. If an outbreak should occur, the combination of AI and the microfluidics technology already present in our bodies means that an antibody therapy should be available almost immediately.

The traditional second-line health care of the past now takes place in care centres that are linked to revalidation centres and specialised treatment centres. Together, these centres form a 'health village', the external arm of which is provided by virtual reality home hospitalisation, home revalidation and follow-up. Third-line care is provided in collaboration with academic research institutions, which focus on developing solutions for the most challenging problems in medicine, which include increasingly far-reaching evolutions in the field of DNA technology and treatment. These are also areas where greater attention than previously is now being given to prevention and the patient is more closely involved in the participative care process.

Specialised DNA centres are now able to carry out DNA corrections at an early stage. In this respect, the mRNA molecule plays a crucial role in the body, by transporting the receptors for the production of various DNA proteins to the part of the cell where the protein synthesis takes place. mRNA can activate or deactivate certain genes, so that conditions such as blindness or sickle cell anaemia can be reversed. With clustered regularly interspaced short palindromic repeats (CRISPR), genes can be permanently changed, so that rare genetic diseases can be prevented or cured, including bone marrow, nervous system and muscular conditions. CRISPR is the work horse, but it is coded and directed by mRNA. Other technological developments include the widespread use of smart health sensors, which offer a wide range of insights into our health throughout our lives, so that AI has become a valuable support tool for doctors. In fact, AI can sometimes take over the role of the doctor, because it can reach the correct diagnosis more quickly – for example, in radiology – and therefore make possible faster and more cost-effective treatment.

Many systems have evolved into 'in-house' or domestic applications. As a result, three-quarters of the treatments that used to take place in hospitals now take place in people's homes. This was the second great shift in health care provision. Following the first shift from hospitalisation to day-hospitalisation, we have now seen a shift to home hospitalisation for an increasing number of care trajectories. Many aspects of health are controlled by consumer diagnostic systems and patient follow-up is now fully digitalised. This kind of participative care means that in most cases the patient is able to make his/her own diagnosis quickly and cheaply. During the last century, the pregnancy predictor was a pioneering example of this kind of participative medicine. Before the predictor was developed, women needed the services of a highly skilled medical professional to find out if they were pregnant or not. An easy-to-use technological aid made it possible for them to establish this for themselves with a high degree of certainty, which resulted in a huge cost saving in the care sector. Through this kind of active care participation and thanks to a growing awareness of the importance of pre-active health behaviour, more and more of these preventive, diagnostic and revalidation techniques are now finding their way into the day-to-day lives of consumers/patients. There are now countless medical matters for which you no longer need to visit a care centre or consult a doctor. This kind of remote diagnosis and follow-up, which makes widespread use of consumer devices (such as digital watches with sensors or digital assistants in people's homes), is much more efficient. At the same time, patients are permanently monitored at distance by health care professionals.

Society is now powered almost exclusively by green electricity. Industry, construction and retail are all based on the principles of the circular economy.

Wide-scale reduction of ecological footprints and greater efforts in the field of nature preservation means that the air we breathe, the food we eat and the water we drink are healthier than ever before.

Types of care centres

Specialised care centres and home hospitalisation

In this world, gigantic-sized hospitals no longer exist. Second-line care now takes place in specialised centres on the basis of single-day admissions. Once treated, the patient can return home or, where necessary, stay in one of the appropriate revalidation centres. Even patients who require intensive care no longer need to be admitted to large-scale institutions, but can be treated in local care hubs or even by at-distance services. For high-tech interventions or treatments, use is made of specific treatment centres, if no mobile alternative is available.

High-tech hospitals linked to 'care villages'

Third-line health care centres focus primarily on the more difficult, non-routine tasks and treatments that require expensive equipment. For example, hadron therapy is a radiotherapy technology that makes use of protons or other charged particles (such as carbon ions) to irradiate tumours with great precision. Building such a centre costs 50 million euros and its annual running costs another 6 million euros each year. Consequently, the number of such centres needs to be limited. For this reason, a hadron laser is used to treat patients within a 300-kilometre radius of the therapy centre on the basis of single-day admissions. If a patient needs to undergo the same treatment repeatedly over a short period, he/she can move with his/her family into the nearest care centre, which will be nothing like the traditional hospitals of the 20th century. These centres are comfortable and offer all the facilities of a hotel-Club Med environment. Patients requiring intensive and state-of-the-art personalised immunotherapy treatment can stay in one of these 'care villages' for months or even years at a time, which avoids the problems of transportation and irregular admission, whilst also allowing their family life to continue to an important degree. These villages accommodate patients of different ages with different conditions and in different stages of treatment, in an atmosphere that strives to be as 'normal' as possible.

Preventative health centres

In these centres, where more than one visit per year is possible, people are treated preventatively to avoid the occurrence of typical ageing diseases. Cancer therapies can also be started in these centres and then further followed up at home via online diagnoses and permanent monitoring through high-tech body implants. Such procedures give additional years of high-quality living to many people, generally known as QALYs: quality adjusted life years. The preventative health centres also have a large following through online communities, where numerous 'tips and tricks' are exchanged about health, vitality and prevention, which can be further individualised by personal AI avatars.

DNA Act of the Millennium and legislation

Much preventative treatment is carried out on the basis of an individual's DNA scan. The DNA Act of the Millennium guarantees all citizens that their DNA information will be stored in a safe manner and only used for approved procedures by people who have the necessary permission and are subject to the necessary controls. This worldwide legislation has drawn a line under the ethical disputes relating to gene-editing, so that it can be used, for example, to add QALYs to people's lives but not to engineer 'designer' babies with blue eyes and a high IQ.

Ageing of the population and life extension

The elderly can remain active and independent for much longer than in the past. Even so, many of them decide to make early use of the preventative health centres. Some also opt from the moment of their retirement (aged 70) to move to one of the many wellness care environments. These are large and comfortable residential complexes, where all the care that is needed now or in the future is available and the atmosphere is one of permanently being on holiday.

Applying scenarios in your organisation: the triple diamond methodology

You have now learned how to construct and describe exploratory scenarios. But what can you do with them? And how do you implement them in your organisation? The scenarios paint a picture of various (and sometimes distant) future worlds, which could one day actually happen. Worlds in which your organisation must ensure that it can still be relevant. In addition to short-term optimisation, the exploration of new markets and the development of new partnerships (horizons 1 and 2), you must also learn to do some things in a radically different way, if you want to answer the new needs of these new worlds. This will take you into horizon 3, the horizon where the long-term vision you have built up through your scenario planning will play a crucial role. This vision will result in the creation of an innovation doctrine, a firm belief that will convince everyone in the organisation that radical innovation is the only way to secure a successful and sustainable future.

The best way to implement scenario thinking is to start at the top. So, begin with your upper echelon managers. Put together a scenario team with a multi-disciplinary composition, taking account of the advice given earlier in the book about the best way to create a successful team. Including a number of young high-potentials is always a good idea. They will be your best ambassadors for spreading the scenario strategy throughout your organisation. The scenario team should consist of between ten and fifteen people, but preferably no more than that. But also no fewer, so that there are enough voices to stimulate discussion. In some organisations, you will soon realise that it is better not to include the CEO. If that is the case in your company, I advise you to set up a steering group that can meet less frequently, but nevertheless repeats each phase of the exercise in brief with the neutral catalyst figures that have been chosen to guide the process. In this way, you will have buy-in and the necessary consensus for the choices that need to be made during the development of the scenarios and their subsequent implementation.

The implementation of scenario thinking as the core of your innovation drive is best done by using the 'triple diamond' method. This involves your scenario team passing through a process that consists of three important phases for divergence and convergence. These phases are:

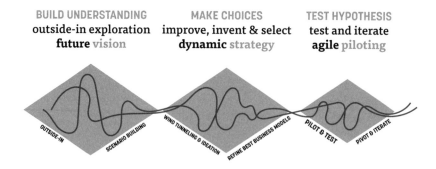

BUILD UNDERSTANDING
outside-in exploration
future vision

MAKE CHOICES
improve, invent & select
dynamic strategy

TEST HYPOTHESIS
test and iterate
agile piloting

Figure 69 – *The triple diamond method to successfully implement scenarios in your organization.*

- **BUILD UNDERSTANDING**
  This involves assessing and better understanding your situation by building scenarios according to the methodology I have outlined in this book: an outside-in approach focusing on the plausible and mapping the most important uncertainties, as a basis for creating probable future worlds. Into this, you need to build customer journeys with personas, eventually arriving at new options, new possibilities, new ideas. This is the phase where your innovation framework for the future is formed.
- **MAKE CHOICES**
  This involves stress-testing your existing business model, developing new options and subjecting them to wind tunnelling. This is the phase where you make choices based on the innovation framework you have defined.
- **TEST HYPOTHESES**
  This involves agile testing via pilots, from RAT (riskiest assumption testing) to MVP (minimum viable products).

You will note that this is not a linear process, but rather a turbulent one that will fluctuate considerably. Remember, however, that discussion and differences of opinion are an added value in scenario thinking. This allows the scenario team members to look at the future in different ways and to find solutions from different angles of approach. This results in a deeper understanding of future possibilities and challenges. In particular, experience shows that the outside-in perspective is crucial for success. Each phase of the process eventually leads to consolidation. You reach conclusions and realign the team before moving on. You can also do the same for the entire organisation by involving them in short scenario exercises.

Following this same trajectory can also be a useful tool during mergers and acquisitions (M&A), as means to align two different cultures within a single future. Similarly, the structuring of fragmented innovations can also be achieved by following a scenario trajectory. So too can making the transition from static forecasting or model-based budget planning to a dynamic, scenario-based rolling strategy.

The duration of this triple diamond process is dependent on a number of factors: the dominating culture (the attitude towards the future, change and risk), the objective (cultural change, M&A, an innovation project), the size of the organisation, its future fitness and its existing level in the six levels of innovation maturity. The amount of time this takes can vary from a few months to

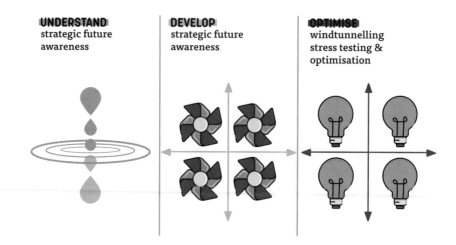

UNDERSTAND
strategic future
awareness

DEVELOP
strategic future
awareness

OPTIMISE
windtunnelling
stress testing &
optimisation

Figure 70 – *Through scenarios you learn to understand the future, you strengthen your organisation and you can innovate better.*

a few years. In this latter eventuality, cultural change is usually involved, but this does not mean that you need to wait that long before starting on the third phase. It simply means working in parallel with different phases.

Understanding the future

The process that you have followed to develop your scenarios is itself an important step forward in better understanding the future. The discussions with and within your team are so beneficial, because they give you a good understanding of what a plausible future might look like. You gradually discover that the contradictions of the past often have their place in a number of different worlds. You can let the opponents of a particular idea think their thoughts freely, before taking them to a different world where this idea has become normal. At the same time, you will also be forced to think about worlds where you would prefer not to go or about which you have never previously thought. Daring to 'think the unthinkable' is an essential part of the process.

The building of strategic awareness and alignment about plausible future scenarios is equally crucial. This works like a drop of water falling onto the surface of a pond. The effect of the drop is felt just as much under the surface as it is on top, creating a series of small ripples that spread across the seemingly smooth water. In scenario planning, your drops are the key driving forces that you allow to fall from your contextual environment onto the smooth water of your future transactional environment. The change that each of your different scenarios imposes on you forces you to see that in the future your company will need to play a completely different role and satisfy very different needs. Understanding your future in this way will also help you to better assess whether or not your current initiatives are future-proof. Why does this idea fail the future test? Why is that one so future-robust? Which elements that have been invisible to you until now might suddenly play a meaningful role in each of the future worlds of tomorrow, and perhaps even create greater value for the customers of tomorrow – assuming they remain the same?

Wind tunnelling, stress-testing and optimisation

Wind tunnelling allows you to test your policy, new ideas, concepts or strategies against the different images of the future provided by your scenarios. How future-robust are they? The term wind tunnelling refers to the wind tunnels that are used to test the aerodynamics of cars. This makes it possible to see whether or not a certain adjustment made to the car will exert an upwards or downwards force or create greater or lesser resistance. And it exactly the same with strategy. Will it make your company more or less stable?

By placing your existing strategy in the wind tunnel of different future scenarios, you will be able to see in which of these scenarios the strategy takes off and in which ones it crashes and burns – or never even gets off the ground. This applies equally to the new ideas or concepts that you extract from these scenarios: do they fly in multiple scenarios or only in one of them? This latter process is sometimes also known as stress testing, but both terms – stress testing and wind tunnelling – are often used interchangeably. In both cases, it is important that your scenarios are sufficiently extreme, whilst also remaining sufficiently plausible. If you only focus on median values on your axes, the results will be too close to your position today, leading to 'business-as-usual' outcomes that will not serve you well. This is a common mistake.

Translating scenarios into implications, options and ideas

It is possible to detect implications in every scenario and to develop ideas (options) around them by discussing or experiencing the scenario with your team. You will discover new and unmet customer needs that will emerge in the future and others that will no longer be relevant. Sketching this evolution will give you a good sense of the road map that you will need to define, if you wish to provide the necessary new solutions to these new needs. It is a good idea to test a number of your early hypotheses and to start with pilots based on agile design that will lead you (hopefully) in the right direction. If targeted testing and questioning prove the validity of a hypothesis, you can continue to invest in it. If this is not the case, put the hypothesis to one side and continue your search for something better. Often, an organisation will find that it does not have the skills required to meet the expectations of the future. That is why it is important to build up an ecosystem around you, so that you can gain access to the knowledge and expertise that will make this possible. I will return to this in more detail later on.

For now, let me illustrate this practically with reference to our hospi-tal-health-hub example. We took as our starting point a core question. Some-times, this is a business idea; sometimes, a concept that needs to be researched. In this case, our subject was the 'hospital of the future'. The aim was to decide with the hospital board what kind of new hospital should be built. Or perhaps, based on the insights gained from the scenarios, to decide what new care ser-vices would need to be developed. To make this assessment, we used the busi-ness model canvas (BMC) devised by Alex Osterwalder.

Business Model Canvas

The BMC is one of the most suitable tools for mapping out your current busi-ness and services. When I use it for commercial companies and non-profit or-ganisations, I refer to it by its standard title. When, however, I use it for gov-ernment and municipal authorities, I prefer to refer to it as the service model canvas. In principle, the methodology is the same in both cases, but in the latter you do not work on the assumption of profit, but rather on the basis of added value for society. Whatever you choose to call it, the BMC is now well known and widely used by many of today's organisations. In case yours is not one of them, you might like to find out how it works by scanning the QR-code to watch a short explanatory film by Strategyzer.

The BMC consists of nine separate building blocks, which require you to think about the basis of your business or organisation. When we make the BMC for a general (non-specialised) hospital, the result will look something like figure 71 on page 282.

As a rule, hospitals deal with patients who have typical pathologies. The value propositions that hospitals offer these patients are good medical treatment, the best possible patient experience and outcomes (leaving the hospital fit and well as quickly as possible), and digital service for patient follow-up. To make good these propositions, hospitals have developed their own resources (management, clinical staff, medical systems and products, personnel, etc) and their own set of activities (specialisations like urology, oncology or A&E, training, database of patient records, etc.). The key partners with whom they work are the medical and pharmaceutical companies, the government, other hospitals in the network, and health insurance institutions. They make themselves known to their patients through information brochures, websites, newspapers, referrals by doctors, etc. They build up their relationships with patients through digital patient records, follow-up visits and prevention advice. Their main expenditure is incurred on personnel, buildings, machines, supplies, maintenance and marketing. Their main revenue comes from invoicing for services, health insurance refunds, e-services and research.

Anno 2022, this is still a typical BMC for a typical hospital. The first thing that strikes you is that there is nothing differentiating about its contents, which seem ill-adapted to respond to future needs or changes. Options are limited. As a hospital board, you might choose to become a specialist facility (for example, a heart clinic) or a regional centre, but that is about all. Even so, it is still worthwhile to make a business model canvas like this, because it allows you to better understand how a hospital today really works. But it becomes really interesting when you translate the BMC into your future scenarios.

Implications from scenarios

Various driving forces will thoroughly change the environment in which a hospital will have to carry out its activities in the different scenarios of its future. The experiencing of each of these scenarios will give you an indication of the changes that will occur and also what the first, second and third order consequences will be, both on your present-day working as a hospital and on the future working of your health-care hub. In this way, the scenario worlds give you insights into the future strengths and weaknesses of your hospital model. Below is a SWOT analysis for the four future worlds in our example.

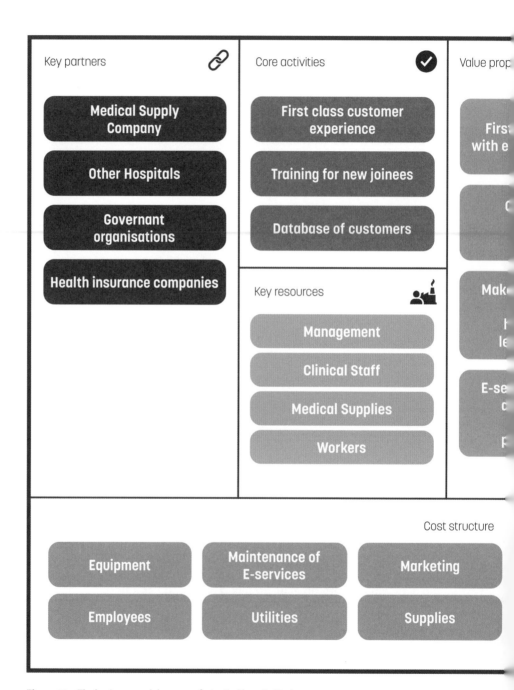

Figure 71 – *The business model canvas of a typical hospital today.*

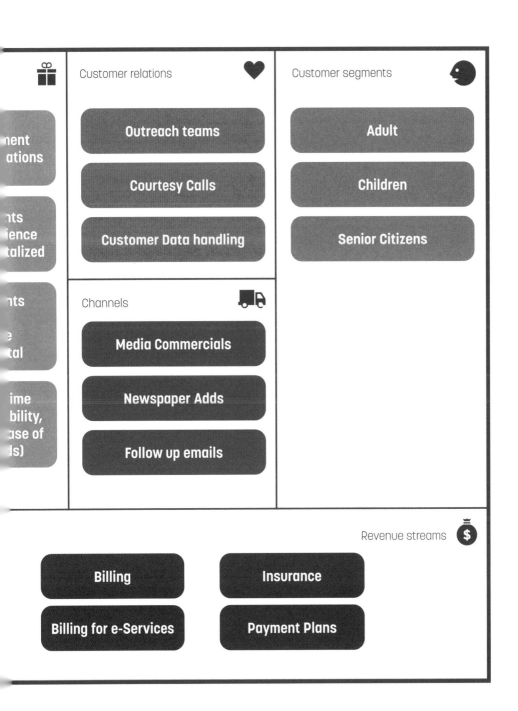

Customer relations

- Outreach teams
- Courtesy Calls
- Customer Data handling

Channels

- Media Commercials
- Newspaper Adds
- Follow up emails

Customer segments

- Adult
- Children
- Senior Citizens

Revenue streams

- Billing
- Insurance
- Billing for e-Services
- Payment Plans

Table 8 – SWOT-analysis.

Care need?	Giant Burger	Paradise	Healthy Wealthy	Dire Straits
S	Co-morbidities High care level	High prevention High budget	High attention for care and prevention	Everyone is sick and thus all the same
W	No prevention No care, only cure	Plenty of competition	High poverty Minimal budget	No budget No real care
O	High budget Comfort-all-in-1 Home hospitalisation	Wellness Prevention Home hospitalisation	Low budget solutions	(Very) low budget solutions
T	Shortage of staff	Affordability?	Low budget Rich-poor divide	No market demand or capital State failure

Based on these results, your scenario team needs to further discuss the strategic implications via the 'implication wheel'. What things strike you in the different worlds and what first, second and third grade consequences will this have for your idea of the future?

Let's take Giant Burger town as an example. It is clear that there will be plenty of co-morbidities. This means that the level of care necessary to deal with all these patients will be extremely high and complex. Diagnosis and treatment will need to be multi-disciplinary, which will require well-equipped centres with a high bed capacity. This is a **first-grade implication**, which indicates what type of services will need to be provided. It also gives an indication of what any future health hub would need to become and what would not be sufficient in that future world.

This leads on to a number of **second-grade implications**; namely, that you will need diverse teams of medics to treat all these patients. Cardiologists, internists, physiotherapists and radiologists will work together in interdisciplinary teams supported by other care personnel, in order to give dignified and effective treatment, further assisted by large amounts of technology and modern medical apparatus. This further implies that the hospital will be less focused on specific diseases and disorders, and also that the patients will constantly need to be brought to the locations where the care is provided. This insight might generate a new idea that it may be better to take the care to patient via home hospitalisation or comfortable revalidation centres.

The high level and complex nature of the care means that a shortage of skilled doctors and nursing staff is likely to occur sooner rather than later, so that it may be necessary to recruit new personnel from abroad. This is a **third-grade implication.**

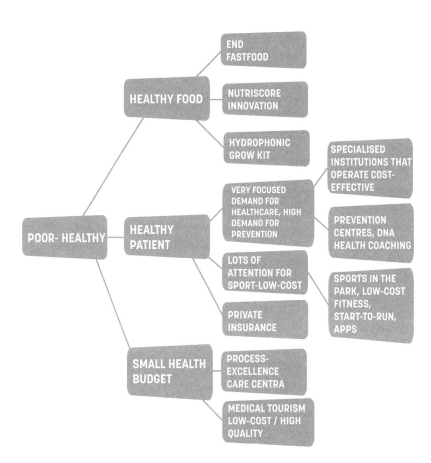

Figure 72 – *An example of implication wheel thinking for the Paradise scenario.*

Using the various implications per scenario, you can test how resistant your current business model is likely to be against the storm of future change. My experience suggests that this will often lead to fierce discussions in your foresight team. How robust is your business model in worlds A, B, C and D? Are you still relevant in each of these scenarios? In any of these scenarios? What are the opportunities and threats in each case? I will illustrate this by wind tunnelling the current hospital BMC in two of our future worlds.

Stress test in the Paradise scenario

In the Paradise world, the hospital of today – the 'as-is' model – will be less suited. Many patients need only a low level of care, so that there is insufficient demand for an old-style large-scale hospital. People in Paradise have both the financial and the technological possibilities to be treated at home. The current model is built too heavily around the concepts of maximum occupancy and bringing the patients to where the care is given. In the Paradise scenario, it is expected that the care will largely come to the patient through home hospitalisation and monitoring. As a result, the level of occupancy in many departments of the traditional hospitals will be too low to make their survival economically viable. Many of the services they provided in the past are now carried out in the patient's home using high-tech sensors, AI analytical systems and only very little physical care. This all means that in this scenario the health care hub of the future will need to invest in this kind of technology, in order to take its services away from hospitals and into patients' homes in radical new ways. In this new world, the ease of the patient is the highest priority. In Paradise, budgets are sufficient and customer expectations about access to health care in the manner they desire is high. Customer experience is therefore centred on providing this care as quickly, as easily and as close to the patient as possible. If we, as a present-day hospital, fail to invest in this future, we can be certain that other alternative organisational forms will emerge to do it in our place.

Stress test in the Healthy Wealthy scenario

This is the world where health is the only luxury. People are very concerned about their health, but society in general is very poor. Customer experience is therefore focused on comfort, luxury and ease, but with the right quality of care at the right price (good value for money). Expensive home hospitalisation trajectories are rare. Mega-hospitals are not necessary, since people are generally healthier in this world. Once again, you can see that the 'as-is' model will

come under pressure. There will be a shift away from general hospitals and towards decentralised care centres that offer everything under one roof at a low
cost. This is only possible with an extreme focus on operational excellence. In
the Healthy Wealthy world, this happens in collaboration with private insurers
and employers, because the government does not have the financial resources
to provide full care for everyone.

This simple act of comparison makes it clear that the existing working model for your hospital would come under pressure in both these future worlds.
Should one of these worlds ever become a reality, you now already know what
your strengths and weaknesses will be. Perhaps there are still no early signals to
say which of these two worlds (or some other) you are likely to find yourself in.
But with these insights you can at least build the necessary flexibility-by-design
into your systems, so that you do not blindly follow the wrong path and invest
in the wrong things. Making use of this aspect of the scenarios has direct value
for every part of your organisation. You get immediate feedback about just how
future-proof your current activities really are, providing your scenarios are constructed in the right outside-in manner and are based on the right axes. All the
more reason for making sure that you conduct your scenario exercise properly.

Options

By exploring and experiencing the scenarios in depth, you not only discover
threats but also opportunities that you can translate into ideas for the future.
In the context of a scenario, we call these ideas 'options'. With the necessary
creativity, you can even convert threats into opportunities. It will require
change and perhaps even radical renewal, but that is the purpose of scenarios:
to give you a wake-up call and transform your fear of the future into a determination to deal with it effectively, reducing your risk of failure by allowing you
to make the right choices from the start.

Note down the options that the scenarios have brought to the surface. The detected future needs of customers can be sub-divided into the categories 'served',
'underserved' and 'new', to which you should then apply design-thinking and
job-to-be-done methodologies, so that you can become FCC: future customer-centric.

The next step is to further categorise your options under horizons 1, 2 and 3. H1
refers to incremental options and therefore often relates to core innovation. H2

options are adjacent ideas and H3 options are radical, transformative ideas. On this basis, you need to decide your strategy, approach and metrics for the future. In traditional hackathons and brainstormings, H1 options predominate. Customers but often also your own staff are interested first and foremost in incremental improvements. However, the long-term value of these improvements is limited. In contrast, H2 and (even more probably) H3 may contain some priceless uncut diamonds. What's more, by applying the scenario method you are often more likely to stumble across them, because scenarios reset your focus away from today and teach you to look at the world through the eyes of the future customer.

In our hospital-health hub example, the stress-testing exercise revealed various options, which we now need to subject to wind tunnelling in those future worlds. In Paradise, those options might include a DNA centre that develops a DNA passport, a care robot or even a health footprint label or score, …

CASE: THE NUTRI-SCORE

A first example to show how this methodology can result in real market innovation is the idea of a health footprint score, a score that would indicate how healthy individual items of food really are. This 'option' was developed during my MBA course in 2009, when the scenarios in our example were first compiled. The idea was tested out in Belgium by the Delhaize supermarket chain under the impulse of its then CEO West Europe, Arthur Goethals. A pilot store was built in our innovation campus and stocked with products bearing a 'quick-and-dirty' prototype label. We knew that our hypothesis had 'bull's-eye' potential but we also knew that it would need government support to get it off the ground. With this in mind, numerous health institutions from around Europe were invited to visit Living Tomorrow, so that they could discover this open innovation concept for themselves. In 2014, the idea was first put into practice in France as the Nutri-Score, under the auspices of the Institut National de la Santé et de la Recherche Médicale. In 2017, the label was introduced in French stores and in 2019 in Belgium and The Netherlands. Delhaize-Food Lion (now Ahold Delhaize) was one of the first international supermarket chains to adopt it for its house brands. By the start of 2021, it had been adopted as standard in seven European countries. After the house brands, many other brand manufacturers also decided to use the idea. Delhaize once again demonstrated its creativity by linking the Nutri-Score to its customer loyalty card: buy healthy food and get a bigger discount. It was a brilliant idea, and one that benefits the customer, public health and Delhaize. In 2017, the similar and successful Yuka app was developed in France by Benoit and François Martin and now has 25 million users. The problem with all this, as we soon discovered when testing our hypothesis in 2009, is the lack of regulatory and policy support. As a result, it is unclear to the customer whether or not he/she can actually trust the label and the app. As a result, it seems likely that the app will be replaced by a European Nutri-Score or will at least have to adjust to reflect it.

What is Nutri-Score?

Nutri-Score is a label with a colour code added to the front of food packaging, indicating the nutritional value of the food or drink it contains. The aim is to help consumers choose healthier products, whilst at the same time encouraging the food industry to improve the nutritional value of its product range. The label has been validated by numerous scientific studies. In general, labels of this kind with specific information about foodstuffs are poorly understood by consumers. However, it is widely accepted that the Nutri-Score helps European consumers to better assess the nutritional value of the products they buy, by allowing comparisons to be made within the same product group or between similar product groups. In this way, people are stimulated to make healthier choices.

Figure 73 - A photo of the Delhaize–Food Lion test store in 2010. The meals had a barcode that indicated a food health score. There was also a prototype shopping trolley that automatically scanned your purchases and also displayed your shopping list, transmitted from the kitchen in the Living Tomorrow House of the Future.

SOURCE: LIVING TOMORROW

CASE: ARAVIND EYE HOSPITALS

A second example will show how you can find good options in even the least attractive of future worlds. In fact, it is often in this kind of world that the most disruptive ideas appear. So, let me take you on a journey to the slums of India...

The Dire Straits scenario depicts a world where no one wants to be. In this world, the normal business model of hospitals no longer functions, as can all too often be seen in harrowing images of the health care situation in many of the poorest developing countries. There is no budget and people have more pressing concerns than prevention and a healthy diet. Yet it is precisely in this kind of environment that it is possible to innovate powerfully with radically different business models. Consider, for example, the success of the Aravind Eye Hospitals in India.

The problem of rapidly escalating and avoidable blindness in India is a major cause for concern. The government is not able to satisfy everyone's health needs in the way it would like, thanks to a paralysing combination of accelerating population growth, inadequate infrastructure, low incomes, demographic ageing, disease in epidemic proportions and illiteracy. It was for this reason that Dr Govindappa Venkataswamy set out to find an alternative health care model that could supplement the efforts of the hard-pressed government and even become self-supporting in due course. The Aravind Eye Hospitals were founded with the mission to 'eradicate unnecessary blindness'. The hospitals offer high-quality and affordable treatment but in a massive volume. Half of the customers are treated free of charge or at highly subsidised low rates, but the organisation continues to keep its head comfortably above the financial waters. Great importance is attached to the idea that every patient must receive the same excellent service and care, irrespective of their economic status. A crucial element in Aravind's new business model is its high patient volume. This attracts doctors from all over the world, who are prepared to come to India to perform operations that are much less necessary in richer countries. In addition, med-tech companies are also interested in testing out their newest and most innovative apparatus in this kind of environment, where a sufficient number of operations take place. In fact, doctors in training and medical companies are prepared to pay Aravind large sums of money for the privilege. The net result is to bring together the best eye doctors in the world and the best medical apparatus in the world at the location with the most practical experience in the world. In consequence, rich patients also come to the Aravind clinics and are prepared to pay whatever it costs to benefit from their zero-fault status. This further contributes to the strong financial basis of the business model, making possible the free or subsidised treatment of the volume of patients.

The unique assembly line approach of Aravind increases productivity by a factor of ten and reduces the cost per operation by the same factor in comparison with prices in Western countries. What started as a hospital with just eleven beds, manned by four doctors, is now the largest eye care facility in the world, with 80 centres that carry out more than five million eye checks and perform half a million operations each year. Aravind also has its own production facility for the intraocular lenses that are implanted during the cataract surgery. In the words of the current CEO, Dr R.D. Ravindran: "It is possible to restore the sight of 70% of our patients. The real challenge is not a technical one, but relates to the fact that we need to get our patients from remote locations to the nearest eye centre. For this reason, we need to invest heavily in remote diagnosis. In this way, we have made eye care accessible to everyone. We have 80 sight centres spread across the country, where patients can be treated via teleconsulting." Since its foundation, Aravind has dealt with more than 65 million polyclinical visits and completed more than 7.8 million operations. The Aravind Eye Care System serves as a model for India and for the rest of the world. At the end of 2020, the Aravind model was rightly rewarded with the award of the Sanford and Sue Greenberg Prize to End Blindness.

By thinking in terms of scenarios, you arrive at new innovative models of this kind. These models are most needed and most applicable when you find yourself in the least attractive scenarios, the ones you would avoid at all costs in normal strategic circumstances. Why does this or that idea no longer work? Where is the bottleneck and can you perhaps free it by turning the idea on its head? That is what Aravind has done - and with success!

By further exploring in the scenario world, you will discover numerous options of your own. It is a good idea to sum them up in a list - before moving on to decide which one(s) you are going to back.

Options – how do you choose the right innovation bets?

In the first instance, you need to ask three questions of each of your available options: Is this what we want? Can we do it? Is it workable? These are the three lenses of innovation – desirability, feasibility, viability – that were first developed by IDEO in their human-centred design model. I have added a fourth lens that takes account of the context or the spirit of the times.

- Customer **desirability**: Is this really what we want? Is our innovation focused on the right customers? Are we solving the problems that people want to be solved?
- Technical **feasibility**: Are we capable of doing what needs to be done?
- Business **viability**: Is this mission workable? Is it profitable? What is the business model?
- Legal **validity**: Is it permissible? Will the regulator allow it? Will public opinion allow it? Does this square with our values? A start-up can try to break the rules; a corporate company will find it more difficult. Legal and regulatory frameworks not only create barriers, but also opportunities. Think of the Nutri-Score versus the Yuka app (foodstuffs), or REACH (chemicals), or the EU's PSD2 (finances), or IP in general.

The important thing is to list your various ideas in order of priority. Scenarios are ideal for putting your options in order of 'future proofness', which you can do by subjecting them to a process of wind tunnelling.

Options – wind tunnelling your innovation bets

You should wind tunnel each of your ideas in each of your four scenario worlds. Give a score for each idea in each world. Do this in a group that is larger than just the people who dreamt up the ideas. Discuss the future value that each option could or would bring to your organisation and to your potential customers of the future. If an option scores 'double minus' in each of the four worlds, scrap it from your list, because it is obviously a loser. One of the options scores 'double plus' in each world? In that case, it is possible you have a winner, but you will need to research further to make sure that the idea does not already exist.

Table 9 – *Wind tunnel options in the scenarios.*

	Scenario 1	Scenario 2	Scenario 3	Scenario 4
Option 1	0	++	--	-
Option 2	+	-	+	0
Option X	++	+	0	++

KEY 7
ECOSYSTEMS: BETTER TOGETHER

Building ecosystems with scenarios: an introduction to the Strategy Map™ and Value Map™

As has already been mentioned, an ecosystem is another name for your transactional environment, the comfort zone in which you work with various stakeholders you know. Today, the concept of an ecosystem has become something of a hype, but if you ask a hundred people what the term means you are guaranteed to get a hundred different answers. The first time that I ever heard the word was in primary school, where we learnt about ecosystems in nature, where different organisms interact freely with each other. In this way, the entire system remains in balance and becomes self-sufficient. This means that every member of the system can benefit from it. Otherwise, it risks becoming weaker and eventually extinct. This kind of ecosystem is therefore a habitat or biosphere with sufficient biodiversity.

Translating this to the business world and to society in general, I define an ecosystem as follows:

A business ecosystem is a targeted collaboration between two or more independent entities (the members) for the purpose of creating and sharing collective value for a common group of customers. Within this system, transactions take place that keep the system in balance and make it self-sufficient, so that it can continue to exist. Some of the members can act as orchestrators. Some accelerate or slow down transactions as catalysts. Some are simply partners in the system. All the members in an ecosystem have an interest in the value of that system.

Ecosystems can also work well for public authorities and organisations for the provision of social services that are not (or at least less) focused on profit creation and permanent growth. An ecosystem equates to your comfort zone: you know your partners and are familiar with them. If you look at your ecosystem from the perspective of your company, these are your customers, suppliers, personnel (permanent and external), lobbyists, peers, competitors, knowledge institutions, rule givers, investors, etc.

Of course, you still need to make every effort to ensure that the business model of your organisation is as unique as it can be within the ecosystem, through the development of differentiating, value creating and bidirectional transactions. This is your organisational strategy. It embodies the things for which you are known and recognised. Your strategy forms the boundary between your small circle – your organisation – and the large circle – the ecosystem.

The innovative aspect of ecosystem thinking is the fact that within an ecosystem – as in nature – you can create a better and stronger value proposition with other members of the system than you could create alone. Just as in nature one player cannot survive without valuable partners, so also in the modern business world: it is now impossible to set up successful transactions without partnerships. In short, you need an ecosystem. All the players in the system collectively wish to create added value for a well-defined target group of customers. They meet the needs of this group by providing them with products and services with an increasingly large transactional value. In today's jargon, this is often referred to as 'customer experience', based on the idea that everything needs to be an experience if you want it to be attractive. This is true – but only up to a point.

Transactions in an ecosystem must be efficient and have value if the natural balance – the success of the system – is to be maintained and further expanded. The difference with a natural ecosystem is that in nature everyone works for everyone else. In a business ecosystem, you focus on a particular target group that you wish to provide with ultimate customer value, from which every member of the system benefits and becomes stronger. In contrast to nature, this process needs to be orchestrated. Some member(s) of the ecosystem (whether in business or society) must take the lead and set out structures for go-to-market, value creation and the sharing of added values. This is the governance framework within which you implement transactions together; the ethical rules for the sharing of costs, benefits and risks.

Let me make this more concrete with a practical example: the car of the future. Imagine that this car is designed by BMW. The innovative ceramic electric motor comes from Bosch. The new generation of metal-air batteries that can be charged in ten minutes come from Panasonic. The connected run-flat tyres come from Michelin. The sat-nav mapping with interactive services such as online searching, reservation making and intelligent wayfinding comes from Google. The entertainment options come from TuneIn, Netflix and Disney+. The online order-and-collect options come from Amazon, UberEats or Hello-Fresh. The option to share the car (and make money) when you are not using it comes from Uber. The trained neural network that makes autonomous driving possible comes from Tesla, while the onboard edge computing comes from Apple. This kind of ecosystem, which focuses on a target group that wants a full CASE mobility experience, can easily consist of a hundred partners or more, who all contribute added value for the end customer. In this instance, the orchestrator might be BMW as the overall designer.

Some of you might be wondering whether or not this is the same as a strategy supply network of the kind that many companies have built up in recent years. Yes and no. Yes, because the partners in such a network work together to create a certain value proposition for a product or service aimed at a specific target group. No, because an ecosystem takes things much further. Each of the partners is now present with their brand in the system's totality and with its strategic development forms an added value both for the other partners and, more importantly, for the whole.

A logical evolution: from R&D, buy-build, open innovation and platforms to ecosystems

In the past, companies often asked themselves whether it was better to build something or buy something that they needed for their product or service. Now it is increasingly a question of finding the right partnerships that can add something to your product or service.

From closed to open innovation

There was once a time when large companies did everything for themselves, including fundamental research. Think, for example, of the now legendary labs of the great global players of the past: the NatLab at Philips, the Xerox

PARC, Bell Labs at AT&T. They developed intellectual property (IP), which was converted in their translation offices into products that could be commercialised. Some of these inventions remained underused or unused, because they could not be scaled up. Think, for example, of the computer mouse and graphic user interface, which were first thought of in the Xerox PARC, from where they were 'stolen' by the more visionary Steve Jobs. In the 21st century, scale is no longer the ultimate advantage for big companies. On the contrary, your legacy – your park of products and services from the past – has become a disadvantage that hinders rapid renewal. Nowadays, even infrastructure is increasingly hired and it is no longer necessary to invest huge sums to get your hands on top technology and massive computing power. Today's large companies are finding it more and more difficult to keep up with the fast pace of change that has resulted from the growth in start-ups. This has made it necessary for them to change the way they work. They need to be lighter: less own R&D and more collaboration. We saw the first steps in this direction some twenty years ago with the emergence of open innovation, a methodology that was described in detail and evangelised by Henry Chesbrough. The core idea was that you no longer needed to make everything yourself, but instead could collaborate with others to develop mixed products. This was made possible by the in-and-out licencing of intellectual property (knowledge, patents, etc.). In time, four different kinds of collaboration emerged, which still exist today.

- Partnerships, whereby external features are added to products.
- Ventures, whereby investment is made in early start-ups with potentially interesting technology. For example, Mercedes invested in Tesla because of the latter's interesting battery technology.
- Acquisitions, whereby promising start-ups are purchased and the new technology becomes the core of your own product. For example, Facebook that buys Instagram.
- Accelerators, whereby the large company makes available technology and experience that will allow a start-up to grow faster. Pfizer gave a boost to BioNTech's mRNA development by making available production facilities, regulatory-commercial skills, and by concluding a purchase agreement.

From open innovation to a platform model

These open innovation collaborative initiatives, which went further than buy-build, eventually developed into successful platform models. These are models in which the other players in your collaboration (your ecosystem) invest time, energy and money in your business model to make it more attractive and more profitable. In theory, there are two main platform models.

The first model involves the development of an own capability through your specific activity, knowledge and data. You then market this capability as a product with which partners can collaborate. A well-known example of this is the Apple AppStore. Thousands of developers provide the millions of apps sold in the App Store, which makes Apple's iPhone platform even more attractive for potential users. Personally, I no longer refer to this kind of venture as open innovation, but see it as a clever example of a closed-open innovation model. Apple created a closed governance framework in which developers are free to innovate openly. In other words, these developers are not truly free in the literal sense of open innovation, as was the case with Linux, for example, which resulted in the development of hundreds of different versions of the original. Instead, tools are made available to them, which they can use as they see fit to innovate. Stripe in the financial sector is another example of the same kind of thing. Via Stripe Connect, money can be accepted from and paid to third parties.

The second platform model is the orchestrator model. The orchestrator ensures that as much friction as possible is removed from between the model's partners and users. In this way, for instance, Airbnb makes it easier to lease or rent a house or room. Similarly, Uber makes it easier to connect supply and demand in the mobility sector.

From platform model to ecosystem

The next step in the progression is from the platform model to an ecosystem. In an ecosystem, the partners are more equal in importance than in the majority of platform systems, where there is often a single main initiator. That being said, with ecosystems there is also a certain degree of hierarchy, to ensure that everything runs smoothly, but it is not as pronounced as in a platform. Ecosystems as they exist today would not be possible without the existence of far-reaching cloud technology. The complex technical, administrative and operational tasks that collaboration makes necessary are much easier (and cheaper) to carry out in cloud systems. Think, for example, of the complexity of integrating the streaming services of Tune-In and Spotify or of the AI-services needed to make autonomous driving possible.

Using scenarios to map ecosystems

You can use scenarios to map out your future ecosystem. Who are the parties with whom you should collaborate in the years to come? Who will be your best partners in each of your plausible worlds? Who will be your real competitors? This is known as a strategy map; a kind of wind rose in which you set crucial elements on the different wind directions, with the aim of seeing in which direction you must travel to make your business idea a success. You plot the different partners on the map, who – according to the insights you have today – you think can help you to achieve this. You can even divide these partners up into horizon 1, horizon 2 and horizon 3 connections. Horizon 1 connections can offer you solutions today and are ready for a partnership now. Horizon 2 connections require further work before you can arrive at a common story. And horizon 3? Who in the future will develop radical solutions, which may be either good or bad for your model?

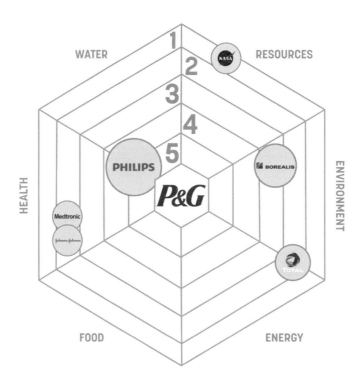

Figure 74 – *An example of a strategy map.* SOURCE: TOMORROWLAB.

The ecosystem strategy map gives you a visual overview of where you might be able to find your partners for tomorrow in different strategic directions. These partners can be either large companies or tiny start-ups, or both. The impact that a partner can have on your business is not always proportional to that partner's size. A start-up with the right technology can sometimes give you a bigger boost than a larger company. Moreover, your strategy map makes it possible for you to measure the vitality or fitness of your ecosystem. You can do this by investigating four specific characteristics in relation to the partners you have placed on the map.

- The first indicator is the number of possible partners in your ecosystem. Are there many or only a few? This is the **density** of your ecosystem.
- A second sign for the vitality of your ecosystem is its **fluidity**. How refreshing and different are the partnerships you can build? If there are not enough young companies or start-ups, there is a risk of falling back into 'business as usual'.
- A third important element is **interconnectivity**. How good are the contacts between the different players? Are these contacts frequent or sporadic? Is their communication dynamic or sluggish?
- The fourth indicator is the **diversity** in your ecosystem. Are your partners varied enough? Or are you always fishing in the same pool?

It is well worth the effort to score your ecosystem in your future worlds on the basis of these four easy-to-measure criteria.

Bonus key: An early warning system as part of a rolling strategy

In our rapidly evolving world with rapidly evolving markets, organisations need to be alert to the early signals of change. What's more, you must know how to interpret these signals correctly and then translate them quickly into your strategy, if you want to stay in the game. But how do you capture these early signals? How do you react to unexpected developments? Or market opportunities? Or changing customer needs and behaviour? You need to keep your eyes and ears open and focused on the outside world. In this respect, the scenario work carried out by your foresight team can be a big help. A scenario exercise that has applied the triple diamond method can be of huge strategic value for the future fitness of your organisation.

Scenario planning not only helps you to see what the future holds in store for you, but also gives you insights into how that future is likely to unfold. During the scenario workshops, your team will have explored different plausible events that could have an influence on the future. It is possible to draw up a list of early signals for each of these events, which could be a sign that something is about to happen. The scenario planning process will also help the team members to become more sensitive to these signals.

As a leader, you are probably familiar with the following feeling: every week someone walks into your office and asks if you have already heard the news. This or that new development has taken place, which, they claim, will undoubtedly have an impact on your company, business model, products, service, staff or ecosystem of partners. Often, this is based on nothing more than the person's gut feeling, but you discuss the development briefly, before quickly forgetting about it – until the next person comes to see you next week with the next new signal...

This reaction is understandable, but perhaps short-sighted. On the basis of your scenarios, you can develop a system to trigger a mental alarm whenever an early indicator of a possible move towards one of your plausible worlds occurs. And the more signals you get that all seem to be pointing in the same direction, the more certain you can be that the signals are reliable and that this is the direction in which you should be focusing. If, by contrast, the signals are all pointing in different directions, it is too early to draw conclusions. I strongly recommend setting up this kind of early warning radar, a tracking system that maps all the signals within your transactional zone.

You have probably heard of the metaphor of a frog in a pan of water. If you drop a frog into a pan of water that is already hot, it will immediately try to jump out. But if you put the frog into a pan of lukewarm water and then gradually increase the temperature, the frog will stay there until it is boiled alive. This is a lesson that can also be important for organisations: you have to learn how to recognise and interpret early signals from the outside world in good time.
Ask the right questions

If you want to detect early signals, you have to ask the right questions. One way to develop the necessary outside-in insight is to use the questions devised by professors George Day and Paul Schoemaker. In their book *Peripheral Vision*, they complied a list of questions that will allow you to detect weak signals in your environment, which could make all the difference between make or break for your organisation. These questions help you to stimulate a future-minded dialogue in your company. Imagine, for instance, that you are active in the car sector and can see the emergence of new kinds of mobility: e-steps, e-bikes, e-drones, self-driving taxis, etc. The following questions are the ones you should ask to decipher what these early signals mean:

- Do we have a *blind spot*? Can we learn from things that have happened in the sector in the past? What happened, for example, when horse-drawn transport was replaced by cars?
- Can we draw *parallels* with other industries? Digital platforms emerged rapidly in the retail sector and dramatically changed the way people shop. Can we expect the same kind of evolution with regard to mobility services?
- Who else in our sector has good *detection skills*, so that they can see changes faster than the rest of us? What are they doing at the moment? Are they doing anything differently? What are they investing in? What strategic partnerships are they concluding?
- What important signals are we *rationalising* or ignoring? Are we going to persist in saying that electric cars will never have a major impact on the sector?
- What can we learn from dissidents and critics, the *odd-men-out*? Is there any truth in what they say? Should we finally free up our real-time data, so that our user community can develop better apps to plan their own journeys?
- What *surprises* could cause us harm? What if the CO_2 taxes levied via the European CO_2 trading system suddenly become ten times more expensive?
- Which *emerging technology* could be a game-changer for our organisation? Will self-driving cars significantly affect our role as retailers? What if pas-

senger drones become a commodity? If the hyperloop can transport us from A to B emission-free at speeds of up to 1,000 kilometres per hour, what does this mean for all forms of long-distance travel?

Be careful with your interpretations

Detecting early signals and placing them in scenarios to understand their possible impact on your business is a good thing, but you need to careful that you don't jump to the wrong conclusions. To avoid this pitfall and develop a robust and dynamic long-term plan of action, you need to develop the following four-phase rolling strategy:

1. Detect signals
You must sense, see and understand changes.
Identify signals that demand anticipation or reaction.
Put signals in an order of priority: = chance x impact x duration.

2. Determine your position
Analyse important signals in more depth.
What is the nature, speed and impact of the change?
How should we anticipate or react?
Should we alter our strategy or organisation?

3. Take action
As soon as the signals give the green light, self-organising teams initiate strategic projects and improvement actions.

4. Manage performance
If the necessary change has been implemented and is working well, optimise your operational systems and further develop the market.

I started this chapter by emphasising that it will continue to be a challenge for organisations to give sufficient attention to their long-term future. I will finish by quoting a remark from Jean-Luc Dehaene, a former Belgian prime minister with whom I often had the chance to discuss the future. He once said: "Urgent things are often not important and important things are often not urgent." That's something worth thinking about...

A PRACTICAL TESTIMONY
FADEL AL FARAJ – Q8 – INNOVATION IS ADDICTIVE

For a number of years, my team and I have been working for Q8. Perhaps it is a good idea for you hear about the impact of our scenario work and the transition it has effected from Q8 North-West Europe and recently Italy's CEO: Fadel Al Faraj. Kuwait Petroleum International, better known as Q8, is the international downstream daughter company of the Kuwait Petroleum Corporation, the national oil company of the Kuwaiti state and one of the largest energy conglomerates in the world.

Mobility is changing rapidly. Companies that sell fossil fuels, like Q8, need to make important and innovative pro-active choices to embrace and deal with the new reality of electric cars, renewable energy and the sharing economy. Fadel Al Faraj, the general director of Q8 North-West Europe, is leading the company through this challenging period of transition. Al Faraj is a highly respected name within the company and within the European oil industry in general. He is a seasoned campaigner in the business world, with 30 years of experience in various areas of the downstream oil sector. During this time, he has booked success after success, but he is still on his guard and takes nothing for granted when it comes to the future. Today, he is in charge of a company in full transformation and aims to get Q8 ready to find a new place in the fast-changing mobility landscape and in the new energy mix.

In 2017, a scenario project was launched as the first step in this transformation journey. Since then, the company has taken giant strides forwards. One example is Q8's decision, taken in 2019, to invest in the SnappCar car share platform, but the company has also collaborated with IONITY (the largest fast-charging network in Europe), has built its own Q8 and Tango electric network, has developed a digital customer experience around its 'Q8 Smiles' and has invested heavily in open innovation with dozens of partners for mobipoints and the services of tomorrow.

Right from the start, the company wanted to know how it could compete with existing and emerging energy suppliers. Was the Q8 strategy sufficiently visionary, well-aligned and robust to satisfy the mobility needs of customers in the future? By exploring the future horizons to 2035 and beyond, the company hoped to get a better picture of precisely where it wanted to go and the scenario exercise certainly helped it to see the uncertainties of the future and offered a number of options for dealing with them. It was on the basis of this exercise that Q8 developed a new strategy for the future that would allow it to become a sustainable mobility player by moving beyond the typical roadside petrol stations with which they are most closely associated today.

Al Faraj: "For us, the meaning of innovation has changed dramatically since the introduction of scenario planning. In the past, innovation for Q8 was a matter of applying new technologies to discover and extract oil and gas reserves more easily. Nowadays, it means changing our business model to become more agile in the market and to better respond to the expanding and changing needs of customers. We now view innovation positively as a way to provide a diversity of mobility services, with a specific focus on sustainable and creative retail options, supported by an intelligent and strongly individualised service approach. We opted to start immediately with lean innovation experiments, a method that has proven its worth and led us to reconsider the value of many of our projects. Our new way of working revolves around experimenting with the needs of the future on the basis of scenario insights. You really need to test things to see if they work."

Today's mobility market is being disrupted by new technologies, changes in the industry, younger customers and new innovative business models. For Al Faraj, this explains a renewed sense of urgency within Q8. "Most oil and gas companies live by very strict processes and procedures, almost like a machine. But now we are suddenly asking whether or not the machine needs to work differently. This is by no means an easy question to ask and that is where visionary leadership has to play its part, by making it possible for creative people to make the difference. That takes courage. Our company has that courage and the necessary willingness to innovate, allowing our best talents to experiment in previously unexplored areas. Sometimes you need to reassure them that it is okay to try new things and even to have the occasional failure. You must encourage your team to act decisively and with confidence in terms of changing the customer experience, otherwise the innovation may turn out to have no value. Q8 is now putting everything in readiness, so that future generations of the company can continue along the path that we have started. Innovation is anchored in our organisation. It is part of our raison d'être. Without innovation, we will become surplus to people's requirements. We need to innovate to remain relevant. Only then will we be able to further ease and support the customer's journey. That is the kind of focus that I wish to ingrain in my people, both now and in the future. Some of them are immediately on board; others are a little more hesitant. In general, however, I see huge commitment, enthusiasm and will to innovate within our organisation, especially when people can see the results of the changes brought about by that innovation. Q8 will continue to reinvent itself, will continue to grow and will continue to serve generations of future customers, as it has done so well during the past thirty years. We will redefine our company as a trusted, reliable and sustainable mobility player. Thanks to our scenario planning and our innovation methodology, we will continue to innovate with passion for the future of our customers, our company and our team."

Via the QR-code you can view the scenarios that were developed for Q8. You can also discover the scenario approach of Skeyes, the Belgian airspace operator. I would like to thank both organisations for their permission to share these videos with all the readers of this book.

Q8 – scenario   Skeyes scenario

'If you cannot fail, you cannot learn.'

ERIC RIES

You can see for yourself how scenarios offer a clear view of the future, both for short and long-term plans and ideas. This makes it possible for you and your organisation to build up and/or maintain leadership in the future. If you apply the principles from this book – thinking far enough ahead about future technological possibilities, monitoring your future fitness, creating ideally matched innovation teams, boosting your innovation output and developing a culture that embraces change rather than rejecting it – then I promise you that your innovation will never fail. On the contrary, it will ensure that you remain ahead of the game, even in an ever-evolving world. In short, you will not be led by change; you will lead it!

FINALLY
A TRIP TO THE FUTURE

Fast forward: now I am 25 years old in 2047.

7.15 a.m.: My virtual assistant wakes me up, gently whispering and nudging my shoulder with soft haptic vibrations. I slept like a baby! Thanks to the emission of deep-brain stimulation waves, I now sleep less than I used to, but better than ever. The 4D printed screen in my bedroom wall opens and I walk through into the bathroom. The screen looks like an old-fashioned sliding door, but without hinges or a hole in the wall. It closes automatically behind me – another example of how my home is constantly adjusting to my needs. Take my windows, for example: larger on cloudy days when I need more light, but smaller on hot days, so that the climate management system hardly needs to use any energy. In the bathroom, the intelligent mirror shows me my health index and suggests a lunchtime cyber workout with my friends in New York. But first I've got that meeting with our potential new customers.

Half an hour later, I am sitting in my home office. Around the table are holographic images of the five people I need to talk to. We are actually separated by hundreds of kilometres, but thanks to the very latest VR technology we can meet virtually in a stylish boardroom with a great view over Brussels. The necessary walls and windows have also been added virtually to my own work room. We can even shake each other's hands, thanks to the haptic feedback from our neurostimulators. And it's all made possible by the smart Meta glasses that we are wearing. These provide the augmented reality in my office, including the 360° surround sound and the projection of my virtual presentation. If needed, I can pass virtual documents across the virtual table to my potential customers and we all have real-time data available to us, when needed. Of course, we all speak in our own language and also hear others in our own language, although with their real voices. In that way, there are no misunderstandings. We also have genuine eye-contact, visible body language and can even experience one another's humour. As the meeting is coming to an end, my glasses inform me that an urgent message is coming in from my friend John. His hologram pops out next to me, although the others can't see or hear him. He asks whether I would be interested in going with him to this evening's Jean-Michel Jarre memorial concert in Nice. We will be back by midnight, he assures me. Why not? I've got nothing else planned. In the background, I hear our virtual assistants arrange the trip, the tickets and our dinner. Meanwhile, the customers signal their approval of the deal and the meeting comes to a close. Our collaboration will start tomorrow. Our team – just one person and a dozen smart AI-bots – will begin first thing in the morning. Our other human specialists are scattered all around the globe, but will be able to work on the project virtually, gaining biometrically authenticated access to all the necessary material.

Goodness, it's lunchtime already! Time for my daily dose of sport. I pull on my sports gear and jog down to the local park. Helen, James and Ursula are running alongside me virtually, although for them this is actually an early morning jog 6,000 kilometres away in Central Park. As we run, we chat about the events of the past week. In the old days, we would have had to wear a set of headphones. Nowadays, of course, I can hear them through the minuscule chip inserted next to my ear drum, which makes direct contact with the auditory nerve in my inner ear. This has lots of other advantages as well. When my virtual assistant speaks to me, it is like she is whispering; music sounds as though it is being played in the same room; and silent self-driving cars make just the right amount of noise to let you know that they are approaching. And if you want real silence, the chip will provide you with some anti-noise. It's a remarkable piece of technology. You can listen very selectively, because the chip can filter in the right sound source from thousands of others. And as was the case in this morning's meeting, you can hear everyone talking in your own language, if that is what you want, while the real speech waves are dampened, so that you don't hear double. Sometimes, you don't even have to speak to your assistant. For some simple tasks, like asking the time, it is enough just to think what you want to happen and the smart lens in your glasses will project a clock somewhere near you.

An hour of sport has done me the world of good! A quick freshen-up and then I have just got time for forty winks in the sun. The garden is looking wonderful, thanks to my garden robot, who mows the lawn, pulls the weeds, prunes the roses, hoovers the swimming pool and even puts a bouquet of flowers on the garden table. While I sit here, my TeslaBot is giving the inside of the house a good clean. After my power-nap, I nip inside, get changed and get my things together for the trip to Nice. My virtual assistant has informed me that I need to be at the landing platform at the end of our street in ten minutes' time. This is where I will get picked up by a self-steering Airbus e-drone. Along with the other two passengers, I fly to Ghent to meet John at the terminal and catch the hyperloop that will take us to the south of France. Fast, easy and environmentally friendly. Travelling at 1,200 kilometres per hour, the small four-person hyperloop shuttles can get you to any part of Europe and back again in no time at all. What's more, their energy use is minimal compared with trains, which are now only used on local 'stopper' lines for commuters. With the emergence of other new forms of self-driving mobility in the air, on the ground, under the ground, in the water and on the water, most of the old main railway lines have disappeared, as have most of the motorways. This has created lots of extra space for green walking routes and sports parks, which are now dotted all across the country.

Of course, in the 2040s we all need much less mobility than we used to. Almost everyone works, shops and learns from home in the new holographic reality that is the Metaverse, which was launched a quarter of a century ago by Facebook. Even so, the majority of people now see each other in person far more often than in the past. We all have so much more free time than back in those days. Humanbots from Tesla, the Coolbot and the Boston Dynamics robot family do a large part of our work in retail, logistics, industry, construction and even in the care sector. Everyone gets a universal basic income from the state, so in theory no one needs to work any more. That being said, most people – like myself – still like to do a couple of days a week, and most of that is person-to-person. But all the old-style office jobs no longer exist, having been taken over by far-reaching AI digitalisation and blockchain innovations.

Fifteen minutes out from Ghent, our hyperloop flashes past Paris. In my parents' day, it took almost three hours to make the same journey. Half an hour later we are in Nice and enjoying the Mediterranean sun. We easily pick up a self-driving taxi and arrive at the concert hall in plenty of time. But first we have a meal at the wonderful restaurant overlooking the beach that was pre-booked by my personal assistant. Boy, she really knows how to pick all the best places, and always exactly what I like. She knows me so well! The restaurant is packed with people from all over Europe, most of whom have come just for the evening to watch the concert. We talk to some of them and I decide to turn off my auto-translator. Every now and then, it's good to practice your French or German or Italian. And if I forget a word or two, I know my assistant will whisper it into my ear.

The concert is spectacular. Jean-Michel Jarre's performance is as good as ever. He is a legend and would have been a hundred years old next year. He almost seems real, even down to the handshake that he gives us in the meet-and-greet we have arranged before the concert starts. The magnificent stage is built out over the sea, with a live orchestra. Is that real or is it another hologram? It's hard to tell any more. There are thousands of people – real ones this time – singing along in the gallery and dancing on the beach. Further along I can see thousands of other virtual people on a grandstand projected out above the water. They even do the Mexican wave with us! At the same time, we know that millions of others around the world are probably doing the same by following the concert live, either in their own homes or in a holopub in the Metaverse. That's the magic of technology!

On our way back to Belgium in the hyperloop, we bump into Gerry and Inga. Gerry is a neighbour of John's and Inga is a friend of his. A friend I rather like. Inga is great fun and we have a fantastic journey. My assistant whispers in my ear that Inga is a perfect Tinder match for me. As if I didn't know already! Inga smiles at me. It looks like her assistant has given her the same message! Not that John and Gerry have any idea what is going on. That makes it all the sexier! We arrange a date for the weekend, simply by thinking it to each other. Our virtual assistants are soon in contact and decide to surprise us with a chic restaurant and an Airbnb in Copenhagen. I am already looking forward to it.

An hour later, the e-drone drops me off at my house. Home before midnight, just as John had promised. My TeslaBot opens the virtual front door, not that it was really necessary, since I can open and close it by thought. But it's nice to be welcomed home in the old-fashioned way. Besides, my bot likes a bit of a chat. "Had a good evening?'"she asks knowingly. "Not now, Tess," I reply. "I'm far too tired. I'll tell you in the morning. Night-night!"

Whether you like or hate this idea of the future doesn't really matter. It is just one plausible scenario of what might happen. Irrespective of the sector in which you are active today, it is an invitation to think about the effect on your organisation of the products and service that will be launched before 2047 ever arrives. Be honest with yourself. Has your company got a role to play in this future world? Not at all? How on earth did you let things get that far? You do have a role? Good – but what role will that be? And is that the role you want? If not, can you change things for the better?

Perhaps it is time to turn the ideas in this book into a holistic vision for the future; a plan for where you want to go with your company in the years ahead. How do you want to improve the world for your children?

I hope that this book will help you to make a start at securing that future. Remember the key principle: build a culture of innovation. And remember the key question: will the future happen to you or be led by you?

You are in the driving seat and now have seven keys that will allow you to innovate successfully, keys that throughout my career have shown me that they are indispensable if you want to find the right path to the future for your organisation:

1. Focus your tech lenses on the future.
2. Avoid innovation obstacles.
3. Structure your organisation according to the six levels of innovation culture.
4. Put together a winning innovation team.
5. Develop a structured three-horizon innovation portfolio.
6. Create and implement a dynamic vision of the future via scenarios.
7. Build a future focused ecosystem.

And the bonus key: Set up an early warning system for a rolling strategy.

Will you keep me informed of your progress? Who in your company or organisation will play a leading role in my 2047 story? I wish you every success. Let's make a date for the future. And that future starts... now!

Joachim

'The greatest DANGER in times of TURBULENCE is NOT the TURBULENCE ... It is ACTING with the LOGIC of YESTERDAY ...'

PETER DRUCKER

FINAL WORD
JOACHIM TALKING

REFERENCES

Abernathy, W.J. and Utterback, J.M. – Patterns of Innovation in Technology, Technology Review 1978.

ASML Investor Day – Company Strategy, 2021 – Peter Wennink.

Elliott Jacques, The Requisite Organisation - https://www.requisite.org.

Forbes, Enrique Dans, 30 Aug 2019 - What Does Tesla's Tentative Move Into Car Insurance Mean For The Sector? https://www.forbes.com/sites/enriquedans/2019/08/30/what-does-teslas-tentative-move-into-car-insurance-mean-for-thesector/?sh=c209dc3148c3.

Fuitsu - Japan's Fugaku Retains Title as World's Fastest Supercomputer for fourth consecutive term, 16 November 2021 - https://www.fujitsu.com/global/about/resources/news/press-releases/2021/1116-01.html.

HBR, How to Live with Risks, 2015 – "Reducing Risk Management's Organizational Drag," by CEB.

IBM, The Era of Open Innovation – 1999 https://www.ibm.com/ibm/history/ibm100/us/en/icons/linux/.

IEEE Spectrum, 2021 – IBM introduces the world's first 2-nm node chip - https://spectrum.ieee.org/ibm-introduces-the-worlds-first-2nm-node-chip.

Kolb, D. et al. (1984). Experiential learning: Experience as the source of learning and development. Englewood Cliffs, NJ: Prentice-Hall.

Managing Your Innovation Portfolio, by Bansi Nagji and Geoff Tuff, HBR, 2012.

MT.be Magazine, Nils Sips, Karin Swiers, 2016 – Cargill omarmt open innovatie.

NewScientist, Jessica Hamzelou, 1 May 2018 - Smart people literally have bigger brain cells than the rest - https://www.newscientist.com/article/2167753-smart-people-literally-have-bigger-brain-cells-than-the-rest/#ixzz7LFtVVzBB.

NYTimes, Japanese Supercomputer Fugaku tops American Chinese machines, 2020, https://www.nytimes.com/2020/06/22/technology/japanese-supercomputer-fugaku-tops-american-chinese-machines.html.

Samsung 6G Vision, 2021 - https://cdn.codeground.org/nsr/downloads/researchareas/6G%20Vision.pdf.

Science Alert - People Running Folding@Home Accidentally Created The World's Biggest Supercomputer - https://www.sciencealert.com/so-many-people-are-running-folding-home-that-it-s-created-the-world-s-biggest-supercomputer -17 April 2020.

Tesla greift jetzt am Strommarkt an – auch in Deutschland – Handelsblatt, 24 August 2021. https://www.handelsblatt.com/unternehmen/energie/energiewirtschaft-tesla-greift-jetzt-am-strommarkt-an-auch-in-deutschland/27530882.html?ticket=ST-18523971-OQecLcaB6NCfI-lOoSam2-ap2.

The Linkages between Crude Oil and Food Prices, Institute of Economics and Finance, Warsaw University of Life Sciences, Monika Roman, Dec 2020.

The Sixth Wave of Innovation – Are We Ready ? - Barbieri, Vasconcelos, Andreassi & Vasconcelos 2010; Desha & Hargroves, 2011; Seebode et al, 2012.

Vice.com, 16 July 2021 - Japan Transfers 319 Terabits Per Second, Setting Internet Speed Record.

Why Sustainability Is Now the Key Driver of Innovation by Ram Nidumolu, C.K. Prahalad, and M.R. Rangaswami, Harvard Business Review, September 2009.

https://www.tesla.com/en_CA/blog/tesla-adds-titanium-underbody-shield-and-aluminum-deflector-plates-model-s

https://www.newscientist.com/article/2167753-smart-people-literally-have-bigger-brain-cells-than-the-rest/

https://www.ibm.com/ibm/history/ibm100/us/en/icons/linux/